T0220929

Conflicts, Crimes and Regulations in Cyberspace

Cybersecurity Set

coordinated by
Daniel Ventre

Volume 2

Conflicts, Crimes and Regulations in Cyberspace

Edited by

Sébastien-Yves Laurent

WILEY

First published 2021 in Great Britain and the United States by ISTE Ltd and John Wiley & Sons, Inc.

ISTE Ltd
27-37 St George's Road
London SW19 4EU
UK

www.iste.co.uk

John Wiley & Sons, Inc.
111 River Street
Hoboken, NJ 07030
USA

www.wiley.com

Library of Congress Control Number: 2021945731

British Library Cataloguing-in-Publication Data
A CIP record for this book is available from the British Library
ISBN 978-1-78630-686-9

Contents

Chapter 2. Cybersecurity in America: The US National Security Apparatus and Cyber Conflict Management   43

Frédérick GAGNON and Alexis RAPIN

Chapter 3. Separation of Offensive and Defensive Functions: The Originality of the French Cyberdefense Model Called into Question?   63

Alix DESFORGES

Chapter 4. The Boundary Between Cybercrime and Cyberwar: An Uncertain No-Man's Land   89

Marc WATIN-AUGOUARD

Chapter 5. Cyberdefense, the Digital Dimension of National Security   107

Bertrand WARUSFEL

Chapter 9. Cyberdefense and Cybersecurity Regulations in the United States: From the Failure of the "Comprehensive Policy" to the Success of the Sectoral Approach.   177

Adrien MANNIEZ

Introduction

Studying Cyberspace Internationally

Why is it necessary to perceive cyberspace from a reflexive point of view? Since it is not a natural or social reality, but a shared system built over time by a multitude of actors, its hybrid nature – it possesses both a technological and a social aspect – does not enable us to use the usual benchmarks that social sciences use to study the social world. Moreover, cyberspace actors are talkative and doctrinaire and produce a host of fairly new strategic concepts (often of little value) that obscure the understanding of the situation[1]. The effort to be reflexive seems all the more necessary. Understanding cyber therefore presumes an approach that takes into account its social and technological dimensions, as well as an ability to distance oneself from the various discourses of the actors, both indispensable conditions in order to make it an authentic object of study. The challenge of this book is specifically to try to contribute to this essential reflection, which is still in its infancy[2], and so we must therefore state for the reader the choices and perspectives that guide it.

The nine chapters of this volume provide a global and, therefore, original dimension of cyberspace. Indeed, it seemed to us to be beneficial to not limit its content, as is sometimes the case, to an irenic vision that only values the collaborative dimension or, conversely, to a cynical vision that reduces cyberspace to a conflictual space. In the spirit of our global perspective, we

---

Introduction written by Sébastien-Yves LAURENT.

1 See Musso (2010).

2 This makes it all the more important to highlight the role of pioneers Loiseau and Waldispuehl (2017) and Loiseau et al. (2021).

chose the title *Conflicts, Crimes and Regulations in Cyberspace*. This book is not directly part of the endless debate between the advocates of cyberwar (Calvo 2014) and those who reject this posture (Gartzke 2013). We note that there are confrontations in cyberspace, involving civilian and military actors, toward various ends that are not always short term. Today, the state of our knowledge strongly exceeds the apocalyptic prognoses of the 1990s and 2000s and this allows us to relativize the quantity and scope of confrontations between state actors, most of which are related to data theft activities, that is espionage (Valeriano and Maness 2018). Thus, we have chosen to describe them as "crimes" or "conflicts" in order to deliberately avoid the term "war"[3], which seems excessive to us and immediately produces a securitization effect.

The 10 authors, whom we thank warmly[4] for their contributions, were each asked to provide a clear definition of what they meant by cyberspace in their text. This is, of course, important since, in this field, diversity prevails; thus, in 2018, the NATO Cooperative Cyber Defense Center of Excellence (CCD COE) in Tallinn identified 29 definitions of cyberspace (Bigelow 2018). We have chosen to adopt the 2006 US definition from the National Military Strategy for Cyberspace Operations since it seems neutral: "[...] an operational domain characterized by the use of electronics and the electromagnetic spectrum to create, store, modify and exchange information via networked information systems and associated physical infrastructures"[5]. The authors gathered here, whether jurists or political scientists, also adhere to the perspective of studying the cyberspace object as a sociotechnical system, that is to say, as a set of social units in dynamic interactions, organized around information and communication technologies, which orientates toward science and technology studies (STS)[6].

Finally, this book is clearly part of an internationalist perspective[7], since its authors believe that the study of cyberspace cannot be confined to the limits of a single country, due to the distributed nature of the system structuring cyberspace and the constant mobility of data. This observation does not, however, invalidate the possibility of studying public cyber policies (see Chapter 2). Adopting this international approach, we make it clear that we will

---

3 For context in the literature, see Gorwa and Smeets (2019).

4 The coordinator also wishes to thank Michel Courty for his work in structuring the manuscript.

5 Quoted by Kuehl (2009).

6 See two particularly successful examples, Balzacq and Cavelty (2016) and Cavelty (2018).

7 See Reardon and Choucri (2012).

not revisit the theoretical debate on whether cyberspace is a component of the international system or whether it constitutes its own autonomous system[8]. In the research paradigm that we have described, we here highlight international cyberspace issues (see Chapters 1 and 8) as well as two countries, the United States (see Chapters 1, 2, 6 and 9) and France (see Chapters 3, 5 and 8). The diversity of cyber actors – state, non-state and individual – is evoked in every chapter of the book, but the chosen approach highlights the first two.

Conflicts, Crimes and Regulations in Cyberspace focuses, on the one hand, on the actors of cyber states, also known as cyber bureaucracies, in Chapters 2, 8 and 9, and, on the other hand, on the tools of cyber states, namely, norms (national and international law), in Chapters 4, 5 and 7, as well as the strategic concepts used by the different actors (cybersecurity, cyberdefense and digital sovereignty[9]). Our approach here is therefore that of the "meso-" level, which is rare, as international approaches to cyber in the academic literature of the Anglosphere rather tend to take into account "macro-" entities (states, international organizations, etc.). Thus, this book intends to contribute to the global academic debate on cyber issues.

References

Balzacq, T. and Cavelty, M.D. (2016). A theory of actor network for cyber-security. *European Journal of International Security*, 1–2, 176–198.

Bigelow, B. (2018). The topography of cyberspace and its consequences for operations. *10th International Conference on Cyber Conflict*. NATO CCD COE Publications, Tallinn.

Calvo, A. (2014). Cyberwar is war: A critique of "hacking can reduce real-world violence". *Small Wars Journal*, June [Online]. Available at: www. smallwarsjournal. com/jrnl/art/cyberwar-is-war [Accessed 18 June 2020].

Cavelty, M.D. (2018). Cybersecurity research meets science and technology studies. *Politics and Governance*, 6(2), 22–30.

Gartzke, E. (2013). The myth of cyberwar: Bringing war in cyberspace back down to earth. *International Security*, 38(2), 41–73.

Gorwa, R. and Smeets, M. (2019). *Cyber Conflict in Political Science: A Review of Methods and Literature*. ISA, Toronto.

---

8 See Laurent (2021).

9 See Türk and Vallar (2017).

Kuehl, D.T. (2009). From cyberspace to cyberpower: Defining the problem. In *Cyberpower and National Security*, Kramer, F.D., Starr, S.H., Wentz, L. (eds). National Defense University Press, Washington.

Laurent, S.-Y. (2021). Ce que le cyber (ne) fait (pas) aux relations internationales. *Études Internationales*.

Loiseau, H. and Waldispuehl, E. (2017). *Cyberespace et science politique, de la méthode au terrain, du virtuel au réel*. Presses de l'Université de Québec, Quebec City.

Loiseau, H., Ventre, D., Aden, H. (2021). *Cybersecurity in Humanities and Social Sciences: A Research Methods Approach*. ISTE Ltd, London, and Wiley, New York.

Musso, R.P. (2010). Le Web : nouveau territoire et vieux concepts. *Annales des Mines. Réalités industrielles*, 4, 75–83.

Reardon, R. and Choucri, N. (2012). *The Role of Cyberspace in International Relations: A View of the Literature*. ISA, San Diego.

Türk, P. and Vallar, C. (2017). *La Souveraineté numérique. Le concept, les enjeux*. Mare & Martin, Paris.

Valeriano, B. and Maness, R.C. (2018). How we stopped worrying about cyber doom and started collecting data. *Politics and Governance*, 6(5), 781–799.

The United States, States and the False Claims of the End of the Global Internet

1.1. Introduction[1]

The end of the 1990s and the 2000s saw a great debate in international social sciences, which focused on the effects of globalization on states. Susan Strange (1996) was the first to write of the irreversible weakening of the state, while others have emphasized its strong resistance (Krasner 1999) to the phenomenon of globalization. Yet others have even suggested that the state is being strengthened (Cohen 2005).

In this chapter, written 20 years later, we would like to revisit this debate, which does not appear to be outdated, by taking as a point of observation one of the manifestations of globalization, namely, the development of information technologies in a global system formerly called the internet, now more extensive and called "cyberspace". Halfway through the 2000s, at a time when the internet was still highly collaborative and barely affected by "cyber insecurity", two American international lawyers, Jack Goldsmith and Tim Wu, put forward the idea of the return of the state to the internet in their celebrated book, *Who Controls the Internet?* (Goldsmith and Wu 2006). Two years earlier, the political scientist Daniel Drezner had indicated that

Chapter written by Sébastien-Yves LAURENT.

1 The author would like to express his gratitude to Daniel Ventre and Benjamin Loveluck for their very attentive proofreading.

the internet was a "tough test for state-centric theories of international relations" (Drezner 2004, p. 479). These authors, and many others after them, postulated on a form of original incompatibility between the state form and the internet.

In this chapter, we return to the attitude of states toward cyberspace, by giving a certain temporal depth to our subject. In order to address this question, we believe it necessary to set out a number of preliminary definitions and semantic clarifications. In this chapter, we will approach cyberspace as a sociotechnical system, that is to say, a social collective "of elements in dynamic interaction"[2], which thus creates a system organized around digital technologies. Indeed, we believe it fundamental to underline from a methodological point of view that what gives consistency to the international dimension of cyberspace is the mobilization of social actors around digital technologies. Whatever the type and diversity of these actors, they organize themselves *de facto* through their interactions as a system whose nature takes a social form (Simmel 1908). Moreover, we will adopt the canonical approach of cyberspace as being composed of the assembly of three layers: the physical (material infrastructures), logical (applications) and semantic/cognitive (meaningful contents) layers, with the "cyber-digital" being the assembly of the three (Ventre 2014a).

1.2. The creation of the internet and the development of cyberspace by the United States

Internationally, management of the old telecommunications systems since the 19th century had taken the form of cooperation between states. In contrast, the internet and cyberspace are international telecommunications systems that originated in the United States and are still under US technical and economic control.

Attempts to transform these sociotechnical systems, under the leadership of the United Nations during the 2000s, have not succeeded in challenging this state of affairs.

---

2 de Rosnay, J. (1975). *Le macroscope. Vers une vision globale*, Le Seuil, Paris.

1.2.1. *The first international telecommunications systems developed by all states*

When technical progress in the 19th century led to the birth of information technologies (electric telegraph, telephone, submarine cables and wireless), the major European states played a decisive role, either by investing in the field, by forcing the private sector to do so or by deciding to set up state monopolies (Griset 1991; Headrick 1991). In Great Britain, France, Italy, Germany and the United States, governments quickly turned these technologies into tools to serve their security needs and their desire for expansion, with police and military administrations being the first to equip themselves with, and to control the new means.

What could be termed the first information and communication technologies (ICTs) were, in fact born from states which were the actors of their internationalization. Indeed, they encouraged the formation of the very first international administrations created specifically to administer ICTs: the International Telegraph Union (1868), the Universal Postal Union (1874), the Central Office for International Transport (1890) and the International Radiotelegraph Union (1906). In the age of nationalism, these international administrations ensured the physical development of technical networks and gave rise to international relational networks around ICTs, which led William J. Drake to speak of the establishment, from that time on, of a NetWorld Order (Drake 2008). From then, international governance of telecommunications emerged, based on state actors. Despite the polarization of the international system at the end of the 19th century, around two major antagonistic alliance systems, international unions and offices accompanied the growth of information flows and fostered the adoption of the first global technical norms and standards. Thus, the international adoption of Morse code in 1865 by states was the first technical standard that structured international information in a lasting way and thus encouraged the first globalization of information and the birth of short time.

1.2.2. *The creation and development of the internet by the United States*

A century later, the situation of international communications is totally different and, from the point of view of the role of states, the contrast is striking. The emergence of a new wave of ICTs, thanks to computers and digital formats that have given rise to what is known as cyberspace, has taken hold without, with the exception of the United States, the involvement of states.

We will not be revisiting the classic works that have established the origins of the internet in detail here (Castells 2001; Goldsmith and Wu 2006; Tréguer 2019); although the origin of the global network was more cooperative than hierarchical and centralized (Schafer and Thierry 2013), it mainly stemmed from the desire of the US military to maintain a technological advantage over the USSR in the field of information processing (Castells 2001). The idea and origins of the internet were American. The US Arpanet of the late 1960s, developed in collaboration with 15 universities, was the matrix of the global internet. Although the individual contributions of British (Tim Berners-Lee), French (Louis Pouzin) and Belgian (Robert Cailliau) computer scientists, for example, were significant, it was the Pentagon's investments and, above all, the dynamics of the IT industry in the United States (Carr 2016) that turned the original military network into a national civilian network, before it was internationalized in a third phase. The states of the other major technological powers did not participate in the development of the internet, which was, until the mid-1990s, a *de facto* US communication system in which European and Japanese scientists participated on an *ad hoc* basis. This reminder allows us to better interpret President Barack Obama's pithy response, during a February 2015 interview: "We have owned the internet. Our companies have created it, expanded it, perfected it in ways that [the Europeans] can't compete."[3] This judgment reflects the dominant view of the perception of the internet by the federal authorities in the United States and sheds light on the relative positions on the subject of managing the internationalization of the internet.

1.2.3. *International management controlled by the United States*

The first American structures that constituted the architecture of the national network have remained those of the global network; sometimes

---

3 See www.recode.net/2015/02/15/white-house-red-chair-obama-meets-swisher.

called Standard Developing Organizations, we have made the analytical decision to characterize them as the "cybersphere core" (Laurent 2015), as is represented in Figure 1.3[4]. Four organizations (IETF, ISOC, W3C and ICANN) ensure ensuring the development of the physical and the software layers. The IETF (Internet Engineering Task Force) was created in 1986 to develop internet protocols. It is organized into more than 100 working groups, active across seven areas[5], and only individuals can participate, which prohibits the presence of states. Members of companies or legal entities can also participate, but only as individuals. The Internet Architecture Board (IAB) is one of the most important committees of the IETF, as it conducts forward thinking on network architecture. Between 1986 and 2020, US engineers produced 55.5% of IETF[6] documents, with Chinese engineers coming in second, but with only 4.21%. Figure 1.1 shows the extent of US domination, which benefits from the dispersion of its competitors. Taking the European countries together, they would be in second place, but still far behind the United States. Moreover, other statistical evidence from the same source indicates that the dominance of US production has remained stable over time; this is therefore a structural effect. Figure 1.2 also shows the large domination of US companies.

In addition, the IETF is able to rely on an association under US law with an international vocation, the Internet Society (ISOC), created in 1992. The ISOC is responsible for raising funds for the IETF, which it gives a legal structure, as well as, in addition to this very important role, promoting the values and founding principles of the internet (see section 1.2.4). It is also the ISOC that edits Requests for Comments (RFCs) for the IETF, thus defining the normative architecture of the internet (Cath and Floridi 2017). The World Wide Web Consortium (W3C) is responsible for developing protocols and encouraging the creation of software for use on the web and, more generally, all web standards. It is a nonprofit organization that brings together only legal entities of the most diverse origins (economic actors,

---

4 We are critical of the notion of a *public core of the internet*, adopted in 2018 by the Global Commission on the Stability of Cyberspace (GCSC) (see www.bit.ly/2DfJN7C). We cannot indicate here the reasons for this due to lack of space.
5 According to the ITEF website the seven groups are the Applications area and general area, internet area, operations and management area, routing area, security area, transport area.
6 This includes final Requests for Comment (RFCs) and RFC drafts.

universities and schools, etc.), with 428 members as of summer 2020[7]. The cybersphere core is finally completed by the *Internet Corporation for Assigned Names and Numbers* (ICANN), created in 1998, which assumes several major operational roles: the functioning of the identification system (allocation of domain names and IP addresses, commonly called the IANA function) (Froomkin 2011) and the management of Domain Name Server (DNS) root servers. It is a private, nonprofit corporation under California law with a signed memorandum of understanding (MOU) with the US Department of Commerce[8]. Although both are different, the ICANN and the IETF are the two main technical infrastructure components of the internet. In addition, some private US companies play a key role, such as Verisign, which administers two of the three DNS root servers. Finally, of the 12 organizations that manage DNS servers, nine are American.

Until the 2000s, the units of the sociotechnical system that is cyberspace thus comprised the United States, the four associations of the cybersphere core and the private companies (first access providers, then content providers, but together rapidly dominated economically by the platforms) that brought the network into the market economy (Castells 2001). Although the structures constituting the cybersphere core give the impression of being global organizations, they are, in fact, an assembly of American structures that have, over time, encouraged a less American and more internationalized composition of their physical members. This has been made possible by foreign contributions to the definition of computer-to-computer communication standards, which has valued the principle of openness (Russell 2014). However, US computer companies and their members have been, and remain, central (Raustalia 2016) to the composition of these various structures, from which states are absent (DeNardis and Raymond 2013). As Laura DeNardis (DeNardis 2016) and Francesca Musiani (Musiani 2018) have clearly shown, the choices of physical and logical infrastructures are political choices.

---

7 www.w3.org/Consortium/Member/List (accessed on 5 June 2020).

8 After 2 years of transition, ICANN took up management of the IANA function at the end of 2016, but, at the time of writing, it is too soon to get a view of the situation since then.

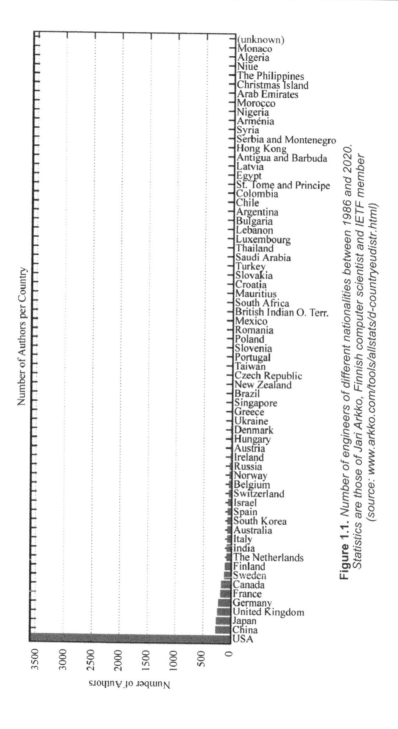

Figure 1.1. *Number of engineers of different nationalities between 1986 and 2020. Statistics are those of Jari Arkko, Finnish computer scientist and IETF member (source: www.arkko.com/tools/allstats/d-countryeudistr.html)*

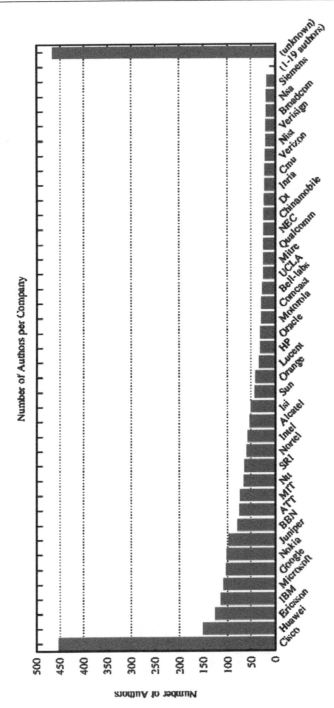

Figure 1.2. *Number of authors publishing with different engineering companies between 1986 and 2020 (source: www.arkko.com/tools/rfcstats/companydistr.html)*

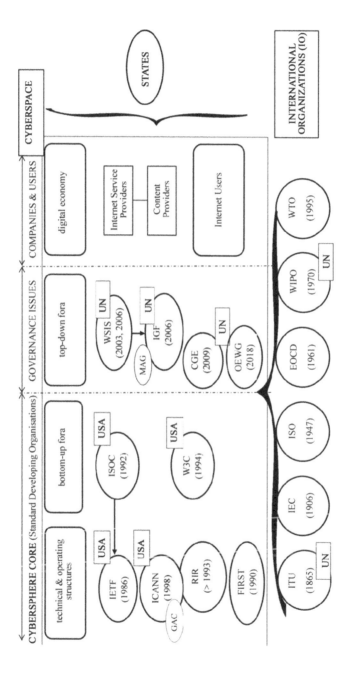

Figure 1.3. *Principal components of cyberspace*

1.2.4. *A sociotechnical system bearing a composite American ideology*

Insofar as the internet is a sociotechnical system, it is a challenge around which values and beliefs have been formed. The technical evolutions of the system of systems that is the internet, and in particular the expansion of the social web from the middle of the 2000s onward, have made it possible to develop the function of communicating content between individuals. From its origins in the 1970s up to the present day, promoters of the system have developed a true vision of the world around the tool, literally constituting an ideology that is profoundly American (Bessone 2011). In our opinion, this is a particular form of ideology that is syncretic in a cultural anthropology sense. Indeed, it incorporates highly heterogeneous elements, which can even be contradictory at times, without this calling into question the unity and power of the ideology of the internet. This syncretic characteristic is essentially due to the great diversity of actors who have carried the innovation of the internet in the United States (Castells 2001; Cardon 2010).

Two technical principles derived from network computing constitute the basis of the ideology: on the one hand, the end-to-end principle, which is linked to the distributed nature of the network (Baran 1962) and, on the other hand, the interoperability of the various network components. The first principle, the absence of centrality, enables the natural growth of the network by the users; the second is the condition of possibility, as it was, insofar as only components that can connect and exchange contents allow networking.

It is these technical foundations onto which a libertarian and antistatist dimension was grafted, of which the *Declaration of Independence of Cyberspace*, published in February 1996 by John Perry Barlow, is probably the strongest illustration[9]. An operating principle has been added to the Californian ideology, derived from the cybersphere core that places the various actors (individuals, companies, states, etc.) on the same plane (thus refuting the very principle of a hierarchy), that is *multi-stakeholder* governance. Finally, the fifth and final element of the internet ideology is informational liberalism (Loveluck 2015), which places an axiological value on the principle of free dissemination of information, constituting *de facto* a

---

9 See www.eff.org/fr/cyberspace-independence.

powerful *soft power* tool for the United States[10]. The practical effect of this element of the ideology is the formation of the idea of net neutrality (Wu 2003), which combines freedom of access and non-discrimination of content according to types of users.

1.2.5. The false recomposition of the global sociotechnical system: the global summits on the information society

The sociotechnical system formed by the different units mentioned (section 1.2.3) was the subject of an external attempt at transformation in the early 2000s, due to the intervention of a new actor, the United Nations.

In December 2001, the United Nations General Assembly (UNGA) approved the holding of a World Summit for the Information Society (WSIS), by voting on resolution 56/183[11]. This apparent UNGA innovation was not, however, an innovation insofar as it was the Russian Federation that had already raised international information-related issues at the United Nations in 1998 (section 1.2.3). It was, in fact, UNESCO that, as early as the 1970s, had promoted a New World Information and Communication Order (NWICO[12]), thereby taking the very first initiative in this area. Countries belonging to the non-aligned movement had taken up this cause at three summits held in 1976 and UNESCO then appointed the MacBride Commission in 1980, from which came the report *Many Voices, One World, which promoted* the NWICO (Frau and Meigs 2012). However, UNESCO was a forum without real capacity for action, weakened further by the withdrawal of the United States and the United Kingdom in 1984 and 1985. The 2001 UN resolution was far from the egalitarian vision of the MacBride report, but it did give rise to the notion of the information society in the largest international forum, entrusting the International Telecommunication Union (ITU) to organize the summit.

The first (held from December 10–12, 2003, in Geneva) was truly groundbreaking in two respects: on the one hand, almost all the states at the time (171 out of 189) participated in this summit. Above all, they adopted a

---

10 "It helped that most of the founding documents of internet culture referred implicitly to the history of the United States: here was the new frontier that belonged to those brave enough to move into it [...]" (Snowden 2019).

11 See www.undocs.org/pdf?symbol=fr/A/RES/56/183 (accessed on 5 June 2020).

12 New World Information and Communication Order.

67 point declaration of principles that developed an entirely new vision of the internet, an alternative to that developed by the United States (see section 1.2.4). In point 48, the declaration stated:

> The internet has become a global public resource and its governance should be an essential agenda item for IT companies. The international management of the internet should be multilateral, transparent and democratic, with the full involvement of governments, the private sector, civil society and international organizations. It should ensure an equitable distribution of resources, facilitate access for all and ensure a stable and secure functioning of the internet, taking into account multilingualism[13].

The characterization of the internet as a "global public resource" at that time contradicted reality in all three layers of a network operated in the orbit of the United States. It was therefore an ideological declaration of a rather performative nature characterized by an open vision of the network, thought of as a dimension of universality and not as an American soft power tool.

Moreover, the conception of an interoperable network (see section 1.2.4) was clearly transformed by the promotion of the idea that multi-stakeholder governance (Lakel and Massit-Folléa 2007) including states was needed, which totally contradicted the US vision centered solely around technical organizations (Mueller 2010; Van Eeten and Mueller 2012). Moreover, the second WSIS, organized in Tunis (November 16–18, 2005), with the same number of states, led to the adoption of a 122 point declaration[14], almost half of which concerned the issue of internet governance. At the WSIS in Tunis, there were heated debates challenging ICANN's dominance. In the short term, the result of Tunis was the creation by the United Nations in 2006 of the Internet Governance Forum (IGF), the ambition of which was to give shape to an alternative governance model to that of the United States. In the longer term, the result of the two WSIS summits was the sectoral intervention of international organizations (see Figure 1.3) on the new international challenge that the internet had become. The global sociotechnical system of the internet (see section 1.2.3) was apparently greatly modified.

---

13 Available at: www.itu.int/net/wsis/docs/geneva/official/dop.html (accessed on 5 June 2020).
14 See www.itu.int/wsis/docs2/tunis/off/6rev1-fr.html (accessed on 5 June 2020).

However, in fact, beyond the symbolic dimension, the scope must be qualified, particularly with regard to the role of states, which has remained minor in the bodies created up to the present day. The IGF has remained what it was at the outset, that is a multi-stakeholder forum that makes it possible to lead a global debate, but without any effect on the structure of the sociotechnical system and particularly on the first and second layers. The multi-stakeholder governance of the IGF is based on the Multistakeholder Advisory Group (MAG), which meets three times a year. Composed of 46 members at its inception in 2006, representing the diversity of internet stakeholders (divided into four categories: technical community, civil society, private sector and government), it had 57 members in 2016[15]. At that time, there were only 18 representatives of states, including only three major technological and economic powers (South Korea, the United States and Russia). It is therefore clear that the United Nations' attempt to transform the balance within the internet's sociotechnical system was not likely to enable an alternative expression to that of the United States.

We can also try to evaluate the influence of states within the significant structure of the cybersphere core that is ICANN. Within ICANN, the Governmental Advisory Committee (GAC) (created in 1999 on the initiative of the European Commission) is the only structure of the cybersphere core that includes legal entities such as states; as of the summer of 2020, there were 178 members and 33 observers[16], bringing together all the states as well as international organizations. However, ICANN is composed of 10 entities and the organization specifies, at the risk of tautology, that in addition to the advisory role of the GAC, it is not a decision-making body[17]. Finally, the internal operating rules of the ICANN organizations are governed by Californian law. It is possible to conclude provisionally at this stage that, apart from the founding United States, the other states have remained on the periphery of the management structures of the global internet.

1.3. Cyberspace transformed by the arrival in force of states

Stable in its composition from the mid-1990s onward, the sociotechnical system of the globalized American internet underwent a very profound

15 See www.intgovforum.org/multilingual/content/mag-members-0 (accessed on 6 June 2020).
16 See www.gac.icann.org/about/members (accessed on 5 June 2020).
17 *Ibid.*

transformation over the following 20 years, mainly due to the rather sudden arrival of states, which formulated discourse and implemented various extreme measures in cyberspace.

1.3.1. *State intentions in "national strategies": a global approach*

In 2003, the United States published *The National Strategy to Secure Cyberspace*, the first national strategy to include the term "cyber" and, three years later, the *National Military Strategy for Cyberspace Operations*. The *UK Cyber Security Strategy: Protecting and Promoting the UK in a Digital World* was published in 2011 by the British government, at the same time as the French cybersecurity agency released its report *Défense et sécurité des systèmes d'information. Stratégie de la France* and the German Ministry of the Interior its *Cyber-Sicherheitsstrategie für Deutschland*. These texts are representative of a vast movement of governmental declarations adopted in the 2010s, making cyber and digital an issue now being defined by states as strategic.

The *Center for Strategic and International Studies* (CSIS)[18] compiled a collection of texts related to what it called "cyber strategy", listing 525 texts between 1974 and 2019[19]. The methodology adopted by the CSIS is open to criticism and undermines the results[20]; however, there is no other inventory and we are forced to rely on this data, while bearing in mind that the results are flawed in terms of orders of magnitude. The breakdown of texts with a digital scope into seven thematic groupings[21] is heuristic; we can see that most of them are concerned with the non-security aspects of digital

---

18 The CSIS is regularly ranked as the leading think tank on defense and national security issues.

19 See   www.csis-prod.s3.amazonaws.com/s3fs-public/Cyber%20Regulation%20Index%20V2%20%28002%29.pdf.

20 The CSIS takes into account as strategies not only strategic texts, but also all texts related to the digital environment, even those without a strategic scope and in particular all legal texts (on digital commerce, etc.). Moreover, there are some curious omissions: there is no mention of the French 1978 legislation or of the 1995 European directive. On the other hand, the American Privacy Act (1974) is not forgotten and makes the United States the first country to initiate an approach in this area, while, in terms of privacy protection, Sweden, a country forgotten by the CSIS, was the first (1973). The valorization of the pioneering role of the United States, even if it is not exact, is in line with what we have shown earlier in sections 1.2 and 1.3.

21 They are themselves open to criticism because of the many overlaps between the categories.

technology and that the security dimension (crime, critical infrastructures and military) represents only 35% of the total production.

	Themes in cyber strategy texts	Percentage
Trade	114	22%
Privacy policy	113	22%
Crime	91	17%
National strategy	78	15%
Critical infrastructures	63	12%
Content	35	7%
Military	31	6%
Total	525	100%

Table 1.1. Themes of digital texts (1974–2019) (source: our calculations based on CSIS data)[22]

The annual breakdown of digital texts (Figure 1.4) clearly shows the three main effects of the structural development of the sociotechnical system: the global expansion of the commercial internet in the mid-1990s (Castells 2001); the 2000s, during which texts on the commercial internet and *privacy* were adopted; and finally the great peak at the start of the 2010s, which saw states claiming global cyber public policies, whether or not they are called strategies.

In any event, all states – including those powers of lesser significance from an economic and technological point of view – have made digital and cyber one of the objectified sectors of their activity, which at this stage of the debate can be described as public policy. We believe it essential to recall once again (Table 1.1) the very broad range of sectors of intervention envisaged by states – we can speak of a global approach – which has made the international object of governance increasingly complex (Kurbalija 2008/2012).

_____

22 See www.csis-prod.s3.amazonaws.com/s3fs-public/Cyber%20Regulation%20Index%20V2%20%28002%29.pdf.

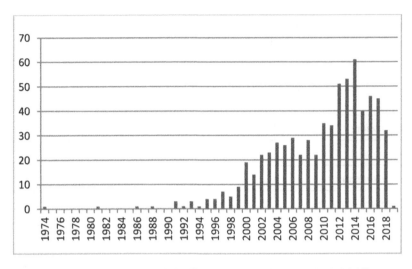

Figure 1.4. *The annual distribution of digital texts (1974–2019)*

1.3.2. *Russian–American structural disagreements on information security and cybersecurity*

However, it is by relying on a common minority theme (Table 1.1), that of cybersecurity, that states have demonstrated their desire to reinvest in the digital component of the international system[23]. The crises that occurred in close proximity to each other, such as the Distributed Denial of Service (DDoS) attacks against Estonia (2007) and Georgia (2008), which were quickly identified as being of Russian origin and skillfully used by NATO and the United States, have helped to put this issue on the international agenda. Nonetheless, national definitions and conceptions of cybersecurity vary widely (Luiijf *et al.* 2013) and thus make it difficult to grasp what cyber insecurity truly means for states.

In fact, the birth of cybersecurity as an international discourse and practice is the result of a confrontation between Russia and the United States at the United Nations (Delerue *et al.* forthcoming; Laurent 2021). In the wake of the end of the Cold War, a period in which the Russian Federation reinvested heavily in the United Nations (Panagiotou 2011; Schmitt 2019), the country took the first steps toward raising awareness of information

---

23 On methodological approaches to cyberspace and the international system, we refer to Laurent (2021).

technology security issues among states by promoting the notion of information security. Indeed, in December 1998, the Russian Federation presented a resolution (A/RES/53/70) entitled: *Developments in the field of information and telecommunications in the context of international security*. This short text[24] was mainly constructed around the idea that information and communication technologies could endanger international stability and security. This immediately placed the issue at the level of states (and not individuals[25]) and established – very securely – a link between these technologies and the international order. The resolution was renewed a year later, with almost identical content (A/RES/54/49), and has been renewed on a regular basis ever since. It can be assumed that the Russian initiative of 1998–1999 is not unrelated to the fact that the UN General Assembly began to discuss this issue in 2001. As for the origin of this decision, it is more than likely due to the observation of the profound imbalance between Russian and American computer capacities and the computer attacks suffered by the USSR in the 1980s. It is feasible that Russia thought that a successful internationalization of the issue (including on the normative level) would have enabled it to compensate for its lack of capacity.

The issue has become clearly bipolarized at the United Nations. Indeed, in October 2005, the United States made its first public statement on the subject by voting against the Russian resolution that had once again been tabled (Maurer 2011). Against the backdrop of growing reciprocal cyber attacks, Russia and the United States then engaged in a bilateral dialog of which there is little public record (Nocetti 2015). It is worth noting, however, the decision that the two countries made to make public part of their dialog conducted within the framework of the "East-West Institute"[26] in 2011. This focused on the crucial issue of critical infrastructure, which was (and remains) the main target of the respective cyber attacks. In 2013, the two countries announced a cybersecurity agreement[27], the culmination of two years of dialog, and the creation of a Bilateral Presidential Commission with three modest measures, limited to securing the modes of information exchange between the two countries. A 2016 bilateral paper provided an

---

24 See www.un.org/ga/search/view_doc.asp?symbol=A/RES/53/70.

25 Yet the object of many forms of digital insecurity.

26 See Russia–US Bilateral on critical infrastructure protection, *Working Towards Rules for Governing Cyber Conflict. Rendering the Geneva and Hague Conventions in Cyberspace*, East-West Institute, January 2011.

27 See www.bit.ly/3gOvSmQ.

update on the extent of the disputes (Working Group on the Future of US-Russia Relations 2016). Since then, no additional information has been made public and this should be seen in the context of the growing competition between the two countries, particularly in the cyber arena. For example, subsequent to the 2013 agreement, four attacks were officially attributed to Russia by the State Department (Corcoral 2019): in April 2016 (Democratic Party), March 2017 (Yahoo), February 2018 (NotPetya) and October 2018 (Democratic Party). Presumably, many other attacks have taken place[28], but the United States has made the political decision not to make them public.

1.3.3. *Discussions on cybersecurity: the symbolic international restoration of the coercive state*

Despite the initial bipolarization of the security issue, one of the effects of the 1998 Russian initiative at the United Nations was the successful multilateralization of cyber exchanges, mainly within the United Nations framework. The process began in 2001 and has continued into 2020.

	Date	GA Res.	Resolution title	Source
1	Jan. 22, 2001	Res. 55/63	*Combating the criminal misuse of information technologies*	www.bit.ly/3gOwadq
2	Jan. 22, 2002	Res. 56/121	*Combating the criminal misuse of information technologies*	www.bit.ly/3jteXYB
3	Jan. 31, 2003	Res. 57/239	Creation of a global culture of cybersecurity	www.bit.ly/3baKNq1
4	Jan. 30, 2004	Res. 58/199	Creation of a global culture of cybersecurity and protection of critical information infrastructures	www.bit.ly/2YPNdFD
5	Dec. 21, 2009	Res. 64/211	Creation of a global culture of cybersecurity and taking stock of national efforts to protect critical information infrastructures	www.bit.ly/32ze21U

Table 1.2. *United Nations General Assembly resolutions on cybersecurity*

---

28 See in particular the sites referencing attacks in real time (www.map.ipviking.com, www.map.norsecorp.com/, www.threatmap.checkpoint.com).

Two UN bodies provide the framework: the General Assembly and the Group of Governmental Experts (GGE). Resolution AG 55/63 of the UNGA, dated January 22, 2001, was the first to express the interest of all the gathered states in cyber issues, with a very clear perspective indicated in its title: "Combating the criminal misuse of information technologies". This resolution was adopted in the same form (as resolution 56/121) the following year, as can be seen in Table 1.2. In 2003, the third cyber resolution (Res. 57/239) adopted by the UNGA was based on the concept of cybersecurity: "Creation of a global culture of cybersecurity". The fourth resolution (Res. 58/199, in 2004) saw the notion of critical infrastructure put forward: "Creation of a global culture of cybersecurity and the protection of critical information infrastructures". The fifth and final resolution to be adopted (Res. 64/211, in 2009) emphasized the stocktaking in this area: "Creation of a global culture of cybersecurity and taking stock of national efforts to protect critical information infrastructures".

Over the past 10 years, the UNGA has not pronounced further on cybersecurity issues, as the debate has been moved to another forum, according to the will of the major technological powers. The debate on cybersecurity now takes place within the framework of an ad hoc and technical body, the GGE. The role of the UNGA is that of a forum and therefore addresses topics with a very broad approach. The resolutions cited in Table 1.2 are extremely brief and include very general incentives. The first GGE[29] was established by UNGA Resolution 58/32 of December 8, 2003. It should be noted that these experts were – exclusively – representatives of their governments and not of the private tech sector (as was the case at ICANN, see section 1.2.5): the GGE did not take into account the multi-stakeholder governance prescriptions on the inclusion of private actors. Thus, it is a manifestation of the arrival of states in cyber governance. This statocentric governance tool was periodically renewed between 2003 and 2017[30], but only three of these were able to agree on a common report (Table 1.3). The fifth GGE failed to produce more results, due to opposition from China, Cuba and Russia to the inclusion of self-defense and the law of armed conflict in the discussions (Delerue et al. forthcoming). Since 2015, the situation within the group, which still includes a representative of each of the five UN Security Council members, has stalled; discussions no longer lead to written outputs and the sixth GGE

29 See www.bit.ly/34NoJR1.
30 A sixth GGE was established in December 2018.

concluded in failure. Noting this, Russia has decided to use the UNGA to create a new structure, an Open-Ended Working Group (OEWG) with a less oligarchic composition than the GGE (Laurent 2019).

GGE number	Report number	Publication date	Ref.	Author (creation date)	Memb ers	Source
1	–	2004	No report	1st GGE (2004)	15	–
2	1.	July 30, 2010	A65/201	2nd GGE (2005)	15	www.bit.ly/32ENe0b
3	2.	June 24, 2013	A68/98*	3rd GGE (2011)	15	www.bit.ly/2EHPLyP
4	3.	July 22, 2015	A70/174	4th GGE (2013)	20	www.bit.ly/3jwpyCb
5	–	2017	No report	5th GGE (2015)	–	–
6	–	–	No report	6th GGE (2018)	25	–

Table 1.3. *List of GGE reports*

Regardless of the conflictual form that relations between states on the issue of cybersecurity may have taken at the United Nations, it should be remembered that security is the foundation of states. We must therefore not only interpret state intervention in cyber matters from a realistic perspective in the sense of international relations, but also as a way of pursuing concrete objectives, such as the reduction of digital insecurity, because it makes it possible, above all, to achieve a symbolic and therefore major objective: that of reaffirming the coercive capacity of the state on an international scale.

1.4. Praxis of state coercion in cyberspace

However, coercion can only be symbolically strong if it is also strong in its practical execution. In this respect, technologically enabled states have a wide range of possibilities for coercive actions in the digital environment, as can be seen in Figure 1.5. In this third section, we will focus solely on civilian coercive actions, which are clearly distinct from the use of digital technology in armed conflict.

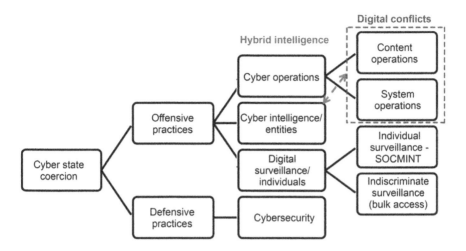

Figure 1.5. *The various forms of state coercion in cyberspace. For a color version of this figure, see www.iste.co.uk/laurent/cyberspace.zip*

1.4.1. *Intelligence and surveillance activities in the digital environment*

Among the offensive capabilities, the collection of information by states is a practice that was once within the limits of electromagnetic capabilities and which has undergone an unprecedented expansion with the worldwide growth of individual digital connectivity[31]. It has two different purposes: for individuals, this episode refers to the notion of surveillance, while for legal entities, it refers to intelligence[32].

When we seek to measure offensive cyber activity, we find disproportions of military and technological power on the global level. Whether referring to information theft – which is the concrete form of intelligence – or surveillance in the digital environment, the United States remains the leading power in these two areas. This can be explained not just by the American invention of the internet and the persistence of its domination (see section 1.2.2), but also by the fact that the United States has been able to draw on the resource constituted at the beginning of the Cold War by an international alliance protected for several decades by secrecy.

---

31 This can be evaluated from: www.internetworldstats.com.
32 Called "espionage" when analyzed from a legal point of view. See the contributions by Fabien Lafouasse and Bertrand Warusfel in this volume.

Originally called UKUSA, and more recently Five Eyes, it was formed in 1947, led by the United States, Great Britain, Canada, Australia and New Zealand. This alliance was based on electromagnetic interception capabilities and on the exchange of contents between the five allies with their worldwide geographical coverage. Its public existence has only truly been well known since 1985, thanks to the publication of a well-documented investigation carried out by two journalists[33]. Five Eyes has accompanied the transformation of ICT and became the first international network of digital content interception, thanks to the development of the internet. The alliance failed to become an international political issue in 2001 with the publication of the report of the European MEP Schmid[34]. However, it was the documents made public[35] by former National Security Agency (NSA) employee Edward Snowden[36], 12 years later, that gave Schmid's observation a much stronger dimension. Where the Schmid report mentioned suspicions and established facts that were unlikely to be disputed, the publication of thousands of classified documents held by the NSA from 2013 onward drew attention to the content and scope of surveillance practices affecting even some heads of allied states, such as Germany.

The use of digital intelligence (which some practitioners call cyber intelligence[37]) based on large-scale collection, which we will call global intelligence, is not exclusive to the United States[38]. Countries possessing sufficient technological capabilities and the will to become powerful also exercise this global intelligence, but without being able to compete with the scale of the technical resources of the Five Eyes. With the expansion of cyberspace and the transition from the analog to the digital world (Warner 2012), the intelligence services of technological powers have, in fact,

---

33 See Richelson, J. and Ball, D. (1990), *The Ties That Bind: Intelligence Cooperation Between the UK/USA Countries*, Unwin Hyman, Boston (first edition 1985).

34 That year was marked by the conclusion of the work of the German MEP Gerhard Schmid on the network (renamed "Echelon" in Europe). Schmid submitted his report in July (Schmid 2001) and the Parliament voted on September 5, 2001 for a detailed resolution establishing the economic intelligence and surveillance activities of the network, as well as a firm condemnation of its practices. The "moral shock" of the attacks in the United States less than a week later prevented the formation of an international "problem" regarding the global surveillance network, dominated by the country that had just been the subject of terrorist attacks.

35 See www.snowdenarchive.cjfe.org/greenstone/cgi-bin/library.cgi.

36 See his memoirs (Snowden 2019).

37 See Mattern *et al.* (2014) and Kalkman and Wieskamp (2019).

38 The Schmid report also clearly incriminated the United Kingdom and France.

become "sociotechnical intelligence systems" (Jackson and Laurent forthcoming), operating within networks. While the *Five Eyes* group is exceptional for its longevity and its multilateral operation, the Europeans have been able to build large-scale technical cooperations. Thus, in 1976, the informal cooperation network Maximator was created on the initiative of Denmark, joined by Sweden and Germany and extended to the Netherlands in 1978 and France in 1985 (Jacobs 2020). This network, which is still active, shares interceptions and diplomatic cryptograms and carries out bilateral cooperation within Maximator to decipher codes.

On a domestic scale, non-democratic countries routinely deploy digital surveillance measures as one of the modern forms of social and opinion control. However, across the world, contemporary digital surveillance is not limited to the means of state coercion. In countries with market economies, private actors also contribute to it. Moreover, in all countries, individuals are the actors, in their daily lives (use of applications and social networks), of what amounts to "sub-surveillance" that only partly contributes to state surveillance (Laurent 2021).

Intelligence services collect information in the software and semantic layers of the internet in search of personal data and metadata, and also the content of exchanged communications, either in a personalized or indiscriminate manner (*bulk access*) (Figure 1.5). The use of personal data and content exchanged on social networks from the 2000s onward and the emergence of the Social Web 2.0 have fostered the emergence of a new category of cyber-based intelligence, social media intelligence (SOCMINT) (Omand *et al.* 2012; Omand 2017; Dover 2020)[39], collected on social networks by domestic intelligence services for the purposes of opinion monitoring or public order (Figure 1.5). For example, in August 2011, the British Metropolitan Police became aware that they were lagging behind in this area during the Tottenham and Birmingham riots, having failed to anticipate the use of social networks, which had been the main means of spreading the violence. It has since transformed its organization by including a social network monitoring function. In Paris, which is chronically subject to demonstrations and social movements, the Police Prefecture's intelligence department is constantly monitoring social networks. For public order, police forces of all major cities have adopted this mode of surveillance, which feeds

---

39 See Omand *et al.* (2012), Omand (2017) and Dover (2020).

from sub-surveillance. SOCMINT is also used by military intelligence services in armed conflicts.

However, military operations across the Western world have, above all, given rise to the invention of new strategic concepts, entirely based on digital technologies. The United States National Geospatial Agency (NGA) thus created the concept of geographical intelligence (GEOINT) in the early 2000s, which proceeds from a fusion of all digital data intercepted on geographic media in order to facilitate the conduct of military operations (Boulanger 2016). Data integration based on the conceptual tool that is GEOINT is only effective if there is genuine processing of the large volumes of data collected. Algorithms backed by computer science occupy a predominant place and appear to represent the only prospect of progress for software solutions used in the production of intelligence. The assumed progress of artificial intelligence (AI) (Ventre 2020), combined with the growth of data volumes to be processed for intelligence services (Lim 2016; Eldridge *et al.* 2018), appears to render this old tool an indispensable part of the modern agenda.

1.4.2. *Non-military cyber operations*

A second form of offensive coercion that reflects the digital praxis of states is what is known in the United States as "cyber operations". We distinguish them from what we have discussed above, insofar as the intention is different: to destroy information, to falsify it or damage information systems over a relatively extended time perspective. Moreover, we will only deal here with offensive operations, as defensive practices appear to us to have a different purpose. Finally, we will leave aside cyber operations carried out in the context of a military conflict insofar as the intention, the legal framework and the actors are clearly different from the cyber operations discussed below, which are conducted outside armed conflict law. This being said, we find ourselves in a context in which the actors are non-military and operate outside of military conflicts, which logically leads some authors to reject the term "cyberwar" (Rid 2012) and even to evoke a "demilitarization" that would be at work in cyber conflicts (Boeke and Broeders 2018), which seems to us to be quite appropriate. In these circumstances, it should be remembered that there is no boundary between the domains of intelligence and cyber operations, as the latter is always preceded and accompanied by intelligence gathering (while the reverse is not true). It is nonetheless important, in our view, to distinguish the difference in intent between the two cases in point, the collection of information (intelligence) and the destruction of information and information systems[40] (cyber operations, see Figure 1.5).

The state organizations that implement these operations belong to very diverse administrative components, which may be military or civilian. Some may be part of the intelligence services, for example the technical directorate of the DGSE (Desforges 2019), which is responsible for conducting what is officially called offensive computer warfare in France. Others are technical agencies that, while belonging to the intelligence community, are not intelligence services in their own right, such as the NSA's Tailored Access Operation (Lolelski 2019) or the Computer Network Operations team of the British GCHQ[41]. However, what seems to us to be of primary importance within the context of this chapter is not the proximity to the intelligence structures, but the state intention which implements and which, depending on the country, is the result of the particular sociogenesis of the administrations in the field of coercion.

The United States formally and publicly adopted the term "operations" to describe all of its activities in 2006 in the *National Military Strategy for Cyberspace Operations* document (Ventre 2014a). The scope of the term appears to have been clarified by the presidency, as evidenced by Edward Snowden's 2013 release of *Presidential Policy Directive/PPD-20 on US Cyber Operations Policy* (October 16, 2012). In this document, the White House distinguished between "cyber collection (collection of intelligence in the cyberspace)", "defensive cyber effects operations (DCEO)" and "offensive cyber effects operations (OCEO)"[42]. The term "operations" allowed an element of euphemization and made it possible avoid using the terms "war" or "warfare", which had fairly rapidly become part of the public debate since the 1990s (Arquilla and Ronfeldt 1993). We also observe that the famous Tallinn Manual, directly inspired by the United States, was, in its first edition (2013), titled *Tallinn Manual on the International Law*

---

40 On analogies between intelligence and cyber operations, see Warner (2017).

41 www.gchq-careers.co.uk/departments/computer-network-operations.html.

42 In comparison, in France, since the 2008 white paper, the terms "defensive computer warfare" and "offensive computer warfare" have become commonplace in public discourse (parliamentary reports, parliamentary hearings, ministerial declarations and Ministry of Defense cyber strategies).

Applicable to Cyber Warfare and became *Tallinn Manual 2.0 on the International Law Applicable to Cyber Operations* for the 2017 edition. Academic literature now uses the term "operations"[43], which has the advantage of avoiding the effects of securitization (Balzacq 2018), which are very prevalent in cyber matters (Laurent 2021). We also note the existence of mixed systems, which associate intelligence resources for the purpose of influence and cyber attacks; this is the case, for example, with the numerous Russian operations conducted after 2016 in an attempt to influence the results of various national elections in the United States and in Europe, for which Gioe (2018) evokes the term *"hybrid intelligence"*.

1.4.3. *Interstate digital conflicts, secrecy and coercive diplomacy*

We must raise the question of the scale of the phenomenon. These operations can only be conducted under two conditions, with appropriate digital means and with the aim of exercising power, which is not the case for all states, including those with powerful technological resources. Despite the adoption of national public strategies (see section 1.3.1) and the claims by certain states of offensive capabilities (the United States, Russia, France, etc.), it is difficult to have a global view of all the states concerned. The only independent census is the one carried out in 2013 by the United Nations disarmament organization (UNIDIR). It is worth noting that this organization usually only deals with issues related to armaments, for which a very precise definition was previously accepted by all states[44].

In 2011, for reasons we have not been able to identify, UNIDIR launched a program of reflection on *"cyberwar"*[45], one of the results of which was the *Cyber Index* report. Drawing exclusively on open sources, UNIDIR's report concluded that 13 states have offensive cyber capabilities (UNIDIR 2013). This included the five permanent members of the Security Council, as well as eight others: three Asian states (North Korea, South Korea and India), three European (Germany, the Netherlands and Poland), one African (South Africa) and one Latin American (Argentina). Insofar as it is based solely on mainstream press sources, the reported number of 13 states may in fact be a

---

43 For example, in international law (Bannelier 2014) and in political science (Loleski 2019).
44 Tulliu and Schmalberger (2003). We thank Julien Ancelin for providing this reference.
45 See www.bit.ly/3bcF6aY.

very low estimate. Statistical assessments of this kind are very rare and it is also necessary to look to the states, although they do not have the constraint of neutrality and prudence of the United Nations. For example, in early 2017, Director of National Intelligence James Clapper sent a letter to the US Senate Committee arguing that 30 states have offensive capabilities (Clapper *et al.* 2017). We believe, however, that technological capabilities are not sufficient for there to be a risk of use, but that the intent to use them as a means of foreign policy must be established.

In this case, non-publicity is the custom, with states seeking in the vast majority of cases to benefit from their ability to commit damage without disclosing its origin. The fact remains that the digital field of activity offers ample opportunity for attackers, while not allowing themselves to be identified, to suggest through more or less complete digital signatures who they might be (Borghard and Lonergan 2017). In so doing, offensive cyber operations would appear to fall fully within the realm of coercive diplomacy (Laurent 2021), while benefiting from the resource of the absence of publicity. In some respects they are similar to a range of actions, covert operations, invented and implemented by the United States since the 1950s (Scott 2004). The recent evolution of covert operations, less covert than during the Cold War (Cormac and Aldrich 2018), has strong analogies with cyber operations. It could be argued that cyber operations are ultimately one of the recent manifestations of covert operations. Partial concealment, or semi-secrecy, holds strong potentialities for an actor who succeeds in controlling it, sometimes more so than total secrecy. This allows him or her to create an environment of uncertainty around his or her objective and to acquire a situation of superiority. If we take into account that the damage is symbolic and economic in nature – including when attacks are on critical civilian infrastructures – we can see how far the intention is from those at work in armed conflict.

Having mentioned the number of actors potentially involved in this manifestation of state resurgence, we believe it important to conclude by attempting to characterize the intensity of cyber operations. However, the secrecy of cyber operations has another major consequence, in that it is very difficult to establish a quantification or even an order of magnitude. We believe this to be essential, as for any insecure phenomenon, insofar as perceptions are often totally removed from reality[46]. However, it seems established that digital attacks on individuals committed by private actors (which are not in the scope of this chapter) are far more numerous – and by a long way – than those carried out by states against state interests[47]. In 2013, Valeriano and Maness conducted an extensive study covering the previous decade, in which they counted 95 cyber conflicts between 20 state actors (Valeriano and Maness 2013). Regardless of the number of states involved, Valeriano, in a 2018 book, counted 192 cyber conflicts over the period 2000–2014 (Valeriano *et al.* 2018).

A third assessment, from a think tank, found just over 500 attacks for the period 2006–2020[48]. These numbers, taken from open sources, are likely to be underestimates, since both the attacking states and their victims have a vested interest in not making the situation known, except for individual state victims. These figures may therefore be low estimates. Nevertheless, they indicate between a little over 9 and 35 numerical conflicts between states per year. From an internationalist perspective, it is not irrelevant in our view to relate this to classical conflictuality. Over the past two decades, there were between 29 and 40 armed conflicts per year[49]. However, this is not a comparison, insofar as armed conflict and digital conflict have significant differences in nature, which, in our opinion, are not yet the subject of sufficient research (Laurent 2021); moreover, we believe it essential to note the existence on this precise point of an important "epistemological obstacle", to use the words of Gaston Bachelard[50].

We must emphasize that the extent of international coercive practice reflecting interstate confrontation has profoundly transformed the original cyberspace, both in its ideology and in its collaborative practices (see section 1.2). What had been shaped by the United States as a space to extend its soft power, and for the expansion of a digital economy that it dominated,

---

46 From this point of view, a comparison could be made with the phenomena of delinquency and their perception: see the classic and very useful work by Roché (1993) and Mucchielli (2011).

47 See the opinion of a computer security expert (www.is.gd/d4DcaP).

48 See   www.csis-prod.s3.amazonaws.com/s3fs-public/200403_Significant_Cyber_Events_List. pdf?.tlmv65Bm5D0d5UVqRtac3qdYqd.BYtLj (accessed on 25 April 2020).

49 See Eriksson and Wallensteen (2004) and Pettersson and Wallensteen (2015). We leave aside here the (nevertheless crucial) question of the technical debate on the casualty thresholds used for the quantitative approach to conflict.

50 See Bachelard (1934/1967).

has become an international space in which non-military interstate conflicts are becoming commonplace.

1.5. The fragmentation of the global internet and the digital sovereignty of states

The exercise of coercion by states in cyberspace is not the only manifestation of their arrival into the sociotechnical system created by the United States. Indeed, it can also be seen that, against the backdrop of the advancement of the idea of digital sovereignty, a significant number of powerful states have attempted and succeeded in controlling the network, and even appropriating it for themselves, by isolating it from cyberspace and challenging the idea of a global network. The term "cyberbalkans" had been raised at MIT, one of the most prestigious research universities in the United States, as early as 1997 in anticipation – very early on – of the expansion of the internet; this piece of language gained momentum around 2013–2014 when it was taken up by internet pioneers, such as Berners-Lee, Cerf and even Kahn (Alves 2014).

1.5.1. *Linguistic balkanization: Digital Babel*

Designed by the United States for a global world that could only be English-speaking, the internet had to necessarily be "united" and "unified"; that is to say, an internet based on tools (notably search engines) and content in English. However, we can see that the share of the English-speaking internet is constantly shrinking: there is an undeniable first level of balkanization, operating on a linguistic level. Indeed, we are witnessing a reduction in the number of English-speaking internet users: from 50% in 2001, there were only 25% in 2011 and 7.5% in 2020. The ability, since 2005, to create domain names in languages other than English, including for non-Western alphabets by being able to use ideograms, has played a large part in the emancipation from English. The following graph, taken from Internet World Stats, shows the effect of this linguistic evolution in 2020. Contrary to popular belief, the English-speaking, Western internet is now in the minority, given that some users in Europe use the Cyrillic alphabet. Although English has become the *lingua franca* in business and everyday life, it is not as widespread as it is believed to be on the internet.

Regions of the world	Number of internet users as of May 31, 2020	Penetration rate (% pop.)	Growth between 2000 and 2020	Proportion in relation to to the world
Africa	526,710,313	39.3%	11.567%	11.3%
Asia	2,366,213,308	55.1%	1.970%	50.9%
Europe	727,848,547	87.2%	592%	15.7%
Latin America/ Caribbean	453,702,292	68.9%	2.411%	10%
Middle East	183,212,099	70.2%	5.477%	3.9%
North America	348,908,868	94.6%	223%	7.5%
Oceania/Australia	28,917,600	67.7%	279%	0.6%

Table 1.4. *Geographic origin of internet users (2020)*
(source: www.internetworldstats.com/stats.htm)

It is also necessary to evaluate the linguistic evolution of the global internet. The connectivity rates indicated by Internet World Stats (see Figure 1.6) enable us to see the high rates of progression by continent and linguistic area.

The three English-speaking continents are three-quarters connected to the internet. North America, which is almost totally English-speaking (despite the presence of nearly 20% Hispanics in the United States, who are largely bilingual), has almost reached its maximum. Moreover, as we have written above, Europe is only partially English-speaking in its use of the internet. Moreover, with 53.6% of connectivity in Asia, the Chinese-speaking internet has a strong margin for growth. This will necessarily continue to accelerate the decline of the English-speaking internet. Moreover, we should not forget the considerable digital importance of the Chinese diaspora and China's soft power. The Chinese-speaking internet extends far beyond the Chinese territory. Finally, the Mesoamerican and Latin American space has a penetration rate of 70%, which allows for a progression of either a Spanish- or Portuguese-speaking internet if the subcontinent wishes to rid itself of North American tools.

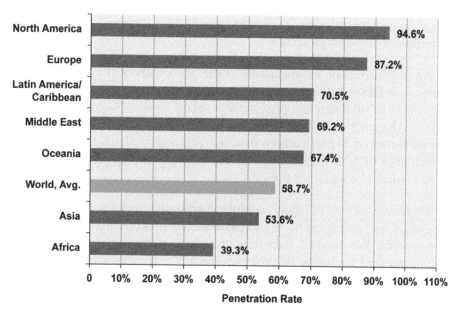

Figure 1.6. *Internet penetration rates (2020)*
(source: www.internetworldstats.com/stats.htm)

1.5.2. Political fragmentation: alternative internets

Many international organizations have identified what they consider to be political fragmentation (WEF 2016). This has often been measured, by the Davos Forum (WEF 2016) or by ISOC (2020), for instance, against the original vision of a free and open internet (see section 1.2.4). From this point of view, both the technical practices of filtering and censoring content and their legal frameworks are relevant.

Since the 2010s, some states have adopted their own data localization legislation for various cumulative reasons, as symbolic aspects of sovereignty, and also for the purpose of personal data protection and for economic reasons. These measures have been termed "data nationalism" (Chander and Lê 2015) or "protectionism" (Mishra 2016). These laws may be global and concern all data, which is mainly the case in non-democratic regimes (China, Russia, etc.). On the other hand, they may be sectoral and relate to only certain types of data, notably personal data; in this regard, the 2018 European General Data Protection Regulation (GDPR) prescribes localization within the territory of the EU or in third countries that offer an equal level of protection. Currently, the EU recognizes 12 countries as providing "adequate" protection[51].

Another aspect of fragmentation is the phenomenon of content control, which is in fact not entirely new. As early as 2006, Goldsmith and Wu noted that 26 out of 40 states practiced content access control (Goldsmith and Wu 2006)[52]. Regardless of the strongly ideological vision developed by the Davos forum, it is indisputable that non-democratic states have made the surveillance of content published on the internet a central element of their public policies of social control.

Moreover, some of these countries with the technological capacity (Russia, China and Iran) have implemented legal and technical measures to circumscribe the national internet and remove it from global cyberspace, putting forward the notion of cyber sovereignty, sovereign internet or digital sovereignty. Iran started to develop a national internet from 2005, which it combines with strict control measures and temporary cuts during periods of crisis. The notion of information security, brought to the fore internationally by Russia (see section 1.3.3), has clearly guided its sovereign policies. In 2011, the Russian Federation issued a *Convention on International Information Security*[53], asserting (Art. 4) that states have sovereignty over their information space, which was a direct challenge to the US "free flow of information" principle. The principle of information sovereignty was also at the heart of the *International Code of Conduct for Information Security*[54], presented to the UN a week before the previous document by Russia, China, Tajikistan and Uzbekistan, under the Shanghai Cooperation Organization (SCO). Russia then went a step further by intervening in the cybersphere core; in 2019; legislation for a safe and sustainable internet was passed with the stated ambition to have an autonomous national DNS registry, not managed by ICANN, by 2021. This legislation requires Russian sites to register with the national registry. China has made digital sovereignty (Creemers 2020) the core of its digital policy, prescribing the territorialization of data and the use of national encryption and cybersecurity resources.

---

51 See   www.ec.europa.eu/info/law/law-topic/data-protection/international-dimension-data-protection/adequacy-decisions_en.

52 Unfortunately, these two authors did not specify their criteria.

53 www.bit.ly/3hHsB9T.

54 www.bit.ly/2YOElQG.

Yet other countries, even those with lower technological capacities, have managed, in times of crisis, such as during the Arab Spring (2011), to temporarily interrupt their connection to the global internet. The old ideology of the free flow of information, which was reactivated and associated with cyber during Hillary Clinton's term as Secretary of State (2009–2013), found an additional limitation. However, despite the arrival of states in cyberspace, the United States has continued to develop a version of a unified internet, even to the point of developing a hyperliberal and libertarian vision assimilating normative provisions with fragmentation (Force Hill 2012)[55]. This vision, which dominates and informs US behavior toward the cyber and digital challenge, appears increasingly atypical and unique, as national cyber policies have steadily gained prominence (see section 1.3.1). On a discursive level, the claim of the notion of digital sovereignty (Türk and Vallar 2017) by democracies (and not only in authoritarian regimes) at international conferences, starting with the Dubai conference (2012), would appear to be a major step, regardless of the debate on whether it is (or is not) an oxymoron.

1.6. The strong constraint of interstate cooperation for all states

The arrival in force of states in cyberspace has largely undermined the US project for the globalized internet. The numerous offensive state actions, the martial discourses and the claims of sovereignty have not, however, led to the "state-ization" of cyberspace. The distributed nature of the system remains prevalent, despite national internets, and states find themselves obliged to cooperate in order to establish minimum standards and ensure the security of cyberspace on a permanent basis.

1.6.1. Interstate agreements on an embryo of international law

The Council of Europe was the first international body to have successfully supported an international treaty for the digital environment. In 1981, Convention 108 laid down the basic rules for the protection of data of individuals (Laurent 2019); signed in 1981 by 10 of the states belonging to the Council of Europe's legal space, all 47 member states and 8

---

55 Many American think tanks are developing indicators of internet freedom in the same spirit as the Davos Forum, equating any form of legislation on content with censorship (www.freedomhouse.org, www.opennet.net, etc.).

non-member states (from Africa and Latin America) have since ratified it, for a total of 55 states[56]. This initial text remained isolated for a long time. However, over the last 20 years, international law applicable to cyberspace has evolved profoundly. Its foundation is the Council of Europe's Convention 185, known as the Budapest Convention, on cybercrime. This international treaty provided for penal harmonization and cooperation between the signatory states. As of July 16, 2020, the convention has been ratified by about one-third of the states (65 in this case), 44 member states of the Council of Europe and also 21 non-members[57].

Despite its deficient record in terms of cybersecurity norms (see section 1.3.3), the GGE's work at the United Nations has also produced a major advance in terms of international law. In 2013, the report of the second GGE[58] endorsed the principle of the applicability of public international law to the digital environment, which in fact distanced itself from ideas in favor of the constitution of a specific law. It is important to note that, of the 15 countries represented at this second GGE, the five permanent members of the Security Council were present, who thus endorsed this major change in principle. Another important text illustrates the result of cooperation in legal matters: the general regulation on personal data, which was adopted in 2016 and came into force in 2018 in the 28 countries of the European Union.

1.6.2. *State dependence on international cooperation for cybersecurity*

The coercive capacity of the state also takes the defensive form of cybersecurity (see Figure 1.5). However, the distributed architecture of cyberspace, despite the effects of political fragmentation that tends to create isolates of centralized architectures, makes the exercise of cybersecurity a primarily cooperative task on an international scale, which brings it closer to the activity of contemporary intelligence agencies (Jackson and Laurent forthcoming). In 1990, the FIRST Forum was created, the international CSIRT/CERT[59] network, ensuring the permanent management of all cyber incidents. The reticular form is essential, given the ubiquitous nature of

---

56 www.coe.int/en/web/conventions/full-list/-/conventions/treaty/108/signatures.

57 www.coe.int/en/web/conventions/full-list/-/conventions/treaty/185/signatures.

58 www.un.org/ga/search/view_doc.asp?symbol=A/68/98.

59 Computer Security Incident Response Team (CSIRT)/Computer Emergency Response Team (CERT).

digital flows and international cybersecurity practices, which rely primarily on the members of FIRST, whose number has been growing steadily and will reach 535 by 2020[60]. CSIRTs and CERTs ensure the reporting of digital incidents between each other and rely mainly on information exchange, leading experts to refer to them as "trust infrastructures" (Skierka *et al.* 2015). It is important to note that CSIRTs and CERTs very often come from the private sector (Kalkman and Wieskamp 2019); thus, the protection of critical infrastructures[61] that the state safeguards in the name of national security is partly dependent on the information provided by private structures.

The cooperation to which the state is bound in the area of cybersecurity is not limited to private actors on its territory. Both the national and public CSIRTs and CERTs must cooperate with their foreign counterparts – both public and private – on an ongoing basis.

1.7. Conclusion

Contrary to the book by Goldsmith and Wu in 2006, there was no return of the states, but rather (apart from the United States) a late discovery in the 2000s and an immediate, massive discursive and practical investment on the part of the new converts. We wanted to show that the internet, including its globalized dimension, was an invention and an undertaking of the United States in order to establish its *soft power* and to reinforce its economic domination (section 1.2). This project was entirely transformed by the arrival of states, which dismantled it and turned the original free, open and collaborative system into a standardized, controlled and conflictual space through their interactions (sections 1.3, 1.4 and 1.5). However, as non-US liberal and authoritarian visions clash, there has not been – except in China, North Korea and Iran – a generalization of the national digital space model, and states (including authoritarian ones) are forced into minimal normative and extensive technical cooperation (section 1.6). The clearest result of this development is the apparent weakening of a global resource for the United States that was conceived and implemented by them in the 1990s. However, we should beware of optical illusions: while alternative Asian internets[62]

---

60 www.first.org/members/teams (accessed on 16 July 2020).
61 Except for the United States and the United Kingdom (Carr 2016), critical infrastructure is predominantly public.
62 Including Russia.

have managed to escape the American grip, the rest of the world is still largely under the influence of a *cybersphere core* dominated by the United States and its digital industry.

1.8. References

Alves Jr., S. (2014). Internet governance 2.0.1.4: The internet balkanization fragmentation [Online]. Available at: www.is.gd/vPuZHj [Accessed 17 April 2020].

Arquilla, J. and Ronfeldt, D. (1993). Cyberwar is Coming! *Comparative Strategy*, Spring, 12(2), 141–165.

Bachelard, G. (1934/1967). *La Formation de l'esprit scientifique. Contribution à une psychanalyse de la connaissance objective*. Vrin, Paris.

Balzacq, T. (2018). Théories de la sécuritisation, 1989–2018. *Études internationales*, 49(1), 7–24.

Bannelier, K. (2014). Cyber-diligence: A low-intensity due diligence principle for low-intensity cyber-operations. *Baltic Yearbook of International Law*, 14, 23–39.

Baran, P. (1962). *On Distributed Communications Network*. Rand, Santa Monica.

Bessone, M. (2011). Culte de l'Internet et transparence : l'héritage de la philosophie américaine. *Esprit*, 376(7), 145–159.

Boeke, S. and Broeders, D. (2018). The demilitarization of cyber conflict. *Survival*, 60, 73–90.

Borghard, E.D. and Lonergan, S.W. (2017). The logic of coercion in cyberspace. *Security Studies*, 26(3), 452–481.

Boulanger, P. (2016). De la géographie militaire au Geospatial Intelligence. *Bulletin de la société de géographie*, Paris, 153–167.

Cardon, D. (2010). *La démocratie Internet. Promesses et limites*. Le Seuil, Paris.

Carr, M. (2016). Public–private partnerships in national cyber-security strategies. *International Affairs*, 92(1), 43–62.

Castells, M. (2001). *La Galaxie Internet*. Fayard, Paris.

Cath, C. and Floridi, L. (2017). The design of the internet's architecture by the Internet Engineering Task Force (IETF) and human rights. *Science and Engineering Ethics*, 23(2), 449–468.

Chander, A. and Lê, U.P. (2015). Data nationalism. *Emory Law Journal*, 64(1), 677–739.

Clapper, J., Marcel, L., Rogers, M.S. (2017). Joint statement for the record to the Senate Armed Services Committee. Foreign cyber threats to the United States, January 5 [Online]. Available at: www.bit.ly/3b76CXC [Accessed 18 February 2020].

Cohen, S. (2005). Les États face aux nouveaux acteurs. *Politique internationale*, 108, 409–424.

Corcoral, M. (2019). L'attribution publique des cyberattaques : sociologie d'une politique déclaratoire américaine. Thesis, Sciences-Po, Paris.

Cormac, R. and Aldrich, R.J. (2018). Grey is the new black: Covert action and implausible deniability. *International Affairs*, 94, 477–494.

Creemers, R. (2020). Comment la Chine projette de devenir une cyberpuissance. *Hérodote. Revue de géographie et de géopolitique*, 177–178, 297–311.

Delerue, F., Douzet, F., Géry, A. (2021). Le droit international et les normes de comportement : entre ambiguïtés et instrumentalisation à des fins géopolitiques. *Études internationales*.

DeNardis, L. (2016). Governance by infrastructure. In *The Turn to Infrastructure in Internet Governance*, Cogburn, D.L., DeNardis, L., Levinson, N.S., Musiani, F. (eds). Springer, New York.

DeNardis, L. and Raymond, M. (2013). Thinking clearly about multistakeholder internet governance. *8th Annual GigaNet Symposium* [Online]. Available at: https://ssrn.com/abstract=2354377 or http://dx.doi.org/10.2139/ssrn.2354377.

Der Derian, J. (2003). The question of information technology in international relations. *Millenium. Journal of International Studies*, 32(3), 441–456.

Desforges, A. (2018). Approche géopolitique du cyberespace, enjeux pour la défense et la sécurité nationale, l'exemple de la France. PhD Thesis, University Paris 8, Paris.

Domingo, F.C. (2016). China's engagement in cyberspace. *Journal of Asian Security and International Affairs*, 3(2), 245–269.

Dover, R. (2020). SOCMINT: A shifting balance of opportunity. *Intelligence and National Security*, 35(2), 216–232.

Drake, W.J. (2008). Introduction: The distributed architecture of network global governance. In *Governing Global Electronic Networks: International Perspectives on Policy and Power*, Drake, W.J., Wilson, E.J. III (eds). MIT Press, Cambridge.

Drezner, D.W. (2004). The global governance of the internet. Bringing the state back in. *Political Science Quarterly*, 119(3), 477–498.

Eldridge, C., Hobbs, C., Moran, M. (2018). Fusing algorithms and analysts: Open-source intelligence in the age of "Big Data". *Intelligence and National Security*, 33(3), 391–406.

Eriksson, M. and Wallensteen, P. (2004). Armed conflict, 1989–2003. *Journal of Peace Research*, 41, 625–636.

Fleury, G. (2008). Internet comme vecteur de pouvoir. *Études internationales*, 39(1), 83–104.

Florimond, G. (2016). *Droit et Internet : de la logique internationaliste à la logique réaliste*. Mare et Martin, Paris.

Force Hill, J. (2012). Internet Fragmentation. Highlighting the Major Technical, Governance and Diplomatic Challenges for US Policy Makers. John F. Kennedy School of Government, Harvard.

Frau-Meigs, D., Nicey, J., Palmer, M., Pohle, J., Tupper P. (eds) (2012). *From NWICO to WSIS: 30 Years of Communication Geopolitics. Actors and Flows, Structures and Divides*, Intellect, Bristol.

Froomkin, M. (2011). Almost Free: An analysis of ICANN's "Affirmation of Commitments". *Journal of Telecommunications and High Technology Law*, 9(2011-01), University of Miami, Department of Legal Studies [Online]. Available at: www.ssrn.com/abstract=1744086.

Gioe, D.V. (2018). Cyber operations and useful fools: The approach of Russian hybrid intelligence. *Intelligence and National Security*, 33(7), 954–973.

Goldsmith, J. and Wu, T. (2008). *Illusions of a Borderless World*. Oxford University Press, Oxford.

Griset, P. (1991). *Les Révolutions de la communication : XIXᵉ–XXᵉ siècles*. Hachette, Paris.

Halpern, C. (2013). Politiques publiques internationales : penser les échelles de la régulation politique. In *Relations internationales. Bilan et perspectives*, Battistella, D. (ed.). Ellipses, Paris.

Headrick, D.R. (1991). *The Invisible Weapon. Telecommunications and International Politics, 1851–1945*. Oxford University Press, Oxford.

ISOC (2020). Internet Way of Networking Use Case. Data Localization [Online]. Available at : www.urlz.fr/egB5.

Jackson, P. and Laurent, S.-Y. (forthcoming). *The Rise of Modern Intelligence.* Bloomsbury, London.

Jacobs, B. (2020). Maximator: European signals intelligence cooperation, from a Dutch perspective. *Intelligence and National Security*, 35(5), 659–668.

Kalkman, J.P. and Wieskamp, L. (2019). Cyber intelligence networks: A typology. *The International Journal of Intelligence, Security, and Public Affairs*, 21(1), 4–24.

Keohane, R.O. and Nye Jr., J.S. (1998). Power and interdependence in the information age. *Foreign Affairs*, 77(5), 81–94.

Krasner, S.D. (1999). *Sovereignty: Organized Hypocrisy.* Princeton University Press, Princeton.

Kurbalija, J. (2008/2012). *An Introduction to Internet Governance.* Diplo Foundation, Geneva.

Lakel, A. and Massit-Folléa, F. (2007). Société civile et gouvernance de l'Internet : la construction d'une légitimité ambigüe. *Hermès. La Revue*, 1(47), 167–176.

Laurent, S.-Y. (2015). Finding a Strategic Horizon in the Cyberenvironment. Presentation, Cyberdefence and Cybersecurity, Saint-Cyr/Sogeti/Thales Chair.

Laurent, S.-Y. (2019). Les gouvernances mondiales fragmentées de l'Internet. Research report, University of Bordeaux, Bordeaux.

Laurent, S.-Y. (2021). Ce que le Cyber (ne) fait (pas) aux Relations internationales. *Études internationales.*

Lim, K. (2016). Big Data and strategic intelligence. *Intelligence and National Security*, 31(4), 619–635.

Lolelski, S. (2019). From cold to cyber warriors: The origins and expansion of NSA's Tailored Access Operations (TAO) to shadow brokers. *Intelligence and National Security*, 34(1), 112–128.

Loveluck, B. (2015). *Réseaux, libertés et contrôle. Une généalogie politique d'Internet.* Armand Colin, Paris.

Luiijf, E., Besseling, K., de Graaf, P. (2013). Nineteen national cyber security strategies. *International Journal of Critical Infrastructures*, 9(1–2), 3–31.

Mattern, T., Felker, J., Borum, R., Bamford, G. (2014). Operational levels of cyber intelligence. *International Journal of Intelligence and CounterIntelligence*, 27(4), 702–719.

Maurer, T. (2011). *Norm Emergence at the United Nations. An Analysis of the UN's Activities Regarding Cyber-security*. Belfer Center, Harvard Kennedy School, Cambridge.

McCarthy, D.R. (2017). *Technology and World Politics. An Introduction*. Routledge, London and New York.

Mucchielli, L. (2011). *L'Invention de la violence. Des peurs, des chiffres, des faits*. Fayard, Paris.

Mueller, M.L. (2010). *Networks and States: The Global Politics of Internet Governance*. MIT Press, Cambridge.

Musiani, F. (2018). L'invisible qui façonne. Études d'infrastructure et gouvernance d'Internet. *Tracés. Revue de sciences humaines*, 35, 161–176.

Neha, M. (2016). Data localization laws in a digital world. *The Public Sphere Journal*, 135–158.

Nocetti, J. (2015). Contest and conquest: Russia and global internet governance. *International Affairs*, 91(1), 111–130.

Omand, D. (2017). Social Media Intelligence (SOCMINT). In *The Palgrave Handbook of Security, Risk and Intelligence*, Dover, R., Dylan, H., Goodman, M.S. (eds). Palgrave Macmillan, London.

Omand, D., Bartlett, J., Miller, C. (2012). Introducing Social Media Intelligence (SOCMINT). *Intelligence and National Security*, 27(6), 809–823.

Panagiotou, R. (2011). The centrality of the United Nations in Russian foreign policy. *Journal of Communist Studies and Transition Politics*, 27(2), 195–216.

Petiteville, F. and Smith, A. (2006). Analyser les politiques publiques internationales. *Revue française de science politique*, 56, 357–366.

Pettersson, T. and Wallensteen, P. (2015). Armed conflicts: 1946–2014. *Journal of Peace Research*, 52(4), 536–550.

Raustalia, K. (2016). Governing the internet. *American Journal of International Law*, 110(3), 491–503.

Rid, T. (2012). Cyberwar will not take place. *Journal of Strategic Studies*, 35(1), 5–32.

Roché, S. (1993). *Le sentiment d'insécurité*. PUF, Paris.

Russell, A.L. (2014). *Open Standards and the Digital Age: History, Ideology, and Networks*. Cambridge University Press, Cambridge.

Schafer, V. and Thierry, B. (2013). Qui a inventé Internet ? Une vraie "fausse question". *Le Temps des médias*, 20, 223–235.

Schmid, G. (2001). Rapport sur l'existence d'un système d'interception mondial des communications privées et économiques, système d'interception ÉCHELON (2001/2098) (INI). Report A5-0264/2001, European Parliament, July 11.

Schmitt, O. (2019). How to challenge an international order: Russian diplomatic practices in multilateral security organisations. *European Journal of International Relations*, 1–25.

Scott, L. (2004). Secret intelligence, covert action and clandestine diplomacy. In *Understanding Intelligence in the Twenty-First Century. Journeys in Shadows*, Scott, L., Jackson, P. (eds). Routledge, London and New York.

Shahin, J. and Finger, M. (2008). *ICANN'S GAC and the Global Governance of the Internet: The Role of the EU in Bringing "Government" Back to Internet Governance*. Global Internet Governance Academic Network (GigaNet), Hyderabad.

Simmel, G. (1908). *Secret et sociétés secrètes*. Circé-Poche, Strasbourg.

Simmel, G. (1908/2013). *Sociologie, études sur les formes de la socialisation*. PUF, Paris.

Skierka, I., Morgus, R., Hohmann, M., Maurer, T. (2015). CSIRT Basics for Policy-Makers. Working paper [Online]. Available at: https://www.researchgate. net/publication/323358187_CSIRT_Basics_for_Policy-Makers.

Smith, A. (2013). L'analyse des politiques publiques. In *Traité de relations internationales*, Balzacq, T., Ramel, F. (eds). Presses de Sciences Po, Paris.

Snowden, E. (2019). *Permanent Record*. Metropolitan Books, New York.

Steel, C. and Stein, A.A. (2002). Communications revolutions and international relations. In *Technology, Development and Democracy: International Conflict and Cooperation in the Information Age*, Allison, J.E. (ed.). New York State University Press, Albany.

Strange, S. (1996). *The Retreat of the State: The Diffusion of Power in the World Economy*. Cambridge University Press, Cambridge.

Tréguer, F. (2019). *L'Utopie déchue. Une contre-histoire d'Internet XVe-XXIe siècle*. Fayard, Paris.

Tulliu, S. and Schmalberger, T. (2003). *Les Termes de la sécurité : un lexique pour la maîtrise des armements, le désarmement et l'instauration de la confiance*. UNIDIR Publications, Geneva.

Türk, P. and Vallar, C. (2017). *La Souveraineté numérique. Le concept, les enjeux*. Mare et Martin, Paris.

UNIDIR (2013). The Cyber Index. International Security Trends and Realities. United Nations, New York and Geneva.

Valeriano, B. and Maness, R. (2013). The dynamics of cyber conflict between rival antagonists, 2001–2011 [Online]. Available at: www.ssrn.com/abstract =2214332 [Accessed 17 May 2020].

Valeriano, B., Jensen, B., Maness, R. (2018). *Cyber Strategy. The Evolving Character of Power and Coercion*. Oxford University Press, Oxford.

Van Eeten, M. and Mueller, M. (2012). Where is the governance in internet governance? *New Media & Society*, 15(5), 1–17.

Ventre, D. (2014a). Impact de la cyberguerre sur les conflits armés. PhD Thesis, University of Versailles Saint-Quentin, Versailles.

Ventre, D. (ed.) (2014b). *Chinese Cybersecurity and Defense*. ISTE Ltd, London, and Wiley, New York.

Ventre, D. (2020). *Artificial Intelligence, Cybersecurity and Cyber Defense*. ISTE Ltd, London, and Wiley, New York.

Warner, M. (2012). Reflections on technology and intelligence systems. *Intelligence and National Security*, 27(1), 133–153.

Warner, M. (2017). Intelligence in cyber and cyber in intelligence. In *Understanding Cyber Conflict. 14 Analogies*, Perkovich, G., Levite, A.E. (eds). Georgetown University Press, Washington.

Working Group on the Future of US-Russia Relations (2016). Toward US-Russia Bilateral Cooperation in the Sphere of Cybersecurity. Working group paper 7, Working Group on the Future of US-Russia Relations.

World Economic Forum (2016). Internet Fragmentation: An Overview. Report, WEF.

Wu, T. (2003). Network neutrality, broadband discrimination. *Journal of Telecommunications and High Technology Law*, 2, 141–178.

Cybersecurity in America: The US National Security Apparatus and Cyber Conflict Management

2.1. Introduction

Although cyber issues have become increasingly important in international security debates over the past decade, much remains unknown about how they are perceived, interpreted and managed by states. In the United States, a major player in the field since the first cyber policies of the mid-1980s, there has been a marked tendency in the literature on national security to adapt or recycle old notions, essentially inherited from the Cold War era and from classical theories of international relations. In recent years, we have thus seen a proliferation in American security debates of ideas and concepts such as "cyberpower" (Betz and Stevens 2011), "cyber deterrence" (Libicki 2009; Nye 2017) and even "cyber security dilemma" (Buchanan 2016). Struggling with a new phenomenon disrupting the international system, the US national security literature seems to seek to integrate the "cyber revolution" into preexisting theories the same way it once integrated the "nuclear revolution" (Kello 2017).

In so doing, such research tends to ignore some important underlying dynamics in understanding cyber conflict. As we witness the emergence of different national conceptions, priorities and strategic cultures regarding the cyber domain (Williams 2019), how do we explain their respective genesis

Chapter written by Frédérick GAGNON and Alexis RAPIN.

and what importance should be given to these disparities? How do states construct their "national interest" in the cyber domain and on the basis of what logic do they defend it? Do they actually do so in a rational manner, or do we witness clear contradictions and suboptimal choices in the way they manage cyber conflict? If one intends to address these questions, it seems essential to also pay attention to the internal dynamics of each state.

In this chapter, we propose to use *foreign policy analysis (FPA[1])* approaches in order to examine state decision-making processes on cyber issues. Inspired by the research of scholars such as Graham Allison (Allison and Zelikow 1999), Morton Halperin (Halperin and Clapp 2006), Valerie Hudson (Hudson 2005) and Amy Zegart (Zegart 2000), our approach aims to shed light on how the United States, at the domestic level, perceives and understands cyber issues and how decisions and policies in this area are elaborated. This method mostly rejects the notion of the unitary state as a central unit of analysis, and rather focuses on the role played by (among others) institutions, organizations and individuals in the formulation of foreign policy. More broadly, such an approach suggests that by focusing on agents, that is to say, the producers of foreign policy, it is possible to better understand why and how they think and act differently from one another – thus rendering any rational explanation of state behavior invalid and unpredictable (David and Rapin 2018).

Using the United States as a case study, this chapter aims to demonstrate how and why cyber conflict management by a state is often distorted and affected by different societal and institutional dynamics, issues of organizational culture and bureaucratic rivalries, as well as disparities in the dispositions and personal positioning of key decision-makers. On the basis of three levels of analysis (societal and institutional, governmental-bureaucratic and governmental-individual), this research will shed light on the mechanisms of competition, negotiation and integration of the different political, corporate and personal agendas that stir up the decision-making

---

1 As an "internationalist" counterpart to policy studies (in the English-speaking world) or public policy analysis (in the Francophone world), foreign policy analysis (FPA) is a field of research that emerged in the second half of the 1950s in the United States. Historically, the birth of FPA is often attributed to a scholarly desire to challenge the dominant paradigms of international relations, a field to which it has remained *de facto* attached ever since. Similar to public policy analysis, FPA aims to be a sociology of state action, but focuses on the internal factors explaining states' external actions in international relations. For a detailed discussion of FPA as a field, see Boucher and Barthe (2018).

process in the cyber domain. From the first policy document adopted by the United States on cyber issues (the *National Policy on Telecommunications and Automated Information Systems Security*, signed by Ronald Reagan in 1984) to the elevation of the US Cyber Command to the rank of unified combatant command in 2018, this chapter draws on various key moments in US cyber decision-making[2]. In so doing, we illustrate how domestic factors give rise to numerous contradictions and dysfunctions in the way the US national security apparatus understands and manages cyber conflict.

2.2. Societal and institutional dynamics

A first set of factors affecting cyber conflict management in the United States unfolds at the societal and institutional levels (for a theoretical overview of these issues, see Halperin and Clapp (2006)). These factors are essentially based on economic, cultural and legislative imperatives and stem from the role played by the private sector, US states and the legislative branch in decision-making on cyber issues. We show here that these factors often contribute to slowing down or constraining federal government decision-making and may occasionally generate suboptimal choices in matters of cybersecurity. At least three significant dynamics can be identified in this regard.

First, cyber issues directly affect the activities of the private sector and are thus subjected to significant efforts by companies (particularly those in the communications technology industry) to prevent the emergence of regulations that may restrict their activities[3]. Through public–private consultation processes, and also through important lobbying channels within the US political system, the private sector has repeatedly shown itself capable of curbing or reshaping various cybersecurity-related measures discussed in Washington. This is particularly true of critical infrastructure protection, which successive administrations have tried to bolster since the mid-1990s, without succeeding in introducing legal cybersecurity standards outside the public sector (Kaplan 2016, pp. 97–101, 275–278). This is despite the fact that cyberattacks on electrical or financial infrastructures are

---

2 See Chapter 9, which discusses the subject from a different perspective than ours.
3 See Chapter 9.

regularly cited as a major threat by US national security actors (Latiff 2018, pp. 3–4).

According to Richard Clarke, former "cybersecurity czar" under Bill Clinton, this inertia is in good part due to the importance of campaign donations in the US political process, as well as the impacts of the "revolving door" phenomenon[4] within the government workforce, which both grant a major influence on cyber policy-making to the private sector. In this respect, he recounts an enlightening anecdote that occurred in 2002 involving himself and President George W. Bush, whom he was advising at the time:

> I had gone to him in the Oval Office with news of a discovery of a pervasive flaw in software, a flaw that would allow hackers to run amok unless we could quietly persuade most major networks and corporations to fix the flaw. Bush's only reaction was: "What does John think?" John was the CEO of a large information technology company and a major donor to the Bush election committee. (Clarke and Knake 2010, pp. 106–110, 263)

In a similar manner, Amy Zegart and Michael Morell (former Deputy Director of the CIA) also note the impacts of the privatization of security within the US government apparatus: "embedded contractors" working within intelligence agencies, for example, frequently tend to prevent or stifle the adoption of new computer programs and systems when these have not been developed by their own companies (Zegart and Morell 2019, p. 92). In other words, despite relatively clear national security imperatives, the private sector regularly succeeds in pushing its profitability and competitiveness priorities into the decision-making process on cyber issues.

Second, because of the decentralized nature of the American political system, there are also important mismatches in the distribution of prerogatives – and therefore resources – between federal and sub-federal authorities (states, counties, etc.) regarding cybersecurity. Richard Andres notes a persistent tendency to recreate and maintain, with respect to cyber issues, the same federal-state organization designed in the past to manage more traditional security issues, thus failing to take into account the

---

4 The revolving door phenomenon describes the back-and-forth movement of personnel between the civil service and the private sector in the United States as administrations change.

particularities and constraints specific to the domain (Andres 2012, pp. 91–92). This has resulted in a number of gaps in capacity and expertise at the state level, where states manage various critical systems and infrastructure (such as electricity or water grids) but are not always equipped to ensure their integrity (Cohen and Nussbaum 2018). A wave of cyber intrusions in 2019 on various power infrastructures in the central and western United States suggests that hackers (suspected of acting on behalf of adversary powers) deliberately targeted small, locally managed facilities, banking on the fact that they would be poorly defended (Smith and Barry 2019).

In addition to this institutional immobility, there are various resistances of a more ideological nature on the part of states to certain federal initiatives. American states, traditionally suspicious of an overly centralized government, tend to forcefully defend their prerogatives against "Washington overreach". This dynamic largely extends to the sphere of national security, where threats highlighted by the federal government are often perceived (and denounced) by states as excuses to legitimize an undue takeover. In cybersecurity, this dynamic was most notably seen in the context of the Russian interference in the 2016 presidential election. Managed on a state-by-state basis, election systems and infrastructure were a cause of serious concern for the Department of Homeland Security (DHS), which feared that voting systems may be subject to hacking. The DHS offered assistance to local election authorities to prevent intrusions, but was starkly rebuffed by several suspicious states (Sanger 2018, pp. 220–221). Georgia's Republican governor, Brian Kemp, went so far as to publicly accuse Washington of wanting to "federalize elections under the guise of security" (Geller 2016). It was later discovered that at least 21 states had had their election systems "visited" without their knowledge by foreign-based hackers (US Senate 2019), further fueling speculations about the integrity of the presidential election. Although avoidable, the incident does not appear to have prompted any significant reform in the management of such risks between federal and state authorities. Three years later, Michael Hayden, former Director of the NSA and then the CIA, lamented the lack of efforts to "cut through the thicket of American federalism to improve the security of state voter rolls and actual election tallies" (Hayden 2018, p. 237). In this case as well, despite a relatively clear cyber threat identified by federal authorities, the weight of domestic political factors generated institutional inertia, ultimately producing a suboptimal response to an act of cyber conflict.

Finally, a third institutional dynamic, circumscribed at the federal level, is rooted in the role of the legislative branch in matters of national security, as well as in partisan rivalries affecting the United States Congress. In the domain of legislative actions, on the one hand, the cross-cutting nature of cyber issues has resulted in a multiplication of decision-making centers. In 2019, one member of the House of Representatives noted that nearly 80 committees and subcommittees claimed jurisdiction over cybersecurity, making the passage of cybersecurity legislation excessively slow and tedious (Corrigan 2019). Yet, legislative institutions seem to be resisting any attempt to further centralize cyber prerogatives for the time being, with the last such initiative breaking down in the Senate in 2017. Kate Charlet thus observes: "No congressional body has the full picture of federal cybersecurity measures, and [...] legislative requirements are spread across many bills, making it more complicated for federal agencies to adapt to threats or adopt new approaches" (Charlet 2018, pp. 17–18). Just like US states, legislative entities jealously defend their turf, ultimately making cybersecurity imperatives subject to the turmoil of institutional rivalries.

In addition to this legislative dysfunction, the extreme partisan polarization afflicting the US Congress represents another significant obstacle to passing the legislations and budgets needed to implement US cybersecurity strategies. Indicators for measuring polarization in Congress (including the DW-Nominate) illustrate that polarization has steadily increased in the House and Senate in recent years (Theriault 2013; Theriault and Edwards 2019). While Congress tends to be less polarized on national security than domestic policy issues (Lindsay 1994), Russian interference in the 2016 US election nonetheless sharpened partisan fault lines on cyber issues. Democrats, on the one hand, gave considerable visibility to the issue of alleged "collusion" by Donald Trump's campaign team with Moscow, preventing a substantive debate on the (less controversial) issues of the hacking of the Democratic National Committee and Russia's internet disinformation campaign (Rapin 2019). Republicans, meanwhile, have continuously curbed initiatives to protect election systems, perceived as implicit challenges to their 2016 victory (Kelly 2019). While several major laws on cyber issues were successively adopted between 2014 and 2015 (such as the *Federal Information Security Modernization Act* and the *Cybersecurity Act*), these efforts to adapt the American legislative framework have slowed down considerably since 2016, particularly in the Senate. In early 2020, a study concluded that the chances of Congress passing meaningful legislation to strengthen the country's cybersecurity were low, finding that only nine bills touching on these issues (among the 300 introduced in Congress since January 2019) had been passed by lawmakers (Brumfield 2020).

2.3. Organizational and bureaucratic dynamics

A second set of domestic factors influencing the American management of cyber conflict unfolds in the administrative sphere of the American national security apparatus and is fueled by organizational cultures and bureaucratic rivalries stirring up the decision-making process (Mulford 2013). We show here how the American foreign policy community, far from functioning as a rational unitary actor, is instead agitated by competing visions and priorities regarding cyber conflict management. Decision-making in the cyber arena is thus often motivated by concerns that are not necessarily in line with national cybersecurity imperatives. Two major dynamics must be considered in this respect.

The first one resides in the frequent clashes between the organizational cultures of each US national security agency. These entities each have different perspectives, missions and priorities, which have a significant impact on how they operate. As per the celebrated Miles's Law – "Where you stand depends on where you sit" (Miles 1978) – national security organizations, when faced with a common challenge, tend to think and act in isolation, competing with each other to assert their vision of the problem and their solution (Zegart 2000). This dynamic very much extends to the cyber domain.

A first antagonism can be observed between the (offensive) priorities of the Department of Defense and the (defensive) priorities of the DHS and the FBI (Zetter 2014, pp. 143–144). In particular, the DHS, which is responsible for protecting US critical infrastructure, shows strong resistance to what it perceives to be the excessive militarization of cyber space[5] by the Department of Defense. In 2010, shortly after the inauguration of the US Cyber Command, Deputy Secretary of Defense William Lynn published an article in the magazine *Foreign Affairs* in which he explicitly presented cyberspace as a "new domain" of conflict in which the Pentagon should now seek to establish military superiority (Lynn 2010). With little taste for this

---

5 On this notion, see Chapter 1.

rhetoric, the DHS responded incisively: Jane Holl Lute and Bruce McConnell, senior officials at the DHS, published an editorial a few months later in *Wired* magazine retorting that "cyberspace is not a war zone [...] but fundamentally a civilian space", in which their agency therefore had an "important role to play" (Holl Lute and McConnell 2011).

Another important illustration of this clash of offensive and defensive organizational cultures concerns the issue of "zero-day" vulnerabilities and the importance of whether or not to publicize their existence. As John Carlin, a former senior Department of Justice official under Obama, puts it:

> Inside the US government, there were often intense philosophical discussions about when and whether companies should be made aware of zero-day vulnerabilities to issue software or hardware patches; often the FBI or the DHS preferred to let companies know quickly, to help them harden their systems, while intelligence agencies might prefer to hold on to them to exploit in their own work. (Carlin and Graff 2019, pp. 181–182)

This antagonism, in 2017, would contribute to the cataclysmic WannaCry ransomware attack, based on a zero-day vulnerability long since identified by the NSA, but publicized too late to be effectively patched (Sanger 2018, pp. 287–291). The above testimony also demonstrates, within the defensive camp, the importance of law enforcement organizations (the FBI and, by extension, the Department of Justice), which oppose militarization with a desire to judicialize cyber conflict management: to identify troublemakers, demonstrate their guilt and initiate international prosecutions against them, notably to dissuade groups or individuals from serving hostile powers. In 2018, US Deputy Attorney General Rod Rosenstein boasted at a major national security forum about the effectiveness of the "long arm of American law" in combating foreign cyber intrusions (Rosenstein 2018).

Within the "offensive" camp itself, two other visions of cyber conflict management also compete: while the armed forces prioritize the kinetic potential of cyber attacks, intelligence agencies emphasize the informational potential of cyber exploitation. The result is an often irreconcilable clash of paradigms, one visible and focused on immediate physical results, the other covert and focused on long-term intelligence collection (Lin 2012, p. 50). This fracture was to complicate the functioning of the US Cyber Command during the Obama administration, in which the military and the NSA were meant to cooperate, but frequently argued over the merits of a given operation. The Secretary of Defense at the time, Ashton Carter, lamented:

> When Cybercom did produce something useful, the intelligence community tended to delay or try to prevent its use, claiming cyber operations would hinder intelligence collection. This would be understandable if we had been getting a steady stream of actionable intel, but we weren't. (Carter 2017)

According to various testimonies, this rivalry affected the effectiveness of the US cyber campaign to defeat ISIS (Sanger 2018, pp. 247–248). In summary, there are thus fundamental shifts across the US national security apparatus between respective perspectives and priorities toward the cyber domain: some organizations see it as a battlefield to be dominated, others as a treasure trove of information to be exploited, still others as a public space to be safeguarded.

The second major dynamic to consider is the bureaucratic competition that marks the functioning of the American governmental machine. Perpetually competing to preserve or extend their prerogatives, resources and prestige in the administrative arena, the national security agencies persistently engage in struggles for influence (Halperin and Clapp 2006, pp. 51–57). This dynamic also visibly extends to the management of cyber issues: as cyber threats pose new security challenges, creating new bureaucratic "markets", intense turf wars are emerging among agencies to extend their mandates. As we will show below, this frequently leads to inertia and even dysfunction in cyber conflict management.

The first antagonism in this area is between the long-established "dominant" agencies (such as the NSA and the FBI) and the more recently created "emerging" agencies (essentially the DHS, inaugurated in 2002). It is a Darwinian competition: the dominant agencies, which have accumulated considerable influence over time, use it to have new missions added to their portfolios, while the emerging agencies struggle to make their mark and survive in the bureaucratic arena. Journalist Breanne Deppisch observes:

> The one corner of government that did note the DHS' apparent ambitions online were the two agencies busy asserting their own authorities in cyberspace: The NSA and the FBI, both

sharp-elbowed bureaucracies that boasted decades of hard-earned reputational prowess and whose influence was buttressed by powerful networks of former officials. (Deppisch 2019)

The issue of protecting American critical infrastructure was to suffer from such rivalries between 2009 and 2016. The DHS (which was theoretically tasked with this mission) "didn't have the money, the manpower, or the technical talent" to fulfill it, but curbed any collaboration with the NSA, for fear that its influential rival would "run the show" (Kaplan 2016, pp. 186–189). The NSA, for its part, worked to prevent Congress from transferring resources that would have allowed the DHS to complete the mission without its support:

Then-NSA Director General Keith Alexander [...] fought fiercely for every inch of territory he could. He regularly pointed out during frequent trips to Capitol Hill how DHS fell short in the talent department. Over and over, NSA leaders pushed the notion that DHS was incapable of effectively combating cyberthreats. (Deppisch 2019)

Deppisch observes that, among other factors, this bureaucratic guerrilla warfare was to complicate and slow the US response to the 2016 Russian interference (Deppisch 2019).

Among the dominant agencies themselves, a second level of antagonism is found between competent agencies (institutionally designated to deal with a given issue) and qualified agencies (which *de facto* possess the adequate means to do so). The former demands the resources necessary to fulfill their mandate, while the latter attempts to extend their jurisdiction. This dynamic can notably be seen in the management of American cyber operations: the NSA has the experience and the talent, but is theoretically not authorized to carry out offensive actions; the armed forces are legally designated to do so, but do not have the expertise. As Richard Clarke recounts, the creation of the US Cyber Command (whose vocation was to integrate the two branches) was to be considerably complicated by this rivalry, with each organization struggling to control the structure:

Many of the other NSA alumni believed NSA should just become the new Cyber Command. To counter the "NSA takeover" of Cyber Command, some in the military argued that

NSA was really a civilian organization, an intelligence unit, and therefore could not legally fight wars [...] the issue of who would run America's cyber wars soon became a battle between military and civilian government lawyers. (Clarke and Knake 2010, p. 38)

Hence, structural dysfunctions emerge in cyber conflict management within the US national security apparatus: agencies authorized to act on certain issues do not yet have the resources to do so, while those that do are struggling to gain authority. Moreover, as we see in the case of the Pentagon and the NSA, territorial rivalries coexist with – and sometimes reinforce – organizational culture clashes between agencies.

2.4. Individual dynamics

A third set of factors influencing US cyber conflict management is unfolding at the governmental-individual level and focuses on key decision-makers, in this case the president. Based on their personal predispositions, world views and experiences, occupants of the Oval Office have their own preferences and priorities that can significantly influence – sometimes positively, sometimes negatively – the management of given issues (Hermann *et al.* 2001; Greenstein 2009). This is demonstrated by a comparison of how Barack Obama and Donald Trump conducted their cybersecurity policies.

First, in the case of Barack Obama, at least two personal characteristics help us understand his approach to cyber conflict. On the one hand, as the first Generation X president, Obama won the 2008 presidential election thanks in part to his extensive use of the internet and digital tools, which allowed him to reach voters directly and raise funds with unprecedented efficiency (Plouffe 2009). John Carlin, who served in his administration, notes:

Obama arrived in office as a new-generation leader [...] more tech-savvy than any president before [...] In his first months in the White House, he hosted an event and speech on cybersecurity that even included a reference to "spoofing and phishing and botnets", terms that were still unfamiliar to nearly all of the country's top decision makers. (Carlin and Graff 2019, pp. 171–172)

Part of this digital sensitivity may also reside in the fact that his 2008 campaign had been hacked by China: "That was our early taste of this problem", Denis McDonough would later confess, Obama's soon-to-be White House Chief of Staff (Sanger 2018, p. 109). This awareness of cyber issues led the 44th US president to show significant leadership, propelling cybersecurity to the top of his administration's agenda: he would reiterate the importance of cyber issues in nearly every State of the Union address during his two presidential terms (Armerding 2017). The president's personal involvement on these issues also allowed for the effective negotiation of a bilateral agreement with China in 2015 to put an end to the massive theft of US intellectual property (Carlin and Graff 2019, pp. 367–368).

On the other hand, a second personality trait helps to understand Barack Obama's vision of cyber conflict: a prudent, "calculating" decision-maker, Obama believes that "force is sometimes necessary" in foreign policy, but above all wishes to use it "cautiously" (David 2015, pp. 915–921), in order to avoid any adventurism that might unnecessarily destabilize the international system. This characteristic explains several of the major decisions taken by the president in the cyber domain. In the case of Operation Olympic Games, for example, Fred Kaplan observes that the idea of hacking the Iranian nuclear program (although inherited from the W. Bush administration) "fits Obama's comfort zone", in that it "both served a national interest, and neither risked American lives" (Kaplan 2016, p. 208). Even so, he would later frequently display doubts about the merits of the operation, fearing that he had opened a Pandora's box of cyber warfare on the international scene (Sanger 2018, p. 10). Moreover, the 44th president's extreme caution would occasionally complicate the American response to acts of cyber conflict. The hacking of Sony Pictures by North Korea, for example, would see Obama reject several means of retaliation envisaged by his advisors:

Ever cautious, Obama came to the conclusion that it wasn't terrorism; it was more like "cyber vandalism", as he said a few days later […] Obama did not want to escalate. But he also did not want to go through another country's networks [in this case, China's] to get inside North Korea. (Sanger 2018, p. 143)

The presidency ultimately opted for a public denunciation of the North Korean regime and economic sanctions, a response that many observers felt was insufficient to deter future similar actions (Carlin and Graff 2019, p. 339).

Barack Obama's successor in the White House, Donald Trump, has also – and perhaps even more so – demonstrated the influence of presidential personal predispositions on US cyber policy. At least three major traits of his personality appear to have had significant impacts in this regard. First, unlike his predecessor, Trump had a reputation for being less interested in the details of public policy: he did not regularly read reports prepared by his advisors, who often seemed to have difficulty getting the president's ear on intelligence and cyber issues (Woodward 2018; Perlmutter-Gumbiner *et al.* 2019). Cyber issues, inherently riddled with technical complexities, never seemed to elicit any particular interest or deep understanding on Donald Trump's part prior to his election in 2016, as demonstrated by Trump's insistence on using his old, unsecured smartphone upon entering the White House.

Trump's policy team did not appear to have subsequently been able to channel any more of his attention or energies into these issues. As Andy Greenberg summarizes on a cyber attack in 2017: "Trump, whose understanding of computers and digital security was notoriously thin, might have ignored the news simply because he tuned out all things 'cyber'" (Greenberg 2019, p. 159). This is also suggested by a conversation between Trump and his former Homeland Security Advisor, Tom Bossert, on the issue of relations with China: when Bossert repeatedly tried to bring up cyber issues, Trump cut the discussion short or refocused on other aspects, especially trade (Woodward 2018, pp. 339–342). Unwilling to engage in in-depth policy debates, Trump does not seem to have devoted much thought to his administration's cyber priorities, thus contributing to leaving several issues on the subject, such as critical infrastructure protection, unaddressed (Hayden 2018, p. 93). In August 2017, eight senior DHS officials announced their resignations to protest "[The president's] insufficient attention to the growing threats to the cybersecurity of the critical systems upon which all Americans depend" (Marks 2017).

A second personality trait of Donald Trump that has directly influenced US cyber security is his impulsive management of the decision-making process. In keeping with the phrase he liked to use when he was running the reality show *The Apprentice*, "You're fired!", Trump's administration has been marked by a particularly high rate of dismissals and resignations (Tenpas 2020). He has not hesitated to dismiss national security advisors, secretaries of defense and homeland security, thus disrupting national security policy-making. In addition to this staffing volatility, Trump also operated several relatively abrupt bureaucratic transformations in the cyber area: he appointed the controversial Rudy Giuliani as his personal cybersecurity advisor, he dismantled the Office of the Coordinator for Cyber Issues in 2017 and then eliminated the position of White House Cybersecurity Coordinator in 2018. These reorganizations and personnel shakeups contributed to making cyber conflict management under Trump a much more informal process subject to presidential moods, with decision-making centers that were sometimes difficult to locate (Tengjun 2018). In the realm of offensive cyber, the 45th US president simultaneously took several steps (regarding the US Cyber Command) in an effort to shorten the chain of command governing the management of cyber operations, presumably in order to make it a rapidly usable foreign policy tool serving the immediate needs of the presidency.

Level of analysis	Key players	Explanatory factors	Major effects
Societal and institutional	Private sector	Lobbying, revolving door	Absence of regulations
	States	Jurisdictional competition (federalism)	Resources mismatch
	Congress	Jurisdictional competition (legislative) Partisan polarization	Legislative inertia
Governmental-bureaucratic	Offensive/defensive agencies	Organizational cultures	Confusion of goals and priorities
	Dominant/emerging agencies Competent/qualified agencies	Bureaucratic rivalries	Inadequacy of resources and mandates
Governmental-individual	Presidents	Personal views and priorities of decision makers	Leadership deficit Politicization of issues

Table 2.1. *The various drivers of dysfunction within the US national cybersecurity apparatus*

Finally, a third Trump personal characteristic that affected his administration's cyber conflict management was his highly politicized (and domestically focused) view of cyber issues, particularly in the wake of the 2016 Russian interference. As mentioned above, the issue of election infrastructure security (and, by extension, much of the critical infrastructure) was continually viewed by Donald Trump as an implicit challenge to his 2016 election victory (Tengjun 2018). This resulted in a certain short-sightedness on Trump's part when it came to cybersecurity: during his first meeting with Vladimir Putin in July 2017, Trump very superficially addressed the issue of interference, only to come around to the idea put forward by his counterpart that Moscow was not involved in the matter (Sanger 2018, pp. 236–237). With regard to the issue of online disinformation, Trump tended to ignore the geopolitical implications of the phenomenon and favored a domestic and partisan perspective: despite constant foreign disinformation campaigns identified by his intelligence agencies, the president often preferred to focus his attention around an alleged bias of the "Big Tech" industry against the American conservative community, the White House going so far as to issue an executive order on the issue in the summer of 2019 (Harding McGill and Lippman 2019). Donald Trump's discursive efforts to downplay the threat of foreign interference have unsurprisingly spilled over into Congress, where Republican lawmakers have frequently echoed the president's arguments and, as noted above, curbed initiatives to address such challenges.

2.5. Conclusion

This chapter attempted to demonstrate that the United States, far from functioning as a unitary and rational actor in the cyber domain, is instead agitated by various internal dynamics that have a considerable impact on cyber conflict management. At the societal and institutional levels, cyber issues, by their very nature, transcend the boundaries between public and private sectors, between federal and state authorities and between institutional jurisdictions, introducing various distortions in the policy-making process. At the governmental-bureaucratic level, cyber issues pit organizations with divergent visions and priorities against each other, resulting in strong competition in priority setting and occasional cacophony in decision-making. Finally, at the governmental-individual level, the personal dispositions of individual presidents may exert a significant influence on their understanding of, and preferences for, cyber issues, occasionally contributing to inconsistencies in the US government's cyber policies.

The involvement and influence of this multiplicity of actors with very different interests, who are often unable to agree among themselves, raise many questions about the existence of a clear and constant American national interest in the cyber domain. As we have seen here, cyber conflict management in the United States sees the overlapping of – and occasional collisions between – different internal forces, whose impacts on decision-making are not so much the product of meticulous cost–benefit calculations as of arbitrations and negotiations with often unpredictable outcomes. Often schizophrenic, sometimes highly politicized, American cyber conflict management appears to not always give primacy to national security imperatives, or at least regularly produces suboptimal choices in this respect. This observation underlines (or rather reminds us of) the importance of opening the "black box" of the state in order to understand its actions, especially if we intend to analyze new forms of conflict that are radically changing the global security landscape.

2.6. References

Allison, G.T. and Zelikow, P. (1999). *Essence of Decision: Explaining the Cuban Missile Crisis*. Longman, New York.

Andres, R. (2012). The emerging structure of strategic cyber offense, cyber defense and cyber deterrence. In *Cyberspace and National Security*, Reveron, D. (ed.). Georgetown University Press, Washington.

Armerding, T. (2017). Obama's cybersecurity legacy: Good intentions, good efforts, limited results [Online]. Available at: www.is.gd/me2sHt [Accessed on 25 February 2020].

Betz, D.J. and Stevens, T. (2011). *Cyberspace and the State: Towards a Strategy for Cyber-power*. Routledge, Abingdon.

Boucher, V. and Barthe, S. (2018). L'analyse de la politique étrangère. In *Théories de la Politique étrangère Américaine*, David, C.P., Gagnon, F. (eds). Presses de l'Université de Montréal, Montreal.

Brumfield, C. (2020). 2020 outlook for cybersecurity legislation [Online]. Available at: www.is.gd/HlySpv [Accessed on 27 February 2020].

Buchanan, B. (2016). *The Cybersecurity Dilemma: Hacking, Trust, and Fear between Nations*. Oxford University Press, Oxford.

Carlin, J.P. and Graff, G.M. (2018). *Dawn of the Code War: America's Battle Against Russia, China, and the Rising Global Cyber Threat*. Public Affairs, New York.

Carter, A. (2017). A lasting defeat: The campaign to destroy ISIS [Online]. Available at: www.belfercenter.org/LastingDefeat [Accessed on 18 February 2020].

Charlet, K. (2018). Understanding federal cybersecurity [Online]. Available at: www.bit.ly/3lsEi6V [Accessed on 7 April 2020].

Clarke, R.A. and Knake, R.K. (2010). *Cyber War: The Next Threat to National Security and What to do About it*. Harper Collins, New York.

Cohen, N. and Nussbaum, B. (2018). Cybersecurity for the states: Lessons from across America [Online]. Available at: www.is.gd/RHwH5J [Accessed on 14 April 2020].

Corrigan, J. (2019). Lawmaker: Congress needs fewer committees with cyber oversight [Online]. Available at: www.is.gd/pXVxkn [Accessed on 11 February 2020].

David, C.P. (2015). *Au sein de la Maison-Blanche. De Truman à Obama : la formulation (imprévisible) de la politique étrangère des États-Unis*. Presses de l'Université Laval, Quebec.

David, C.P. and Rapin, A. (2018). Les théories bureaucratiques du processus décisionnel. In *Théories de la Politique étrangère américaine*, David, C.P., Gagnon, F. (eds). Presses de l'Université de Montréal, Montreal.

Deppisch, B. (2019). DHS was finally getting serious about cybersecurity. Then came Trump [Online]. Available at: www.is.gd/UMhFAs [Accessed on 18 February 2020].

Geller, E. (2016). Elections security: Federal help or power grab? [Online]. Available at: www.is.gd/YbMcm2 [Accessed on 19 February 2020].

Greenberg, A. (2019). *Sandworm: A New Era of Cyberwar and the Hunt for the Kremlin's Most Dangerous Hackers*. Penguin Random House, New York.

Greenstein, F. (2009). *The Presidential Difference: Leadership Styles from FDR to Clinton*. Princeton University Press, Princeton.

Halperin, M. and Clapp, P. (2006). *Bureaucratic Politics and Foreign Policy*. Brookings Institution Press, Washington.

Harding McGill, M. and Lippman, D. (2019). White House drafting executive order to tackle Silicon Valley's alleged anti-conservative bias [Online]. Available at: www.is.gd/AA5b1N [Accessed on 2 March 2020].

Hayden, M.V. (2018). *The Assault on Intelligence: American National Security in an Age of Lies*. Penguin Books, New York.

Hermann, M., Preston, T., Korany, B., Shaw, T. (2001). Who leads matters: The effect of powerful individuals. *International Studies Quarterly*, 34(3), 83–131.

Holl Lute, J. and McConnell, B. (2011). Op-Ed: A civil perspective on cybersecurity [Online]. Available at: www.wired.com/2011/02/dhs-op-ed/ [Accessed on 13 February 2020].

Hudson, V.M. (2005). Foreign policy analysis: Actor-specific theory and the ground of international relations. *Foreign Policy Analysis*, 1(1), 1–30.

Kaplan, F. (2016). *Dark Territory: The Secret History of Cyber War*. Simon & Schuster, New York.

Kello, L. (2017). *The Virtual Weapon and International Order*. Yale University Press, New Haven.

Kelly, M. (2019). Congress is running out of time to secure the 2020 elections [Online]. Available at: www.is.gd/lUd2Fr [Accessed on 27 February 2020].

Latiff, R.H. (2018). *Future War: Preparing for the New Global Battlefield*. Vintage, New York.

Libicki, M.C. (2009). *Cyberdeterrence and Cyberwar*. RAND Corporation, Santa Monica.

Lin, H. (2012). Operational considerations in cyber attack and cyber exploitation. In *Cyberspace and National Security*, Reveron, D. (ed.). Georgetown University Press, Washington.

Lindsay, J. (1994). *Congress and the Politics of U.S. Foreign Policy*. John Hopkins University Press, Baltimore.

Lynn III, W.J. (2010). Defending a new domain: The Pentagon's cyberstrategy. *Foreign Affairs*, 89(5), 97–108.

Marks, J. (2017). Trump cybersecurity advisers resign in "moral" protest [Online]. Available at: www.is.gd/mUXHxU [Accessed on 1 March 2020].

Miles, R.E. (1978). The origin and meaning of Miles' Law. *Public Administration Review*, 38(5), 399–403.

Mulford, L.A. (2013). *Let Slip the Dogs of (Cyber) War: Progressing Towards a Warfighting US Cyber Command*. National Defense University, Norfolk.

Nye, J.S. (2017). Deterrence and dissuasion in cyberspace. *International Security*, 41(3), 44–71.

Perlmutter-Gumbiner, E., Dilanian, K., Kube, C. (2019). On Trump's calendar, just 17 intelligence briefings in 85 days [Online]. Available at: www.is.gd/w4Anf9 [Accessed on 6 February 2019].

Plouffe, D. (2009). *The Audacity to Win: The Inside Story and Lessons of Barack Obama's Historic Victory*. Viking Press, New York.

Rapin, A. (2019). La collusion, cet arbre mort qui cache la forêt de l'ingérence [Online]. Available at: www.is.gd/bTIPl3 [Accessed on 6 February 2019].

Rosenstein, R. (2018). Deputy Attorney General Rod J. Rosenstein delivers remarks at the Aspen Security Forum [Online]. Available at: www.is.gd/OJbQ5G [Accessed on 7 April 2020].

Sanger, D.E. (2018). *The Perfect Weapon: War, Sabotage, and Fear in the Cyber Age*. Broadway Books, New York.

Smith, R. and Barry, R. (2019). Utilities targeted in cyberattacks identified [Online]. Available at: www.is.gd/55lZXS [Accessed on 14 April 2020].

Tengjun, Z. (2018). The cybersecurity policy adjustment of the Trump administration. *China International Studies*, 72, 128–144.

Tenpas, K. (2020). Tracking turnover in the Trump administration [Online]. Available at: www.brook.gs/2FKYknT [Accessed on 1 March 2020].

Theriault, S. (2013). *The Gingrich Senators: The Roots of Partisan Warfare in Congress*. Oxford University Press, Oxford.

Theriault, S. and Edwards, M. (2019). *Congress: The First Branch*. Oxford University Press, Oxford.

US Senate (2019). Report of the Select Committee on Intelligence United States Senate on Russian Active Measures Campaigns and Interference in the 2016 U.S. Election. 116th Congress, 1st Session, Senate Report 116-XX.

Williams, A. (2019). A methodology for the comparative analysis of strategic culture and cyber warfare. In *European Conference on Cyber Warfare and Security*, Cruz, T., Simoes, P. University of Coimbra, Coimbra.

Woodward, B. (2018). *Fear: The Trump White House*. Simon & Schuster, New York.

Zegart, A. (2000). *Flawed by Design: The Evolution of the CIA, JCS, and NSC.* Stanford University Press, Redwood City.

Zegart, A. and Morell, M. (2019). Spies, lies, and algorithms: Why US Intelligence Agencies must adapt or fail. *Foreign Affairs*, 98, 85–96.

Zetter, K. (2014). *Countdown to Zero Day: Stuxnet and the Launch of the World's First Digital Weapon.* Broadway Books, New York.

Separation of Offensive and Defensive Functions: The Originality of the French Cyberdefense Model Called into Question?

3.1. Introduction[1]

In the aftermath of the attack on Estonia in 2007, France assessed the challenges posed by cyberattacks for national security and implemented an ambitious and proactive strategy. The 2008 *Livre Blanc sur la Défense et la Sécurité Nationale* (LBDSN) (White Paper on Defense and National Security) consecrated information system security as part of the first-circle "domain of sovereignty" (SGDSN 2008, p. 318). It should be noted that in France, the term "cyberdefense" is not exclusively used to describe the capabilities of the Ministry of Defense. In fact, cyberdefense refers to "all the resources put in place by a state in cyberspace to defend information systems deemed of vital importance, which contribute to ensuring cybersecurity" (Journal Officiel de la République française 2017).

From the beginning, the French cyberdefense strategy has been organized according to a model separating the defensive (*lutte informatique défensive* (LID)) and offensive (*lutte informatique offensive* (LIO)) cyber warfare functions. On the one hand, the defense and security missions of the state's

Chapter written by Alix DESFORGES.

1 The author wishes to express his thanks to Sébastien-Yves Laurent, Frédérick Douzet, François Delerue and Aude Géry for their attentive proofreading and their enlightened comments.

computer networks have been entrusted to a newly created interministerial agency, the National Information Systems Security Agency (*Agence Nationale de Sécurité des Systèmes d'Information* (ANSSI)), while the offensive capabilities are entrusted to the Ministry of Defense and the intelligence services. Specifically, this is not a separation of civilian and military capabilities, since the Ministry of Defense is responsible for both the security of the Ministry's networks and for the LIO in the context of military operations. This choice of organization is particularly different from the Anglo-Saxon organizational models, although they are similar in their perception of threats. Indeed, in the United Kingdom and the United States, it is the technical intelligence agencies that combine the defensive and offensive functions of cyber warfare.

Ten years later, however, the   *Revue stratégique de cyberdéfense* (SGDSN 2018), a strategic orientation document for French cyberdefense, pointed out the limitations of a "very strict separation between offense and defense"[2]:

> While it is not compensated by a very strong coordination between its defensive and offensive parts, the French model may present, in terms of effectiveness, the disadvantage of a overly assumed bipolarity. (SGDSN 2018, p. 45)

The document published by the French General Secretariat for Defense and National Security (*Secrétariat Général à la Défense et la Sécurité Nationale* (SGDSN)) also considers that this model "does not sufficiently take into account the contribution of certain national cyberdefense actors and does not fully reflect the different purposes of cyberdefense" (SGDSN 2018, p. 52). The document then proposed a new structuring of French cyberdefense organization, which tended to mitigate this separation without, however, calling it into question. In January 2020, the director of ANSSI, Guillaume Poupard, declared: "in years to come, the offensive and the defensive will have to work together" (Adam 2020), while stressing that this cooperation would be aimed at reinforcing defense and that it did not call into question the French model. Since the end of the 2000s, French strategy and cyber capabilities have evolved considerably, in line with the new threats and security issues raised by digital technology. However, the

2 Hearing of Guillaume Poupard before the armed forces national defense committee of the French National Assembly, January 31, 2017; available at: www.is.gd/wBOLtc.

separation between offensive and defensive capabilities has remained the central pillar of cyberdefense organization.

However, the threat context has changed significantly in recent years, putting the strict separation model to the test. Like France, many states have also developed offensive capabilities, even engaging in a cyber arms race, in which the private sector is also participating. The proliferation of powerful offensive tools, some of which are now available to a large number of actors with varying motivations and capabilities, has become a real threat to the stability and security of cyberspace and, more globally, of the international order (Douzet and Géry 2020). The increasing complexity and globalization of cyberattacks challenges the organization of states in terms of cyberdefense. Ensuring an effective defense requires a very advanced knowledge of the state of the threat in order to anticipate and prevent all the risks that the state, as well as companies and, in particular, critical infrastructure operators (*Opérateurs d'Importance Vitale*, (OIVs)), have to face. However, without exchanges with intelligence services and the military, ANSSI can only have a fragmented vision of the state of threats.

Moreover, as early as 2013, French strategy envisaged responding to a large-scale cyberattack that "could [...] constitute a real act of war" (SGDSN 2013, p. 49). As such, the white paper specified that France could respond, including by mobilizing the graduated use of the Ministry of Defense's resources. A response requires the identification of the source and the person responsible for the attack and therefore an attribution. However, the attribution of a cyberattack is often complex to formally carry out using the individual technical elements collected during the attack. Indeed, they can be misleading or intentionally manipulated in order to accuse a third party. The attribution therefore needs additional elements, in particular those from the intelligence services. For example, the United States relied on intelligence gathered by the National Security Agency (NSA) to attribute the attack on Sony Pictures to North Korea in 2014 (Sanger and Fackler 2015).

In this context, a strict separation of the defensive and offensive parts seems to contradict the fundamental missions of cyberdefense as defined by French strategy. While it is praised by all the actors of French cyberdefense, can France maintain its cyberdefense organization model?

After reviewing the origins and advantages of the French model, we will question its limits in light of the evolution of the geopolitical context.

Finally, we will see how France has been trying to mitigate its drawbacks for several years without crossing the red line.

The argument of this chapter is that while France has been bringing together the actors responsible for the defensive and offensive parts for several years in order to improve cyberdefense, the separation of functions remains real, at least for the moment.

3.2. A model designed and developed in response to the threats and challenges of the early 2010s

In 2008, the new *Livre Blanc sur la Défense et la Sécurité Nationale* (LBDSN), a document that sets the strategic orientations for France's defense and national security, presented information systems security (ISS) as one of the "capabilities necessary to maintain the nation's strategic and political autonomy". ISS was even listed alongside nuclear deterrence elements among the first-circle technologies for which "France must keep a domain of sovereignty" (SGDSN 2008, p. 318). Until then, ISS had been confined to the state's IT services, but it was now making a remarkable entrance onto the French strategic landscape.

For more than 10 years, France has deployed considerable political, financial and human resources in order to achieve this ambitious objective. Its resources have been concentrated around two main actors, ANSSI and the Ministry of Defense, and it has made the conscious choice to separate the offensive (Ministry of Defense and intelligence services) and defensive (ANSSI and Ministry of Defense for its own networks) functions. In contrast to the models implemented by Anglo-Saxon partners, this model is praised by French actors for its ability to generate trust, especially with the private sector and critical infrastructures.

3.2.1. *An organizational model apparently based on two main actors*

ANSSI and the Ministry of Defense are the two leading figures in the organization of French cyberdefense, but the intelligence services, although more discreet, are also involved in the system. Since 2008, France has invested a lot of resources to increase the power of these actors. ANSSI's budget has thus increased from 43 million euro in 2010 to more than

100 million in 2017. On the side of the Ministry of Defense, too, investments are considerable, with 1 billion euro over the 2014–2019 period devoted to the implementation of an action plan dedicated to military cyberdefense.

3.2.1.1. A defensive player: the National Information Systems Security Agency

In order to increase France's power in terms of cybersecurity, the 2008 LBDSN recommended the creation of an "agency in charge of information system security" (SGDSN 2008, p. 182). Created in 2009, ANSSI, which reports to the Secretary General for Defense and National Security, who is himself placed under the authority of the Prime Minister, is part of the interministerial system. This affiliation gives it a strategic position to impose itself as a central actor in French cyberdefense. The political will to make ANSSI the main agent of cybersecurity in France has first of all been achieved through the provision of considerable financial and human resources. When ANSSI was created in 2009, it had a staff of 130 people, compared to more than 560 in 2019, a threefold increase in its workforce. In 2011, it was designated as the "national authority for information systems security"[3], giving it the power to define the security standards to be observed by the state systems under its responsibility. Its mission is exclusively defensive and it watches over the state's cybersecurity.

The agency has quickly seen its role grow with private actors and, more particularly, with critical infrastructure operators. Among these companies, whose complete list is classified, are financial, energy management, transport and telecommunications operators. In 2013, the LBDSN considered that the threat of cyberattacks against these operators now required the state to impose "security standards to be observed" (SGDSN 2013, p. 106). A few months later, the 2014–2019 Military Programming Law (*Loi de programmation militaire* (LPM)) gave ANSSI new powers over critical infrastructures. Article 22 of this law establishes, among other things, that ANSSI sets the cybersecurity rules that critical infrastructures must implement, that it certifies the tools they use to detect cybersecurity incidents and that they must notify ANSSI of any incident without delay. Finally, the article specifies that in the event of a major crisis, ANSSI may be required to impose measures on critical infrastructures.

---

3 Decree No. 2011-170 of February 11, 2011, amending Decree No. 2009-834 of July 7, 2009, creating a department with national competence called the National Information Systems Security Agency.

Today, the agency has established itself as the central player in French cyberdefense and has managed numerous crises (among the most well-known were Areva (Haquet 2011) and MINEFI (ZDNet.fr 2011) in 2011, TV5 Monde (Untersinger 2017) in 2015 and Saint-Gobain (FranceInfo 2017) in 2017) that have established its know-how and skills. It is also a source of regulations and expertise and develops the national prevention policy against cyber risks for the general public and companies.

3.2.1.2. *A defensive and offensive actor in military operations: the Ministry of Defense (excluding intelligence services)*

While ANSSI is in charge of interministerial coordination of French strategy, one ministry has a special place in the French system: the Ministry of Defense. Like ANSSI, it has seen a sharp increase in its workforce since 2010, from a dozen agents to more than 3,000 "cybercombatants"[4]. It has a dual defensive and offensive function, supporting military operations. Through delegation and in coordination with ANSSI, the Ministry of Defense ensures the protection of its own information systems. However, since 2008, it has also taken responsibility for developing offensive capabilities within the operational framework (SGDSN 2008, p. 207).

In February 2011, in order to achieve the objectives set out by the LBDSN, Rear Admiral Arnaud Coustillière was appointed as Cyberdefense Policy Officer at the Joint Chiefs of Staff before being appointed, a few months later, as General Officer for Cyberdefense[5]. Reporting to the Deputy Head of Operations of the Joint Chiefs of Staff and under the dual supervision of the Head of the Joint Chiefs of Staff and the Minister's military chief of staff, the Rear Admiral took over the direction of the Cyberdefense Cell. This historical attachment to the operational chain is fundamental because it has allowed a great deal of freedom in adapting to threats, which have been evolving very quickly. For Admiral Coustillière, the integration of cyberdefense issues into military operations, rather than into the information and communication system (ICS) or plan chain, is the "DNA" of French military cyberdefense strategy[6]. It is therefore through the operational dimension that the Ministry of Defense has historically approached military cyberdefense. In 2017, the ministry underwent a

---

4 In the words of the Department of Defense.

5 Biography of Arnaud Coustillière, vice-admiral; available at: www.is.gd/uxGdwb.

6 Interview with the author on May 22, 2018.

reorganization that led to the creation of the Cyberdefense Command (*Commandement de la Cyberdéfense* (COMCYBER)), placed under the authority of the Joint Chief of Staff. In 2019, the Armed Forces ministry published two documents outlining the military LID (defensive cyber warfare) and LIO (offensive cyber warfare) strategy.

3.2.1.3. *The intelligence services: a discreet but fundamental player within the French cyber offensive organization*

Although the role of the intelligence services is assumed within the French cyberdefense organization, it is nevertheless subject to great discretion. These services are in fact in charge of the development of France's offensive capabilities, mainly entrusted to the technical directorate of the Directorate-General for External Security (*Direction Technique de la Direction Générale à la Sécurité Extérieure* (DT DGSE)), the French external intelligence services. The offensive tools are designed within the framework of intelligence services missions. It is difficult to evaluate French offensive capabilities because "the volume of forces, their organization and the ambitions set out are information that fall under defense secrecy", but Admiral Coustillière estimated in 2018 that France is not "lacking"[7]. In 2014, documents made public by Edward Snowden revealed that Canadian intelligence services suspected their French counterparts of being behind the Babar malware, discovered in 2009 and designed for espionage purposes. In 2015, two cybersecurity researchers linked Babar to another espionage malware, Evil Bunny (Marschalek 2015; Rascagnères 2015). The Canadian suspicions would be publicly confirmed in June 2016 by Bernard Barbier, director of the DT DGSE from 2006 to 2013[8].

However, as early as 2013, the participation of intelligence services in the issue of attribution and response to attacks was addressed in the LBDSN. The document described intelligence services as one of the cornerstones of French cyberdefense strategy: "[The] development of intelligence activities in the cyber domain and associated technical resources", with the aim of "better identifying the origin of attacks, assessing the offensive capabilities of potential adversaries and, if necessary, responding to them" (SGDSN

---

7 Hearing of Rear Admiral Arnaud Coustillière before the national defense and armed forces committee of the French National Assembly, June 12, 2013; available at: www.is. gd/69ZvYa.

8 CentraleSupélec Symposium, June 18, 2016, lecture by Bernard Barbier; available at: www.youtu.be/s8gCaySejr4.

2013, p. 73), is among the priorities of the 2013 white paper. Beyond its mention in a strategic document, the collaboration between ANSSI and the intelligence services in terms of attribution was illustrated in the management of the attack suffered by the Élysée during the inter-round of the 2012 presidential election. At the time, the directors of ANSSI and the DT DGSE went together to the headquarters of the NSA to demand explanations from their American counterparts, whom they suspected of being behind the attack (Follorou and Greenwald 2013b). Civilian and military intelligence agencies have been participating in cyberdefense missions since at least 2013, exchanging information with ANSSI.

Although there are few public elements, the proximity between the defensive and offensive parts is evident in the successive appointments of officials within ANSSI and COMCYBER. Indeed, several personalities have made the move in one direction or the other, starting with the first Director of ANSSI, Patrick Pailloux, who was appointed in 2014 as Technical Director of the DGSE. On the Ministry of Defense side, Vice Admiral Arnaud Coustillière's replacement in September 2017 at COMCYBER, Brigadier General Olivier Bonnet de Paillerets, came directly from intelligence as he was number two to the DT at the DGSE, where he worked with Patrick Pailloux. In 2019, he returned to the DGSE. The number two at ANSSI, appointed in November 2016, Emmanuel Germain, also worked at the DGSE before joining the agency.

The French cyberdefense organizational model is historically based on the three actors briefly presented above, even if over the last 10 years other ministries have also taken an increasing part in it (Foreign Affairs, the Interior and the Economy). These three actors share the defensive and offensive missions of cyberdefense, according to their respective prerogatives. Only COMCYBER combines the two functions in support of military operations. According to Admiral Coustillière, former Cyberdefense General Officer, deontological and ethical reflections are being carried out within the Ministry to limit the ambiguities raised by the concentration of defensive and offensive functions[9], which are often emphasized in the speeches of French actors to defend their organizational model, in contrast to that of their Anglo-Saxon allies.

---

9 Interview with Rear Admiral Arnaud Coustillière conducted by the author on May 22, 2018.

3.2.2. *The commitment to a strict offensive/defensive separation*

All French state actors consider the functional separation between the offensive and the defensive to be "healthy"[10] and even "virtuous" (Adam 2020). The French argument about the advantages of this organization is based on one main tenet. The separation of offensive and defensive activities, inherited in part from a historical positioning of state actors in IT security in France, would "facilitate a work of trust between ANSSI and business" (D'Elia 2017, p. 116).

3.2.2.1. *A model in contrast to the ambiguities of the Anglo-Saxon model*

French cyberdefense actors like to recall this originality of the model compared to their foreign counterparts, especially the United States and Great Britain. In these two countries, which are among the most advanced in terms of cyberdefense, offensive and defensive capabilities have been entrusted to the same services. The logic that prevailed was to entrust all these prerogatives to the entities that had first developed skills and knowledge of the threats. These are the technical agencies of the intelligence services, which very early on seized the potential of computer networks and the internet (cyberattacks for the purpose of espionage), but which also perceived threats in the context of their missions. Guillaume Poupard, Director of ANSSI, reminded us of this in 2017: "[Our] Anglo-Saxon allies chose to entrust cyberdefense to those who initially knew how to do it, that is to say, to the technical intelligence agencies, who had been the first to develop these skills"[11].

In Great Britain, the Government Communication Headquarters (GCHQ), the technical intelligence service of MI6 (the foreign intelligence service) and MI5 (the domestic intelligence service), manages both aspects of British cyberdefense strategy. In the United States, it is the powerful NSA that is responsible for both protecting the government's networks and carrying out offensive activities. In the United States, the concentration of power is even greater, since the military aspect of cyberdefense is managed by the US

---

10 Hearing of Rear Admiral Arnaud Coustillière on June 12, 2013.

11 Hearing of Guillaume Poupard, January 31, 2017, before the national defense and armed forces committee of the French National Assembly; available at: www.is.gd/ wBOLtc.

Cyber Command (USCYBERCOM) which, although different from the NSA, is headed by the same person.

For French actors, the concentration of both functions in the hands of the same entity or person represents a form of schizophrenia. Indeed, this situation raises the question of the objective pursued in the first place. The concentration of defensive and offensive prerogatives leads to contradictory objectives, since the people in charge of protecting networks from attacks and raising the level of cybersecurity are also the ones in charge of undermining these same protections and developing tools to break down defenses. This duality of contradictory objectives is particularly illustrated by the question of the policy of notification of the vulnerabilities discovered by these services. As part of their offensive activities, intelligence services are able to search for vulnerabilities in networks, systems or software themselves, or else to buy them from private companies[12]. In the hypothetical case where intelligence agencies discover a vulnerability, do they choose to defend or attack? Do they notify the security vendors and the company that designed the product, system or software affected by the vulnerability in order to raise the level of cybersecurity, or do they prefer to keep it secret for offensive purposes in future operations? For a security service, the temptation to exploit a vulnerability can be great in terms of the benefits that can be gained from an attack exploiting that vulnerability. Intelligence services are particularly fond of zero-day vulnerabilities, that is to say, those that are not yet known and therefore have not been patched. Their exploitation within an offensive operation is therefore almost certain to succeed, giving the operation a high chance of success. To guide the trade-offs between defensive and offensive vulnerabilities, the NSA and GCHQ have implemented vulnerabilities equities process (VEP) policies.

The dual responsibility for offensive and defensive components within a single entity thus raises the issue of what Ben Buchanan calls the "cybersecurity dilemma" (Buchanan 2016). This concept, derived from the security dilemma, establishes that an increase for one state in its cyberoffensive capabilities can lead other states to perceive it as a threat and to also acquire offensive capabilities. These perceptions thus lead to an arms race between states, which then creates a security threat. By reinforcing their offensive capabilities, services such as the NSA or GCHQ undermine their

---

12 Several companies trading in vulnerabilities have been in the news following revelations in the press (Hacking Team and Vupen, for example).

secondary mission, which is to protect systems. This situation is all the more prevalent in cyberdefense issues, given the links between intelligence and offensive activities (Buchanan 2016, p. 26).

In addition, it poses a problem of trust between the agencies responsible for cybersecurity and their interlocutors, whether private or state-owned, both in potential interventions (such as remediation of an attack) and in the exchange of information about the threat. "In the United States, when the NSA [...] comes in, you never really know who is behind it. Moreover, I think that the NSA itself does not know exactly what its mission is"[13], says Guillaume Poupard, Director of ANSSI. The French argument for a separation of offensive and defensive prerogatives thus highlights the clear positioning of ANSSI without any conflict of interest: "[In] France, we know that ANSSI has a purely defensive and protective mission, it does not carry out intelligence or attacks"[14].

3.2.2.2. A model for building trust, especially with the private sector

Although it is a conscious choice, this separation is also the result of a historical heritage that has separated the offensive and defensive functions of cryptology since the Second World War. In the context of an occupied France and the organization of a liberation movement from outside France, the coordination between intelligence services distributed between France, Algeria and London was subject to political rivalries (Laurent 2001). The offensive functions of cryptology (code breaking) were entrusted to the intelligence agencies, while the defensive functions (protecting state secrets) were entrusted to the Cipher Technical Directorate, created in Algiers in 1943 and the historical predecessor to ANSSI.

The separation of offensive and defensive forces is perceived as a factor of coherence between the civilian and military in the defensive aspects. For Louis Gautier, former Secretary General for Defense and National Security, this choice is "useful both for our individual and public freedoms"[15]. "This allows us to avoid excesses like those of the NSA" (Duquesne 2014), according to Bernard Barbier, referring to the abuses of the American

---

13 Hearing of Guillaume Poupard, January 31, 2017, before the national defense and armed forces committee of the French National Assembly; available at: www.is.gd/wBOLtc.

14 *Ibid.*

15 Louis Gautier, October 15, 2015, at the ANSSI strategy presentation; available at: www.is.gd/apgAkj.

agency revealed by Edward Snowden from 2013. The intense communication of French actors on the separation of offensive and defensive functions fulfills two objectives: to position France as a global player in cyberdefense, but above all to make ANSSI the central actor of the defensive aspect at the national level, including for private actors.

The main argument put forward to justify this choice of organization is that of generating trust between ANSSI and its interlocutors. The main objective of this choice is more specifically to provide a framework for exchanges between ANSSI and private actors, first and foremost the critical infrastructure operators. The aim is to position ANSSI as a trusted actor for the private sector, which is the main victim of cyber attacks. Companies must be able to share information related to the attacks they suffer and which is generally sensitive from a strategic point of view (product design, business plans, R&D, etc.), without fear that this information will be reused for intelligence purposes. This positioning aims not only to support companies in the event of a crisis, but also to improve the general level of IT security for all French actors by sharing information on the threats and risks they face.

At the beginning of the 2010s, the issue of protecting critical infrastructures was an emerging subject, but one that was taken very seriously by specialists. In the United States, an attempt at legislation in 2010, called the Protecting Cyberspace as a National Asset Act, aimed to provide for the disconnection of American critical infrastructures from the internet in the event of a major attack. The bill was strongly opposed. Its detractors considered that the American president had too much power within this framework and denounced the idea of a total "kill switch" for the internet (Hoover 2010). In a statement, the American Civil Liberties Union, a US civil liberties group, expressed concern about the role of the NSA in protecting civilian networks: "A role that would likely mean less transparency about cybersecurity activities."[16] In the face of criticism, the bill was finally abandoned. However, the issue of protecting critical infrastructures would become increasingly urgent with the revelations about the origin of the Stuxnet worm, in 2012, which had struck Iranian nuclear power plants 2 years earlier. The *New York Times* revealed that Stuxnet had been designed by the NSA in collaboration with the Israeli intelligence services (Sanger 2012). It is in this context that the 2014–2019 Military

---

16 American Civil Liberties Union, Civil Liberties Issues in Cybersecurity Bill, June 23, 2010.

Programming Law was passed in France at the end of 2013, giving ANSSI the power to define the minimum level of cybersecurity for critical infrastructures.

Designed to generate trust, and although touted by French actors, the offensive/defensive separation model needed "clarification of its operational organization, as well as better consideration of objectives related to intelligence missions and judicial actions" (SGDSN 2018, p. 45), according to the 2018 *Revue stratégique de cyberdéfense* (RS Cyber). Finally, it "requires, in order to be more effective and coherent, a greater fluidity of exchanges within the cyberdefense community" (SGDSN 2018, p. 45).

The first part of this chapter has shown that, while there is a separation of offensive and defensive functions, which at the beginning was reflected in a desire to display limited communication between the actors of the two parts, since 2012 there has been, at the very least, an increasingly assumed collaboration, particularly on issues of attribution and reaction to cyberattacks. However, despite the growing strength of the French system, Guillaume Poupard estimated in January 2020 that "for the attackers, the game is beautiful" (Adam and Poupard 2020). As such, and in order to contribute to better defense, he considered it necessary to implement closer cooperation between the defensive and offensive parts "so that it is not too easy and too comfortable for those who attack us"[17].

3.3. A strict separation of offensive and defensive functions and missions: an obstacle to better defense?

The evolution of threats, and the affirmation of the French strategy aiming at attributing cyberattacks and potentially responding to them, has led to exchanges of information between the actors in charge of cyber offensive and cyber defensive dimensions.

Indeed, the 2010s have seen an increase in the threat and the complexity of attacks (TV5 Monde, WannaCry, NotPetya). In order to protect themselves against these attacks, defense actors, and in particular ANSSI, need the information held by intelligence services more than ever – namely, the status of other states' capabilities and information on possible attacks in

17 *Ibid.*

progress against France or other states. Indeed, a strict separation presents real obstacles to the implementation of an effective defense in the accomplishment of cyberdefense missions. This is what the *Revue stratégique de cyberdéfense* points out by highlighting the problems of the lack of efficiency of the French model (SGDSN 2018, p. 45).

While the separation of defensive and offensive functions is claimed by all French actors, in reality, exchanges between actors from both parts already take place. In 2018, the *Revue stratégique de cyberdéfense* proposed to formalize a new French cyberdefense organization, which tends to mitigate the strict separation to promote exchanges and cooperation between defense and offensive actors (SGDSN 2018).

French actors assert that this is not a questioning of the French model: "[We] will remain very clear on the fundamentals" (Guiton 2020), said the Director of ANSSI in January 2020. The aim of the rapprochement is to reinforce and intensify exchanges between responsible actors from the two parts, each in their respective missions. The RS Cyber recognizes that the two defensive and offensive parts work together on cyberdefense missions as defined in the document. Moreover, a note to the definition of cyberdefense in the *Journal Officiel* of September 19, 2017 specifies that "cyberdefense implements, in particular, defensive and offensive cyber warfare" (*Journal Officiel de la République française 2017*). This participation of offensive missions in defense is also made explicit in the *Éléments Publics de Doctrine Militaire de Lutte Informatique Offensive* (Public Elements for the Military Cyber Warfare Doctrine), published by the Ministry of the Armed Forces in January 2019 as part of the ministry's missions (Ministère des Armées 2019a, p. 6).

3.3.1. *A rapidly changing context: an increasingly significant threat from the most advanced states*

For the past 10 years, the geopolitical context and the evolution of cyber threats have tested the French cyberdefense organization model. Cyberattacks are becoming more and more targeted and sophisticated, requiring the use of significant technical, financial and human resources, which can only be provided by states that have developed advanced capabilities. These attacks are much more difficult to counter than those carried out by opportunistic criminals.

In 2013, Edward Snowden revealed several cyberespionage operations conducted by the NSA against several heads of state and government, including France, and international organizations, on a regular basis as well as during international events, such as during the G20 in Toronto in 2010 (Follorou and Greenwald 2013a; Shane 2013; Weston 2013). The NSA's espionage is also aimed at economic and strategic targets. Snowden's revelations showed the extent of the NSA's offensive capabilities and that of its Tailored Access Operation (TAO) unit, which is in charge of operations for espionage purposes. They also perfectly illustrated the duality of contradictory objectives of the American and British intelligence services, which are also in charge of defending their country's networks. Indeed, documents showed that these agencies have the ability to break most encryption systems (Ball *et al.* 2013). For example, in order to guarantee their capacity, the NSA and GCHQ used their status as cybersecurity managers within international standardization organizations (ISOs) to push cryptographic standards that they were able to break (Perlroth *et al.* 2013).

In 2016 and 2017, the Shadow Brokers group published several offensive tools stolen from the NSA. Some of these tools were used within weeks of their release in the WannaCry attack in 2017. This attack was a ransomware that encrypted systems and aimed to extort money from victims, in exchange for the promise of the return of their data. WannaCry had a global impact, through its extremely rapid spread and the number of its victims, listed in 150 countries (Pixel 2017). This attack illustrates the ambiguity of vulnerability management by the NSA and therefore its responsibility at the global level of cyber insecurity (Delerue and Géry 2018).

Many states, including France, have taken responsibility for the development of advanced offensive capabilities. These capabilities often take a prominent place in the strategy of these countries. As an example, in 2018, the US Cyber Command announced its new strategy, calling for "achieving and sustaining superiority in cyberspace" (USCYBERCOM 2018). In the face of the evolving threat, the document promoted the implementation of a strategy of "persistent engagement", which consisted in having "the continuous ability to anticipate the adversary's vulnerabilities and formulate and execute cyberspace operations to contest adversary courses of action under determined conditions". Due to its very offensive nature, this strategy fully participates in the increase of threats. Indeed, it operates the levers of the cybersecurity dilemma (Buchanan 2016) and risks participating in the reinforcement of the cyber arms race or resulting in an escalation of tensions, or even open conflict.

The pursuit of a cyber arms race is leading to an intensification and to the growing complexity of attacks, which are becoming increasingly difficult to counter, even when the significant resources available to states are exploited. In this context, the separation of defensive and offensive functions, by limiting exchanges between the two parts, does not allow for an effective response to these threats.

3.3.2. *Limits that have become obstacles to accomplishing cyberdefense missions*

As part of the definition of French cyberdefense strategy, the RS Cyber lists six missions for the French cyberdefense system: prevention, anticipation, protection, detection, attribution and reaction (SGDSN 2018, p. 48). However, in this context of increasing threat complexity, the strict separation of offensive and defensive missions and functions constitutes an obstacle to the realization of all these missions contributing to French cyberdefense, rather than merely a limitation. Whether it is missions upstream of the discovery of an attack (prevention, anticipation, protection and detection) or downstream (attribution and reaction), principal French cyberdefense actors need to work closely together.

For a long time a taboo subject in order to ensure ANSSI's reputation for integrity, since 2017 exchanges on the state of threats and in terms of attribution between ANSSI and the intelligence services have been carried out. During a hearing at the National Assembly, Guillaume Poupard declared that his agency exchanges "with all services, especially technical services. We are fully responsible for these links and I am happy with all the elements that the intelligence services can bring concerning attacks in progress or in preparation, or in terms of attribution"[18]. Beyond the existence of exchanges between the two parts, the defensive function requires operational capabilities that can be used for both defensive and offensive purposes. This is why, even before the 2018 RS Cyber, the French organization had begun

---

18 Hearing of Guillaume Poupard, January 31, 2017, before the national defense and armed forces committee of the French National Assembly; available at: www.is.gd/wBOLtc.

to relax the initial arrangement in order to provide ANSSI with resources to accomplish its defensive mission.

3.3.2.1. *Prevent, anticipate, protect and detect*

The defensive part needs to have very detailed knowledge of the state of threats in order to carry out its missions. This knowledge can be held by the actors of the offensive part, and can also come from the analysis of attacks handled by ANSSI.

Through their assessment of the cyber capabilities of malicious actors, whether state or non-state (cybercriminal groups or terrorists), intelligence services possess some of the knowledge necessary to implement a more effective defense strategy. However, the model of strict separation, even if it does not tend *a minima* to limit exchanges between the two parts, forces them to remain informal outside of any regulatory framework. The previous sections showed that these exchanges existed before the 2018 RS Cyber. They were also intended to intensify them by systematizing and formalizing these practices, while respecting the separation of defensive and offensive functions.

Furthermore, from an operational point of view, there is a proximity between the tools designed for offensive, as opposed to defensive, purposes. In IT security, the tools used for security audits and penetration tests, which aim to improve cybersecurity, are the same as those that can be used by attackers. Similarly, stopping and investigating an attack may lead the defender to use offensive tools. Finally, the tools used to monitor the network in order to detect an attack can also be used for intelligence purposes. This dual purpose of tools that blurs the lines is reinforced by use that can be both civilian and military (Géry 2018).

Originally, the policy framework of ANSSI's defensive mission did not allow its agents to possess the tools necessary to analyze the computer codes of cyberattacks they were dealing with, thus preventing them from learning more about the modus operandi of the attack and being able to prevent possible future attacks. It would be necessary to wait for the 2014–2019 Military Programming Law, in which article 21 allows ANSSI agents to hold and use these reverse engineering tools.

On the detection side, the 2019–2025 Military Programming Law gives ANSSI the power to place probes on private operators' networks "when it is aware of a threat likely to affect the cybersecurity of public authorities, critical infrastructures and essential service operators"[19] (art. 34 LPM 2019-2025). These "devices implementing technical markers" must be deployed "for the sole purpose of preventing and characterizing the threat affecting the cybersecurity of the aforementioned actors" (art. 34 LPM 2019-2025).

Thus, prevention, anticipation, protection and detection missions require close cooperation between defensive and offensive actors of French cyberdefense, as well as the provision of resources that can fulfill the offensive objectives for the benefit of defensive actors.

3.3.2.2. A need to attribute and respond

Following the discovery of an attack, accomplishing attribution and reaction missions also requires close collaboration between the entire French cyberdefense community. In terms of attribution, the contribution of intelligence agencies and their knowledge has been evident since at least 2012.

From 2013, the LBDSN provided for an increase in France's efforts in the development of military cyberdefense capabilities. This "marked effort" would center around two main axes. The first was aimed at the "implementation of a robust and resilient posture for protecting state information systems, essential operators and strategic industries". The second concerned the development of "a global and adjusted governmental response capacity [...] calling first and foremost on all diplomatic, legal and law enforcement resources"[20]. This capacity was to be based on two elements: offensive cyber capabilities and intelligence capabilities through "cyber threat intelligence" (*renseignement d'intérêt cyber*).

Then, in the framework of a "possible and proportionate response to an attack" (SGDSN 2013, p. 73), offensive cyber warfare (LIO) capabilities must enrich "the range of possible options available to the state" (SGDSN 2013, p. 107). In this respect, the LBDSN specifies that France will not prohibit "the gradual use of resources under the authority of the Ministry of Defence, if national strategic interests are threatened" (SGDSN 2013, p. 107),

---

19 "Operators, public or private, offering services essential to the functioning of society or the economy and whose continuity could be seriously affected by incidents affecting the networks and information systems necessary for the provision of said services" (Article 5 of Law No. 2018-133, February 26, 2018).

20 For legal issues, see Chapters 4 and 5.

and may therefore generate a potential military response. The 2014–2019 Military Programming Law thus confers response capabilities against cyberattacks "that target information systems affecting war or economic potential, security or the survivability of the nation". Article 21 of the 2014–2019 LPM, which allows ANSSI to possess reverse engineering tools, also permits it to penetrate an automated data system without authorization, with the aim of "carrying out the technical operations necessary to characterize an attack and neutralize its effects by accessing the information systems that are at the origin of the attack". The collection of technical markers or identifying elements of an attacker may require penetration of the attack system set up by the attacker, which may potentially be located abroad. This article helps to meet the goal of developing a response capability for cyber attacks as discussed in the 2008 and 2013 LBDSN. It thus provides defensive services with a new capability that serves the objective of protecting information systems during an attack by enabling them to stop it.

3.3.2.3. The need to pool resources

Beyond accomplishing cyberdefense missions, the strict separation of defensive and offensive missions has created situations of duplicate investment, both in terms of tool design and human resources. However, in both cases, these resources are scarce and costly.

With regard to human investment, despite the increase in funding and the opening of positions, the Ministry of Defense and ANSSI very quickly encountered recruitment difficulties. Indeed, there are few training courses in France in the field of cybersecurity and the public sector has to compete with the private sector to recruit students graduating from these courses. The demand and needs, whether in the public or private sector, are much greater than the number of students graduating each year. As early as 2012, Patrick Pailloux, Director General of ANSSI, estimated that France was training a quarter of the cybersecurity experts it needed[21]. The observation was still true in 2017, as evidenced by ANSSI Deputy Director Emmanuel Germain's remarks: "[Unfortunately] we are facing a war for talent because demand is higher than supply" (La Nevé 2017) Moreover, the salaries offered by the private sector are more attractive than those of the public sector. The DGSE, COMCYBER and ANSSI have therefore set up *modus vivendi* in order to

---

21 Speech by Patrick Pailloux at the 2012 Monaco Security Assises, October 6, 2012; available at: www.youtu.be/Jn0YOAHeThM.

identify and recruit the rarest profiles[22]. The issue of human resources management is identified as the "weak point of the entire French system"[23].

In terms of tool design, Claire Landais, Secretary General for Defense and National Security, recognized in 2019 that the separation of offensive and defensive functions requires "the development of distinct tools, in order to avoid any confusion in the event of detection on networks, but at the cost of investments that are sometimes duplicated"[24]. While all the services in charge of offensive functions (civil and military) plan to develop common offensive tools, technical mutualization is also taking place with ANSSI for the creation of a "technical pool" participating in the attribution of attacks[25].

This search for mutualization of technical tools brings the actors of the offensive and defensive parts a little closer together and tends to attenuate the organizational model of French cyberdefense as it was originally proposed. The creation of this technical pool in order to attribute an attack shows that the separation of offensive and defensive functions is no longer as marked as before.

3.3.3. *An institutionalized rapprochement of the actors of defensive and offensive parts in the name of cyberdefense missions: from mitigation to obliteration?*

The organization of the French cyberdefense community proposed by the 2018 *Revue stratégique de cyberdéfense* aims to reduce the impacts of a strict separation of the actors of the two parts. It is the result of interministerial work and aims to formalize practices that were already in place. The distribution of all missions and cyberdefense organization reflects the rapprochement of the actors in charge of the defensive and offensive parts. They contribute together to accomplish both the defensive and offensive aspects of cyberdefense missions.

---

22 Intelligence on line (2019), Les services de renseignement en quête d'économie dans le cyber, March 20.

23 Intelligence on line (2018), Les chantiers de Bonnet de Paillerets au Comcyber, August 29.

24 Intelligence on line (2019), Le secrétariat général à la Défense clarifie sa politique d'attribution des cyberattaques, May 29.

25 Intelligence on line (2019), Les services de renseignement en quête d'économie dans le cyber, March 20.

As previously mentioned, the 2018 RS Cyber defined six missions for French cyberdefense. Figure 3.1 shows the contribution of the different state actors to cyberdefense missions. Cooperation between the defensive and offensive parts is necessary in at least three missions out of six.

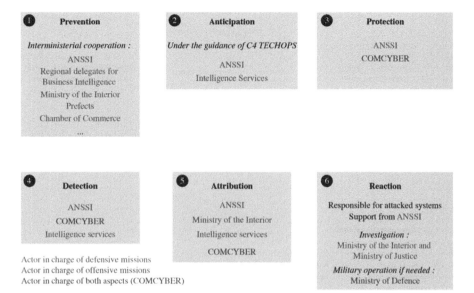

Figure 3.1. *The six missions of French cyberdefense (source: SGDSN 2018; design: A. Desforges, A. Géry; production: G. Marotte). For a color version of this figure, see www.iste.co.uk/laurent/cyberspace.zip*

In order to contribute to the realization of these six missions, the 2018 RS Cyber advocated clarifying the general organization of French cyberdefense by structuring it around four operational chains. The RS Cyber also recommended "strengthening the mechanisms of technical coherence" (SGDSN 2018, p. 52). The four operational chains (protection, military action, intelligence and judicial investigation) would be coordinated at the highest level of the state by the cyber steering committee. Co-chaired by the President's military Chief of Staff, the national intelligence and counterterrorism coordinator and the Prime Minister's Chief of Staff, the cyber steering committee would also monitor the implementation of the National Defense and Security Council's decisions on cyberdefense.

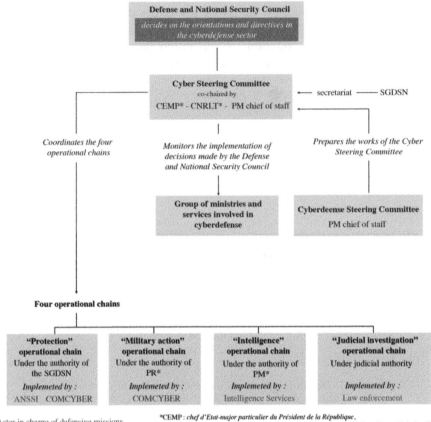

Figure 3.2. *Cyberdefense organization in France in 2018 (source: SGDSN 2018; design: A. Desforges, A. Géry; production: G. Marotte). For a color version of this figure, see www.iste.co.uk/laurent/cyberspace.zip*

Since 2018, French authorities have been communicating more and more about bringing offensive and defensive actors together. In January 2020, the Head of ANSSI assumed that "by 2025, [...] we will be obliged to have common platforms [bringing together defenders and attackers] in order to react effectively to the worst threats" (Guiton 2020). With this in mind, ANSSI has already announced the opening of a branch in Rennes, alongside the Ministry of the Armed Forces, which has made it its main branch in the provinces. However, these announcements are always tempered by the assurance that the French model separating offensive and defensive forces will not be called into question.

However, this operational example given by Guillaume Poupard raises the question of whether the multiplication of these cooperative ventures, some of which have operational objectives, does not risk calling into question the French model. Similarly, the announcements concerning the pooling of technical tools raise questions about the capacity of the French state to maintain this historical model in the execution of cyberdefense missions, as defined by the SGDSN (2018). In these examples, the indication of a model separating offensive and defensive functions has its limitations. However, the Director of ANSSI still remains optimistic: "The frequency of cases where we will have an interaction, without confusion of genres, between offensive and defensive, will develop."[26]

3.4. Conclusion

Although it has been thoroughly revised, France has so far managed to maintain its original cyberdefense organizational model, separating the offensive and defensive functions. Rather than bringing the two functions closer together, for the moment it is more a question of bringing the actors of the defensive and offensive parts together for the benefit of defense. However, the latest announcements seem to advocate a much more advanced operational rapprochement that could call this model into question. Future developments in the announced collaboration between the defensive and offensive parts will show whether France has succeeded in maintaining its model, or whether it is just a communication argument. Especially since the separation of offensive and defensive missions produces positive externalities, it contributes in particular to international stability and security. By entrusting an exclusively defensive mission to certain actors, the French model contributes, without ambiguity, to the general rise in the level of global cybersecurity.

---

26 *Ibid.*

3.5. References

Adam, L. (2020). Guillaume Poupard : "Dans l'avenir, l'offensif et le défensif devront travailler ensemble". *ZDNet*, February 20 [Online]. Available at: www.is.gd/ignAXo [Accessed on 4 April 2020].

Ball, J., Borger, J., Greenwald, G. (2013). Revealed: How US and UK spy agencies defeat internet privacy and security. *The Guardian*, September 6 [Online]. Available at: www.is.gd/KdYEtP [Accessed on 6 April 2020].

Buchanan, B. (2016). *The Cybersecurity Dilmena. Hacking, Trust and Fear Between Nations*. Oxford University Press, Oxford.

D'Elia, D. (2017). La cybersécurité des opérateurs d'importance vitale : analyse géo-politique des enjeux et des rivalités de la coopération public-privé. PhD Thesis, Paris University 8, Paris.

Delerue, F. and Géry, A. (2018). Prolifération des cyberarmes et droit international de la responsabilité, MasterClass. *International Cybersecurity Forum 2018*. Lille, January 23.

Douzet, F. and Géry, A. (2020). Le cyberespace, ça sert, d'abord, à faire la guerre. Prolifération, sécurité et stabilité du cyberespace. *Hérodote*, 177, 329–349.

Duquesne, M. (2014). DGSE : un costume plutôt bien fit pour Patrick Pailloux, en partance de l'ANSSI. *L'Informaticien*, January 22 [Online]. Available at: www.is.gd/k3MUjL [Accessed on 30 April 2018].

FranceInfo (2017). Ce que l'on sait (et ce que l'on ne sait pas) sur la nouvelle cyberattaque mondiale. *France Info*, June 28 [Online]. Available at: www.is.gd/p0um65 [Accessed on 2 April 2020].

Follorou, J. and Greenwald, G. (2013a). How the N.S.A. spies on France. *Le Monde*, October 21 [Online]. Available at: www.is.gd/IDhEo3 [Accessed on 4 April 2020].

Follorou, J. and Greenwald, G. (2013b). Comment Paris a soupçonné la NSA d'avoir piraté l'Élysée. *Le Monde*, October 25 [Online]. Available at: www.is.gd/XAMlWR [Accessed on 4 April 2020].

Géry, A. (2018). Droit international et prolifération des cyberarmes. *Politique Étrangère*, 2, 43–54.

Guiton, A. (2020). Cyber à la française : l'attaque et la défense, de la "separation" à l'"interaction". *Libération*, January 30 [Online]. Available at: www.is.gd/4f8km4 [Accessed on 28 March 2020].

Haquet, C. (2011). Areva victime d'une attaque informatique de grande ampleur. *L'Express*, September 29 [Online]. Available at: www.is.gd/Ql9m8T [Accessed on 27 March 2020].

Hoover, J.N. (2010). Senators say cybersecurity bill has no "Kill Switch". *Dark Reading*, June 24 [Online]. Available at: www.is.gd/s9zWef [Accessed on 6 April 2020].

Journal officiel de la République française (2017). Texte n°45. 0219. Document, Journal officiel de la République française, 19 September.

La Neve, S. (2017). Administration recherche "hackers" de confiance. *Acteurs publics*, November 28 [Online]. Available at: www.is.gd/oTtFk6 [Accessed on 1 April 2020].

Laurent, S.-Y. (2001). Les services secrets gaullistes à l'épreuve de la politique (1940–1947). *Politix*, 14(54), 139–153.

Marschalek, M. (2015). Shooting elephants [Online]. Available at: www.is.gd/RIBSpk [Accessed on 2 April 2020].

Ministère des Armées (2019a). Éléments publics de doctrine militaire de lutte informatique offensive [Online]. Available at: www.bit.ly/2G3ygsW [Accessed on 4 April 2020].

Ministère des Armées (2019b). Politique ministérielle de lutte informatique défensive [Online]. Available at: www.bit.ly/3jqGPMW [Accessed on 4 April 2020].

Perlroth, N., Larson, J., Shane, S. (2013). N.S.A. able to foil basic safeguards of privacy on web. *The New York Times*, September 5 [Online]. Available at: www.is.gd/ZWyOdk [Accessed on 14 April 2020].

Pixel (2017). 200 000 victimes, 150 pays : le premier bilan de la cyberattaque mondiale. *Le Monde*, May 14 [Online]. Available at: www.is.gd/zz5Q3y [Accessed on 27 March 2020].

Rascagnéres, P. (2015). Babar: Espionage software finally found and put under the microscope [Online]. Available at: www.bit.ly/3be1oJM [Accessed on 2 April 2020].

Sanger, D. (2012). Obama order sped up wave of cyberattacks against Iran. *The New York Times*, June 1 [Online]. Available at: www.is.gd/1Tf28C [Accessed on 14 April 2020].

Sanger, D. and Fackler, M. (2015). N.S.A. breached North Korean networks before Sony attack, officials say. *The New York Times*, January 18 [Online]. Available at: www.nytimes.com/2015/01/19/world/asia/nsa-tapped-into-north-korean-networks-before-sony-attack-officials-say.html [Accessed on 14 April 2020].

SGDSN (2008). *Livre blanc sur la défense et la sécurité nationale*. Odile Jacob, Paris.

SGDSN (2018). Revue stratégique de cyberdéfense [Online]. Available at: www.is.gd/QEJ3U2 [Accessed on 27 March 2020].

Shane, S. (2013). No morsel too minuscule for all-consuming N.S.A. *The New York Times*, November 2 [Online]. Available at: www.is.gd/FDlenW [Accessed on 15 April 2020].

Untersinger, M. (2017). Le piratage de TV5 Monde vu de l'intérieur. *Le Monde*, June 10 [Online]. Available at: www.is.gd/ZArRKo [Accessed on 28 March 2020].

USCYBERCOM (2018). Achieve and maintain cyberspace superiority [Online]. Available at: https://www.cybercom.mil/Portals/56/Documents/USCYBERCOM %20Vision%20April%202018.pdf?ver=2018-06-14-152556-010) [Accessed on 15 April 2020].

Weston, G. (2013). New Snowden docs show U.S. spied during G20 in Toronto. *CBC News*, November 27 [Online]. Available at: www.is.gd/CqUJUZ [Accessed on 15 April 2020].

Zdnet.fr (2011). Sécurité : Bercy victime d'une attaque informatique de grande ampleur. *ZDNet.fr*, March 7 [Online]. Available at: www.is.gd/t5vtYk [Accessed on 27 March 2020].

The Boundary Between Cybercrime and Cyberwar: An Uncertain No-Man's Land

4.1. Introduction

The history of humankind could be studied through conquests of spaces. After land, sea, airspace and outer space, humans are currently investing in cyberspace[1]. However, the process is not the same. Can we speak of conquest when cyberspace, unlike the others, is built *ex nihilo*? The other spaces pre-existed and impose their physical, spatial and temporal constraints. Humans have discovered, mastered and exploited them and resisted the whims of nature as best they can. Cyberspace or "digital space" is, on the other hand, manmade, without any real plan and without any spatiotemporal limit. More than just a "free" space[2], it is a substrate that permeates, irrigates and reformats all other natural environments. Each innovation affects its foundations, modifies its architecture and upsets its equilibrium with a speed that exceeds that of human perception and understanding. Since the beginning, humans have created value in the spaces they have discovered or appropriated. All experts agree on the immense

Chapter written by Marc WATIN-AUGOUARD.

1 The term appears for the first time in a collection of short stories, *Burning Chrome*, by William Gibson, and then in his book *Neuromancer* (1984, Ace Books, New York). Today, we prefer the term "digital space" or, better, "digital substrate". On the notion of cyberspace, see Chapter 1.
2 This is what John Perry Barlow believed when he published his *A Declaration of the Independence of Cyberspace* (https://www.eff.org/cyberspace-independence).

potential of the digital space in terms of freedom, access to knowledge, communication, economic growth and scientific progress, particularly in the health domain. However, everyone must also admit that no newly conquered space escapes predators, delinquents, terrorists, mercenaries or warriors. As soon as humans tamed the sea, they encountered pirates and made war. The libertarian utopia of the pioneers of cyberspace is being undermined by those who have understood that the relationship between risk-taking and expected gain is very favorable to looters, raiders and hawks. The "global village" (McLuhan 1967) needs governance, but this governance is failing to impose itself. The efforts undertaken by the UN have so far resulted in failure[3]. The regional conventions (Budapest in 2001, Malabo in 2014) may have taken place, but they were only ratified by a limited number of states (64 for the aforementioned 2001 Council of Europe convention). Europe seems to be waking up since the 2017 Tallinn summit, with, more particularly, the adoption of the June 2019 Cybersecurity Act. However, in the absence of a global agreement, the states find themselves in the front line. They are being put to the test by individuals and legal entities who are asking them to fulfill their regulatory security and defense missions in the digital space.

The defense–security continuum (Watin-Augouard 1992a, 1992b) is now a matter of course in the real world: terrorism, piracy and large-scale trafficking call for hybrid responses that combine the actions of the armed forces and those of internal security actors. In cyberspace, this continuum is even more apparent. Crime and delinquency are transferring to the immaterial world, which is becoming a new terrain of conflict. In this borderless space, there is no "battlefield" or "priority security zone". The mesh construction of the network and the development of mobility give threats a polymorphous and ubiquitous character.

The symbiosis between the fight against cybercrime and cyberdefense is a perfect illustration of this continuum, which associates the delinquent, the terrorist or the "warrior" in the same gray area. The boundary between what is ordinary – internal security – and what is extraordinary – cyberdefense – is particularly porous because of the connection between the actions.

---

3 Failure of the ITU summit (2012), failure of the Group of Governmental Experts (GGE) in 2017; the world is split in two, with some states wanting absolute control of exchanges between individuals in the name of national security.

The continuum has only one limitation: the coming into force of the law of armed conflict. As long as this law cannot be invoked, common law applies, including for the most serious attacks, which may target what in France are called operators of vital importance (*Opérateurs d'Importance Vitale* (OIV)), for example critical infrastructures, or the armed forces. These are offenses (attacks on automated data processing systems, espionage, sabotage, etc.), notably provided for and punished by the Godfrain Act. Cyberdefense, which aims to protect critical systems, combines its effects with the fight against cybercrime. Both are essential components of cybersecurity strategy. Cyberwar, or the use of cyber in warfare, is governed by other rules of international humanitarian law.

The evolution of cybercrime raises the question of the glass ceiling, which, from the outset, does not reveal any legal discontinuity; it is pierced when cybercrime departs from common law to become a form of armed conflict. At what point is it broken? The field of cybercrime enters that of cyber conflict, an "infra-war" that does not have the characteristics of war and cannot be qualified as such. It stops as soon as a cyber attack can be qualified as armed aggression. The crossing of the boundary is thus conditioned by the ability to attribute cyber attacks with disastrous consequences. This quasi-war calls for a strategy of cyberdeterrence, which draws from dissuasion and coercion by abandoning the utopia of passive defense.

4.2. The field of cybercrime up to the limits of the glass ceiling

Cybercrime is not defined in international law, except in certain regional conventions. This is undoubtedly because states do not all have the same approach, particularly due to differences that may exist with regard to public liberties.

In France, as in other member states, a consensus is nevertheless emerging. Cybercrime is the crime of the 21st century, to quote the theme of the first International Cybersecurity Forum[4], organized in 2007. Due to its

---

4 The International Cybersecurity Forum (*Forum International de la Cybersécurité* (FIC)) was created by the National Gendarmerie. It is held every year. In 2020, it brought together more than 12,500 participants and 450 companies from 112 countries. It is not only a place of exchange but also an opportunity for ministerial or European authorities to give structuring speeches on cyber strategy.

origins, its intensity and its targets, it differs from traditional crime in its paroxysmal manifestations.

4.2.1. *The field of cybercrime: an attempt at delimitation*

Cybercrime does not have a universal definition. In 1986, Professor René Gassin (1986) distinguished between:

– cases in which computers are the very object of delinquency;

– cases in which computers are instruments, the means of fraud;

– cases in which computer technology provides the opportunity for crime.

At the time, this definition was visionary, as the internet was still in its early stages of development.

In 1986, the Organisation for Economic Cooperation and Development (OECD) defined a cybercrime as "any illegal, unethical or unauthorized conduct involving automatic data processing and/or data transmission". This definition included:

– computer manipulations;

– computer espionage;

– computer sabotage;

– computer time theft[5];

– embezzlement through the use of computerized means;

– undue access to systems and networks.

The Council of Europe Convention on Cybercrime of November 23, 2001 does not provide a definition but lists the offenses that fall under it:

– violations against the confidentiality, integrity and availability of data and computer systems, in the field of information systems security (ISS);

– computer crimes: computer forgery, computer fraud;

– content-related offenses involving child pornography;

– infringements of intellectual property and related rights.

---

5 That is to say the misuse, for the benefit of the predator, of the calculation capacities of the target computer.

The UNODC, for its part, has, since 2013, explicitly recognized the difficulty of agreeing on a definition:

> The way cybercrime is defined depends mostly on the purpose of the term in the context in which it is used. A limited number of attacks on the confidentiality, integrity and availability of data or information systems constitute the quintessence of cybercrime. However, other actions, such as the use of computers for financial or other gain or harm, including some forms of identity theft and attacks on computer content (all of which fall under the broadest definition of "cybercrime"), do not facilitate efforts to legally define the term in its entirety[6].

In 2011, according to ANSSI[7], a national authority on cybersecurity in France:

> cybercrime consists of acts that contravene international treaties or national laws, using networks or information systems as a means of committing a crime or an offense, or targeting them. It includes:
>
> – traditional crimes and offenses facilitated by the use of new technologies: money laundering, pedophilia, organized crime, terrorism, etc.;
>
> – new crimes and offenses directly linked to the use of information and communication technologies: credit card forgery, identity theft, tagging or defacement of official websites, denial of service attacks or botnets[8], data theft, theft of computer

---

6 United Nations Office on Drugs and Crime (UNODC), "In-depth Study on the Phenomenon of Cybercrime and the Measures Taken by Member States, the International Community and the Private Sector to Address It", UNODC/CCPCJ/EG.4/2013/2, p. 2.

7 ONDRP 2011 report, note by Philippe Wolf, project manager for the ANSSI director general, and Luc Vallée, engineer at the ANSSI operational center (COSSI).

8 According to ENISA ("Botnets: Detection, Measurment, Desinfection and Defence", 2011), a botnet is a network of advanced malware that often incorporates viruses, worms, Trojans and hostile stealth programs designed to spread and embed themselves in a foreign system and then reconnect to a central server or other infected systems, allowing the attacker to control the operation of the affected system.

resources, phishing[9], carding (illegal sale of credit card numbers), etc.;

– the rapid misuse of new technologies for criminal and terrorist purposes: the use of cell phones to set off homemade bombs, increasingly accessible GPS devices coupled with communication resources to manage explosive devices, commercial drones, the Internet of Things, etc.

What is simpler and probably more effective is the definition used by the report of Attorney General Marc Robert (2014), which repeats the conclusions of the Breton report of 2004 (Breton 2004): "Cybercrime includes all criminal offenses attempted or committed against or by means of an information and communication system, mainly the internet." This definition is very similar to that of the European Union in 2007, for which "cybercrime should be understood as criminal offenses committed with the help of electronic communications networks and information systems or against these networks or systems"[10]. This definition focuses on the legal qualification of the facts, in that it retains the target and the tool without the risk of getting lost in a classification according to the authors, the motives or the modes of action. In the absence of a universal definition, the domain of cybercrime can be delimited by deduction, by referring to the penal corpus. This resembles a millefeuille, formed by incremental sedimentation as the uses, and therefore the misuses, multiply. The logic of codification does not promote a global vision of a legislation, which is nowadays divided between several codes[11].

---

9 Phishing is a method of recovering personal data by impersonating public or private legal entities, large corporations or financial institutions. A hypertext link refers to a page that is a carbon copy of an official page. This method allows for the fraudulent collection of personal data, especially banking data.

10 "Vers une politique générale en matière de lutte contre la cybercriminalité", Communication COM (2007) from the Commission to the European Parliament, the Council and the Committee of the Regions, May 22, 2007.

11 Criminal Code, Code of Criminal Procedure, Customs Code, Post and Electronic Communications Code, Commercial Code, Consumer Code, Post and Electronic Communications Code, Intellectual Property Code, Monetary and Financial Code, Defense Code, Internal Security Code, etc. See Chapter 5.

4.2.2. Cybercrime, the "21st century crime"

The digital transformation of society has been accompanied by a transfer of criminality from the field of the real to that of the immaterial. Predators are changing their behavior. If they are migrating to cyberspace, it is because they have never found a better ratio between the expected gain and the penal risk. Thanks to the shrinking of the space-time framework, they have never been so close, so invisible or so unidentifiable to their victims, through concealment, anonymization and even identity theft. Often acting from cyber rogue states, they have never been so distant from their judges, if only because of legal borders and the slowness of judicial cooperation compared to the speed of the internet.

Cybercrime is growing in frequency, although a highly significant "dark figure" prevents us from knowing the exact measure of it[12]. The statistics published by security providers, insurers and *ad hoc* organizations (such as Cybermalveillance in France) each year are highlighting a growth that is more exponential than linear. Increases in the number of internet users (4.7 billion in 2020), connected systems (80 billion in 2020) and in the attack surface with the massive deployment of poorly protected connected objects explain this dynamic. Following a period notable for small-scale, individual cybercrime, "script kiddies" and isolated hackers, the transition to an industrial and collective stage is becoming the new trend. The more that cybersecurity measures are developed, the more powerful the attack must be, transposing the "cannon–armor" duel to the digital space. We are now in an era of organized, targeted cybercrime, which is violent both in its intensity and its results. The industrial concentration of human and technical resources does not, however, exclude the persistence of individual actions, which can also produce devastating effects. Since 2007, the year of the massive cyber attack in Estonia, the rise of the aggressors has become a reality.

4.2.3. Cyber conflict at the edge of the glass ceiling

In addition to the migration of offenders, there is also the migration of states, all of whom are eager to exploit the strategic opportunities of the digital space on political, economic, cultural and ideological levels. Competition or

---

12 The dark figure for cybercrime is one of the highest, often because the natural or legal persons targeted are unaware of the facts or do not dare to reveal them.

peaceful confrontation in cyberspace is now a reality. However, antagonisms can also lead to a form of conflict. Some states have understood that the digital space is an ideal place to settle their accounts. Digital banderillas are replacing gunboat policies. To avoid any attribution leading to the condemnation of a coercive intervention by the international community, these states most often call upon mafia, paramilitary and hacktivist groups, whose activity is related to organized crime. These organized, structured criminal groups, not without any link to their sponsors, can play the role of third-party attackers; they are ready to provide a service, so long as they have an interest in it, even if the cause is alien to their core business. The so-called advanced persistent threat (APT) groups fall into this category. In some cases, their relationships with states are implicitly established when they are located in public buildings. Collusion between structured groups and states is already a feature of the continuum in the real world.

Cybercrime is not only growing in frequency but also in quality, in the virality of its manifestations and its intensity of impact. In its most extreme form, cybercrime is likely to undermine national security and the fundamental interests of the nation[13], which justifies a cyberdefense policy that, along with ISS and the fight against cybercrime, contributes to cybersecurity. In France, the the two issues of the *Livre blanc sur la défense et la sécurité nationale* from 2008 and 2013, as well as the "cyber" dimension of the military programing laws and the recent legislation on terrorism, intelligence and the fight against organized crime, illustrate the mobilization of public authorities against this phenomenon.

Some writings, some of them official[14], suggest a trilogy of "cybercrime–sabotage–espionage", which would seem to restrict the scope of cybercrime to criminal offenses. This is a legally erroneous approach, since sabotage and espionage are offenses provided for and punished by the penal code and therefore fall under cybercrime. This distinction undoubtedly reflects the difficulty of legally understanding a cyber attack of state or parastate origin, which is more akin to the use of force, or even an act of aggression, than to a traditional crime or offense. The multiplicity of actors, and in particular the lack of clear demarcation between state agents, terrorists, delinquents, patriots and isolated developers of malware acting on their own behalf, may explain this difficulty in categorization.

---

13 As defined in Book IV Title I of the Criminal Code.

14 For example, the 2018 *Revue stratégique cyberdéfense* (available at: www.sgdsn.gouv.fr).

Interpretations sometimes contrast the fight against cybercrime with cyberdefense, whereas the two are composed of each other. For example, in his 2012 report, Senator Jean-Marie Bockel drew a line between cyberdefense and cybercrime:

> Cyberdefense is particularly distinct from the fight against cybercrime [...], which has been deliberately left out of the discussion in order to focus on computer attacks likely to harm the fundamental interests of the nation [...][15].

However, these attacks are indeed offenses (espionage, theft or modification of data, hindrance, sabotage, etc.), provided for and punished by Book IV of the Criminal Code, which is specifically devoted to the fundamental interests of the nation and to terrorism. In addition, since the Godfrain Act[16], attacks on automated data processing systems, "thefts", destruction and modification of data are subject to criminal sanctions[17]. Except in the case of an armed conflict, attacks falling within the scope of cyberdefense also fall within the competence of the judiciary and the specialized services of the police and gendarmerie. In a report from June 8, 2015, the Assembly of the Council of Europe Parliament considered that "Member states should agree on a common level of criminalization of large-scale cyber attacks [...]"[18]. The draft Council conclusions on a framework for a joint EU diplomatic response to acts of cybermalware[19] support this analysis:

> Cybermalicious activities directed against information systems, as defined by Union law, constitute a criminal offense [...] and the effective investigation and prosecution of such offenses remains a common effort by member states.

---

15 Bockel, J.M. (2011–2012), La cyberdéfense, Information Report No. 681 on behalf of the Senate Committee on Foreign Affairs, Defense and Armed Forces.

16 Law no. 88-19 of January 5, 1988, on computer fraud.

17 The offenses defined by the Godfrain Act may be acts of terrorism within the meaning of Article 421-1, 2° of the Criminal Code.

18 Report of the Committee on Culture, Science, Education and the Media. Reporter Hans Franken. Doc. 13802 of June 8, 2015.

19 Draft Council conclusions on a framework for a joint EU diplomatic response to acts of cyber-malware ("cyber-diplomatic toolkit", No. 9916/17, June 7, 2017, auj. Council Regulation EU 2019/796, May 17, 2019, on restrictive measures against cyber attacks that threaten the Union or its member states).

The intensification of cyber attacks brings cybercrime closer to the glass ceiling, which is broken when an armed attack is characterized. In this uncertain frontier zone, the transparent and contradictory judiciary tends to fade away and give way to other more secret modes of action, while remaining legal[20]. The intelligence techniques, resulting from the legislation from July 24, 2015[21], are part of this. The DGSI, the first-circle intelligence service, possesses judicial competences and is systematically involved in cases of cyber attacks on OIVs. Within the DGSI, a bridge has been established between judicial action and that of intelligence techniques. The criminal, internal security and defense codes contain provisions that exclude the criminal responsibility of cyberdefense or intelligence actors when they commit acts in the execution of their functions. This is proof that, following the government's will, the legislator considers that the field of cybercrime penetrates the field of cyber conflict in a gray zone that is supracriminal but infra-warlike and that it is appropriate to protect state actors who do not have the status of combatants, in the absence of a recognized armed conflict. Being unable to define what is beyond, a barrier is erected, a "firewall" is created.

4.3. War in cyberspace, cyber in war

In a borderless space that challenges the Westphalian order, states are seeking to re-establish their sovereignty, a stake in power and even economic or cultural domination. Cyberspace then also becomes a place of competition and the struggle for influence and confrontation. It reproduces and amplifies the rifts and antagonisms that divide or fragment the real world. In this context, tensions can reach a paroxysmal level, likely to undermine national security and lead to cyberwar; but is it a war in cyberspace or the use of cyber means in war?

4.3.1. *Cyber in war, a daily reality*

Cyber in warfare does not raise any conceptual difficulty. Since the Kosovo conflict and, later, the conflict between Russia and Georgia (2008), all military operations have been using cyber weapons before, along side or after the use of conventional means. This is not cybercrime, but an act of war that must respect

---

20 See the Act of July 24, 2015, on intelligence and legalizing intelligence techniques.
21 Act No. 2015-912 of July 24, 2015, relating to intelligence.

the rules set by international humanitarian law (principles of humanity, discrimination, proportionality, non-perfidy and neutrality). It should be noted, however, that Article L.4123-12 of the Defense Code was amended by the 2019–2025 Military Programming Law to establish the principle of the criminal irresponsibility of a soldier who, in compliance with the rules of international law and within the framework of an operation mobilizing military capabilities, executes or orders digital coercion measures. This is clear proof that legislators wish to avoid the risk of application of common law.

4.3.2. Autonomous warfare in the cyber world: the test of the law of armed conflict

Autonomous warfare in the cyber world raises more difficulties as to its qualification. Jean Giraudoux questioned: "Will the cyberwar of the Trojan horse take place?" In 2007, when Estonia was massively targeted by a distributed denial of service attack (DDOS), the media talked about cyberwar. It was a title that certainly sold, as sensationalism aroused interest. Does this neologism give in to the trend that adds the prefix "cyber" to any real-world concept, or does it cover a new form of conflict? "Cyber Pearl Harbor" and "Cybergeddon" are examples of this temptation to create expressions or words before having really defined their meaning and scope. Announced in 1993 by John Arquilla and David Ronfeldt, in their article "Cyberwar is coming!" and then, in 1999, through the concept of war without limits by the Chinese co-leaders Qiao Liang and Wang Xiangsui, cyberwar is also contested by other authors, such as Thomas Rid (2013) and Martin Libicki (2012). War in cyberspace, which is independent of military operations conducted in the real world, has not yet been observed *de jure* because, in order to qualify as a cyberoffensive, two cumulative conditions are required. War refers to the notion of armed aggression, which must reach a certain magnitude and have physical (destruction) and human (death and injury) consequences, and be part of an international or non-international armed conflict in the sense given to it by international public law (the Law of The Hague, the Geneva Convention and its additional protocols, etc.)[22]. Thus, for there to be a war, that is to say, an armed conflict arising between

---

22 The Hague Law deals with *jus ad bellum*: The Hague conventions of July 29, 1899, and October 18, 1907. Humanitarian law deals with *jus in bello* and is based on the four Geneva Conventions of August 12, 1949, and the two additional Protocols of June 8, 1977. Arms control law concerns the prohibition or limitation of certain weapons.

two or more states, the conditions laid down in Articles 2 and 3[23] and in Article 1 of Additional Protocol II[24] (1977) of the Geneva Conventions must be met. Article 2, drafted in identical terms in the four conventions, defines international armed conflict between two or more states. Article 3 refers to non-international conflict, the definition of which is specified by the second Additional Protocol. Thus, a non-international armed conflict is one in which, in the territory of a state, "its armed forces and dissident armed forces or organized armed groups which, under responsible command, exert such control over a part of its territory as to enable them to carry out sustained and concerted military operations"[25]. The second Protocol excludes situations of internal disturbance or tension, such as riots and isolated or sporadic acts of violence, which fall within the scope of common law and therefore of cybercrime. The ICRC is in line with this approach, as it considers that computer warfare concerns only those means and methods of warfare used to conduct cyber operations equivalent to armed conflict, or conducted in the context of an armed conflict, within the meaning of international humanitarian law (IHL)[26].

Whatever the hypothesis, the aggression must produce particularly serious effects to be characterized. The massive attack that hit Estonia on April 27, 2007, did not result in any deaths or injuries. However, for several weeks, denial of service attacks blocked government sites, banks, the media, emergency services, etc., 85,000 computers having been hacked. In 2010, in Natanz (Iran), and 2012, at Saudi Aramco (Saudi Arabia), massive destruction of equipment was observed without any loss of life. Under these conditions, it is difficult to qualify as cyberwarfare facts that are not however without consequences. These events do not constitute armed aggression, but

---

23 Geneva Convention for the Amelioration of the Condition of the Wounded and Sick in Armed Forces in the Field, Geneva Convention for the Amelioration of the Condition of Wounded, Sick and Shipwrecked Members of Armed Forces at Sea, Geneva Convention Relative to the Treatment of Prisoners of War, Geneva Convention Relative to the Protection of Civilian Persons in Time of War of August 12, 1949.

24 Additional Protocol to the Geneva Conventions of August 12, 1949, and relating to the Protection of Victims of Non-International Armed Conflicts, June 8, 1977.

25 The International Criminal Tribunal for the former Yugoslavia (ICTY), in the trial of Duško Tadić, clarified "that an armed conflict exists whenever there is recourse to armed force between states or prolonged conflict between government authorities and organized armed groups or between such groups within a state".

26 ICRC Expert Meeting (2018), The Potential Human Cost of Cyber Operations, November 12–16, Geneva.

a form of e-conflict. It would be different if cyber attacks on critical infrastructure were leading, directly or indirectly, to large-scale loss of life and property.

The aggression, if it is characterized, must be imputed to a perpetrator. How do we qualify cyberwarfare facts if we cannot identify the aggressor? This is the problem of attribution, of imputation, which in France is the prerogative of the President of the Republic. In the case of Estonia, Konstantin Goloskokov, a member of the Russian youth group Nashi[27], claimed responsibility for the attacks in the name of civil disobedience, but there was never a signature, notably because there was no conventional commitment to reveal the identity of the aggressor[28]. Only one Russian-speaking Estonian was arrested, betrayed by his IP address. Russia referred to the initiatives of patriotic groups and was never legally implicated.

Due to a lack of confounding evidence, agressors may respond with plausible deniability. The search for anonymity is the first precaution of a stealthy aggressor, except when he or she uses cyberspace for propaganda or subversion, but can we describe an action that is not claimed as a cyber attack as subversive warfare? For these reasons, the hypothesis of an autonomous war in cyberspace is unlikely today. Cyberwar is uncertain, even if it is possible. Let us always think about it and act as if it were inevitable – because defeats are the result of refusing to believe the worst – but let us only talk about it wisely, with the conditional tense, as was used in the 2013 *Livre blanc sur la défense et la sécurité nationale.* This is a continuation of the previous paper (2008), but it more explicitly takes into account the risks linked to cyber attacks: "They constitute a major threat, likely to paralyze entire sectors of the country's activity, to trigger technological or ecological disasters and to result in widespread casualties, which could constitute a real act of war"[29]. NATO, especially since the Newport summit (September 4 and 5, 2014), considers that: "cyber attacks may reach a threshold that could threaten the prosperity, security and stability of states and the Euro-Atlantic zone. Their impact on modern societies could be just as damaging as that of a conventional attack".

---

27 Group formed by Vladimir Putin.

28 The attack followed the removal of a monument erected in 1947 on Tonismäe Hill in Tallinn in memory of Soviet soldiers in Second World War. Russia has, of course, been suspected without formal evidence.

29 *Livre blanc sur la défense et la sécurité nationale,* 2013, p. 49.

4.3.3. *Digital cyber persuasion*

In an uncertain environment where cyber conflict is developing, drawing from war and cybercrime, the fight against cyber attacks calls for both preventive and reactive measures[30]. Today, France has clearly chosen to equip itself with offensive means. On December 12, 2016, in Bruz, Jean-Yves Le Drian, then Minister of Defense, opened the new buildings of the DGA-MI and announced the recruitment of 4,500 cybercombatants by 2022 and 4,400 cyberdefense reservists, as well as the creation of a "fourth army". Decree No. 2017-743 of May 4, 2017, created COMCYBER, responsible for the design, planning and conduct of military cyberdefense operations, under the authority of the "Operations" Deputy Chief of Staff. As the French Armed Forces Minister, Florence Parly, indicated at the 2019 International Cyber Security Forum:

> If there is one threat that affects us all and does not care about borders, it is the cyber threat. So, we must create a common culture, stronger ramparts and act together, including the use of offensive computer warfare [...] The cyberwar has well and truly begun. We will not be naïve or blind, we will prepare for it.

In an article recently published by *Le Monde*, three eminent authors (Barbier *et al.* 2020) proposed a strategy of "counter-cybercoercion" with strategic coordination at the highest level of the state[31]. They defined cybercoercion as "the action of one state to influence and weaken the leadership of another state by implicitly demonstrating that it can cause, in a way that is difficult to attribute, serious disruption in public services or important industrial activities". The authors add that "this state must be convinced that France has the capacity and the will to retaliate against attempts at cybercoercion". This "counter-cybercoercion" – to use their vocabulary – must apply international law, which the Group of Governmental Experts (GGE)[32] proclaimed in 2013 to be applicable in

---

30 See Chapter 3.

31 It already exists at the level of the President of the Republic (NSDC) and the C4 (see SGDSN 2018).

32 GGE (2013), Applicability of international law to cyberspace and, in particular, the United Nations Charter: state responsibility, due diligence.

cyberspace and which was very clearly explained in a document published in September 2019 by the Armed Forces Ministry[33]. This law provides for the possibility that a state invokes a situation of necessity, distress and force majeure. The state may take retaliatory (diplomatic, embargo, etc.) measures, unfriendly measures, lawful in themselves, taken in response to unfriendly behavior. In the case of armed aggression, self-defense may be invoked, but the double condition mentioned above must be verified. The authors rightly dismiss the concept of cyberdeterrence. The basis is the law of politico-strategic hope, formulated by General Lucien Poirier, one of the "four generals of the Apocalypse"[34], with regard to nuclear weapons: the risk incurred by the adversary is greater than the expected advantage. The aggressor may suffer damage in return that is far greater than what is at stake. However, the digital response cannot satisfy this inequality. The physical and particularly the psychological impacts can be mitigated in non-democratic states. Deterrence is based on weapons that are not used, but whose use is deemed probable by the adversary. Cyber weapons are single-use weapons, often developed and owned by private actors[35]. The technical credibility of nuclear weapons can be demonstrated[36]; cyber weapons, on the other hand, are not publicly demonstrated, except when they are used. The answer lies rather in a strategy of cyberpersuasion, of "cyberdiscouragement"[37], which can be guessed at and which is surrounded by a halo of certainty and uncertainty. This state strategy is based on nine pillars:

– its real or assumed capacity to act in a coercive, adapted and proportioned manner, including below the threshold of armed conflict;

– its R&D capabilities, particularly in the area of forensics, to improve attribution criteria;

– the sovereign nature of its cyberdefense industrial fabric;

---

33 International Law Applied to Operations in Cyberspace, September 2019. Available at: www.defense.gouv.fr. See Chapter 1 in this volume.

34 See Poirier (1988).

35 They are notably covered by the Wassenaar Arrangement and are included in the list of dual-use (DU) items.

36 The purpose of nuclear testing is not only to verify technical credibility, but also to prove it to the rest of the world.

37 A more defensive term than "cyberpersuasion".

– its organization with regard to cyber risk (ANSSI, COMCYBER, etc.), including the ability to develop public–private partnerships;

– its human resources skills (does it train and retain enough specialists?);

– the robustness of its civilian and military cyberresilience, verified during cyber attacks;

– the relevance of its legal corpus;

– its resistance to information manipulation;

– the solidarity of the alliances of which it is a member and the areas of co-action in which it is involved (e.g. the EU).

Without doubt, we are more concerned with preventing cyber risk than with retaliatory action. However, it is undoubtedly a way to keep control of one's degrees of freedom in the uncertain zone where cybercrime and cyber conflict overlap.

4.4. Conclusion

Is cybercrime drifting, due to its intensity and the objectives pursued, toward cyber conflict? Is the latter merging with the former by passing under the glass ceiling of armed conflict? Whatever the hypothesis, the hybrid nature of "unfriendly" actions makes the fight more complex. Judicial investigations are reaching their limits, while the coercive response cannot find its basis in the law of armed conflict. The boundary is therefore uncertain. National and international law can make progress in removing doubts and clarifying situations. The Paris Appeal of November 12, 2018, for trust and security in cyberspace, invites us to react with a desire for stabilization and peace. However, for now, the solution is undoubtedly more national than international, more political than legal, more clandestine[38] than open, in a digital world where the balance of power often prevails over the law. Today, "the sword is passing before the toga".

---

38 One thinks of the clandestine action capabilities of the DGSE.

4.5. References

Barbier, B., Gergorin, J.-L., Guillaud, E. (2020). Cybercoercition : un nouveau défi stratégique. *Le Monde*, January 28 [Online]. Available at: https://www.lemonde.fr/idees/article/2020/01/28/cybercoercition-un-nouveau-defi-strategique_6027444_3232.html.

Boyer, B. (2020). *Guérilla 2.2 – Guerres irrégulières dans le cyberespace*. Éditions de l'école de guerre, Paris.

Breton, T. (2004). Chantier sur la lutte contre la cybercriminalité. Report, Marc Watin-Augouard.

Castets-Renard, C. (2020). *Enjeux internationaux des activités numériques*. Éditions Larcier, Brussels.

Delerue, F., Douzet, F., Géry, A. (2020). *Les représentations géopolitiques du droit international dans les négociations internationals*. IRSEM, Paris.

Gassin, R. (1986). *Le droit pénal de l'informatique*. Dalloz, Paris.

Libicki, M.C. (2012). *Cyber Space Is Not a War Fighting Domain*. Oxford University Press, Oxford.

Limonier, K. (2018). *Ru.net, Géopolitique du cyberespace Russophone*. L'Inventaire, Paris.

McLuhan, M. (1967). *The Medium is the Message*. Bantam Books, New York.

Poirier, L. (1988). *Des stratégies nucléaires*. Éditions Complexe, Paris.

Rid, T. (2013). *Cyberwar Will Not Take Place*. Oxford University Press, Oxford.

Robert, M. (2014). Protecting Internet users. Report, February 2014.

Salamon, Y. (2020). *Cybersécurité et cyberdéfense : enjeux stratégiques*. Ellipses, Paris.

SGDSN (2018). Revue stratégique cyberdéfense [Online]. Available at: www.sgdsn.gouv.fr.

Watin-Augouard, M. (1992a). La gendarmerie et la défense. *Revue Administration*, 154, 43–45.

Watin-Augouard, M. (1992b). Le continuum. *Armées d'Aujourd'hui*, 171, 32–35.

Cyberdefense, the Digital Dimension of National Security

5.1. Introduction

The notion of cyberdefense continues to develop as French official statements and documents affirm its strategic necessity. In 2019, in particular, the French Ministry of the Armed Forces confirmed that its cyberdefense strategy includes both defensive (Ministère des Armées 2019a) and offensive (Ministère des Armées 2019b) dimensions[1].

This rise of cyberdefense as an operational concept is not surprising. It is part of a broader movement that has seen the scope of information systems security (ISS) evolve toward what is now called cybersecurity[2], with, in particular, a decompartmentalization of the concerns around public and private information systems security. However, it is also the current political and legal affirmation of national security practices (whether it be the intelligence or external operations legal frameworks) that makes it more necessary to define a legal regime for cyberdefense, so that it can be fully integrated into French national security law, which is gradually being built. After repositioning cyberdefense within the digital security continuum, we highlight some aspects of its legal regime and the place it now holds in the legal and operational system of national security.

Chapter written by Bertrand WARUSFEL.

1 See Chapter 3.

2 See Chapter 1.

5.2. Cyberdefense in the political and legal framework of digital security

Article 1 of the recent French law of February 26, 2018[3], gives us a definition of what it calls networks and information systems security (and what we more generally call cybersecurity). This consists of the ability of these networks and systems to "resist, to a given level of confidence, actions that compromise the availability, authenticity, integrity or confidentiality of data stored, transmitted or processed, and related services that these networks and information systems offer or make accessible".

5.2.1. A definition of cyberdefense

However, while cybersecurity, thus defined, targets the resilience of all digital systems, cyberdefense – as the official vocabulary presents it – is only concerned with systems considered of vital importance, which contribute to cybersecurity and which the state defends[4]. The notion of essential information systems considered to be of vital importance refers us directly to the French Defense Code, in which Article L.1332-6-1 indicates that these are the systems of the "operators of vital importance", the public or private operators whose "unavailability could significantly diminish the war or economic potential, or the security or survival capacity, of the nation" (according to Article L.1332-1 Cdèf).

We can therefore deduce a double differentiation between the concepts of cybersecurity and cyberdefense:

– on the one hand, cybersecurity has a universal scope, since it is about ensuring the resilience of all digital systems, whereas cyberdefense only focuses on ensuring the security of vital systems whose failure could harm the nation;

– on the other hand, while cybersecurity is the business of all system and network managers, cyberdefense is a fully sovereign activity, which is

---

3 Law No. 2018-133 of February 26, 2018, containing various provisions for adapting to European Union law in the field of security (transposing, in particular, the NIS Directive).

4 It is in fact defined as a "set of resources put in place by a state to defend in cyberspace the information systems deemed to be of vital importance, which contribute to ensuring cybersecurity" (JORF (2017), Defense vocabulary: Cyberdefense, September 19).

carried out by various state actors, or at least under the state's direct responsibility and by virtue of the specific powers given to it by law.

Moreover, we can revise the initial definition somewhat to clarify the underlying logic: cyberdefense is the set of resources put in place under the responsibility of the state to defend information systems in cyberspace[5], the attack of which would affect the war or economic potential, or the security or survival capacity, of the nation, that is to say, national security. In so doing, we move away from a primarily organic approach to a logic based on the nature of the threats to be dealt with, which makes it possible to better position cyberdefense in the graduality of French security concepts. Indeed, since 2009 and the new drafting of Article 1111-1 Cdéf, a new conceptual hierarchy has been introduced into French law, based on the supreme notion of "national security". This concept differs from other aspects of internal security in that it focuses exclusively on the anticipation and treatment of threats and risks that could affect national life. We can therefore consider that cyberdefense, which only aims to ensure the security of digital systems of vital importance to the nation, is a national security concept, or that, more precisely, it constitutes the cyber dimension of national security.

5.2.2. *Linking cyberdefense to national security strategy*

This proposed interpretation of the notion of cyberdefense is confirmed if we look at what cyberdefense implies in terms of the legal and operational resources to be deployed by the state and operators of vital importance. It has been written that "national security corresponds to a very specific dimension of the general interest, which has the attribute of being able to justify the implementation of special prerogatives by executive powers, leading to limitations in the exercise of public freedoms" (Warusfel 2018). However, what clearly distinguishes cyberdefense from the rest of cybersecurity is that it justifies the implementation by the state of several special prerogatives, the most restrictive of which – and the most derogatory to freedoms, including those of commerce and industry – are, as we shall see, found in the Defense Code. Moreover, the official 2017 definition of cyberdefense, which we have taken as a reference, also mentions that "cyberdefense implements, in particular, defensive and offensive computer warfare". Yet both of these dimensions of cyberwarfare fall under the special means of the state. "Defensive computer

---

5 On this notion, see Chapter 1.

warfare" (*Lutte Informative Défensive* (LID) in the Ministry of the Armed Forces vocabulary) is more specifically related to intelligence actions, since it "mainly covers the missions to anticipate, detect and react, and completes the missions to prevent, protect and allocate"[6]. It is planned and conducted by COMCYBER, in coordination with ANSSI (*Agence nationale de la sécurité des systèmes d'information*, the French national infosec authority) and the intelligence services[7].

Offensive computer warfare (*Lutte Informatique Offensive* (LIO)) is defined as "a coordinated set of actions carried out in cyberspace by a state against information or data systems in order to disrupt, modify, degrade or destroy them"[8]. It is therefore directly related to military defense, since "the primary objective of LIO is to contribute to military superiority in cyberspace"[9].

Here again, conformity with the logic of national security is obvious. The specialized intelligence services have, among other things, the mission of collecting information relating to "threats and risks likely to affect national life"[10], while, even more explicitly, "the public intelligence policy contributes to the national security strategy"[11]. For its part, "defence policy aims to ensure the integrity of the territory and the protection of the population against armed aggression" and "contributes to the fight against other threats likely to affect national security"[12]. However, just as national security is defined in this way, the French cyberdefense doctrine includes a specific subset dedicated to the implementation of military resources when the nature of the attack justifies it. While cyberdefense is therefore an integral part of the French national security system, the legal framework for its use needs to be specified.

---

6 Ministry of the Armed Forces (2019), Politique ministérielle de lutte informatique défensive (LID).

7 *Ibid.* On the different structures, see Chapter 3 in this volume.

8 It is in fact defined as a "set of resources put in place by a state to defend in cyberspace the information systems deemed to be of vital importance, which contribute to ensuring cybersecurity" (Jorf (2017), Defense vocabulary: Cyberdefense, September 19).

9 Ministry of the Armed Forces (2019), Politique ministérielle de lutte informatique offensive (LID).

10 Article L.811-2 of the Internal Security Code (from the Intelligence Act of July 24, 2015).

11 Art. L.811-1 CSI.

12 Art. L.1111-1 Cdéf mentioned above, 3rd paragraph.

5.3. The emergence of a coherent legal regime for cyberdefense

Various French and European texts[13] have contributed over the last 10 years to the densification of the legal system, allowing the highest authorities of the state (and first and foremost the Prime Minister) to implement cyberdefense actions that may be required to protect national security. As we are in the field of national security, it is important to distinguish between special prerogatives that are intended to be permanently applied, as soon as a national security objective is at stake, and those that are exceptional, that can only be used temporarily to respond to a crisis or a conflict.

5.3.1. *The legal basis of the permanent cyberdefense posture*

The permanent legal resources of cyberdefense are all the provisions allowing the state, through its national authority for information systems security (ANSSI), to impose preventive cybersecurity measures on various major actors in the digital society.

First of all, the Defense Code imposes obligations on operators of vital importance (whose central role in cyberdefense we have already mentioned), who must comply with the "security rules" set by ANSSI, which "may, in particular, prescribe that operators implement qualified systems for detecting events likely to affect the security of their information systems" and call on service providers also qualified by ANSSI[14]. In 2018, more than 1,000 qualified IT systems of vital importance were listed, distributed among more than 350 operators. However, the transposition of the European Network and Information Security (NIS) Directive of July 6, 2016, by the French Act of February 26, 2018, and the Decree of May 23, 2018, has expanded the ability of the security authority to also impose obligations on essential service operators and digital service providers. The 2018 Military Programming Law completed this by enabling the authorities to require electronic communication operators to install cyber attack detection probes that are

---

13 While it might seem surprising that European law should intervene in an area concerning the national security of the member states (which retain exclusive competence according to Article 4.2 TEU), it must be admitted, however, that, indirectly, European Union law is increasingly incorporating security issues that are reasonably combined with strictly national measures (see our analysis (Warusfel 2014)).

14 Art. L. 1332-6-1 Cdéf.

under the direct control of ANSSI on their networks[15]. In addition to these rules for preventing vulnerabilities and anticipating threats, which constitute a permanent derogatory right justified by the national cybersecurity imperative, there are, logically, provisions intended to come into force only during a crisis.

5.3.2. *Exceptional instruments for responding to a crisis*

As a recent parliamentary report on cyberdefense indicates, "the French model is based on four main actors, which form the first circle of cyberdefense" (Assemblée nationale, 2018). Each of these four levels has its own branch of the national response to cyber attacks.

The first level of response is simply for the state to trigger, if necessary, the judicial investigations and associated sanctions that are provided for in the French Criminal Code and that punish cybercrime. Since their introduction into French law in 1988 with the famous "Godfrain Act", the quantum of penalties under Articles 323-1 to 323-7 of the Criminal Code has increased and their scope of application has widened. On the one hand, since the end of 2014, Article 323-3 Cpen[16] also prosecutes the fact of "fraudulently extracting, holding, reproducing, transmitting, deleting or modifying data", which provides better protection against acts of cyberespionage. However, on the other hand, the same 2014 reform provided that an attack on any "automated personal data processing system implemented by the state" constitutes an aggravating circumstance of all these offenses, which increases the penalties incurred in Articles 323-1 to 323-3 Cpen and allows, when committed by an organized group, a maximum penalty of 10 years in prison and a €150,000 fine[17]. Even if we may wonder why the legislator chose to only target the processing of personal data, and not all government information systems (which can be extremely sensitive – especially in technical areas – aside from any personal data processing), this renunciation is clearly a political signal and a legal mechanism aimed at responding to major attacks targeting the key structures of dematerialized administration. This legal response could also be transnational, since French criminal provisions

---

15 Art. L. 2321-2-1 Cdéf. created by the Military Programming Act of July 13, 2018.

16 Precisely since Act No. 2014-1353 of November 13, 2014 (which amended Article 323-3 Cpen), strengthened the provisions relating to the fight against terrorism.

17 Art. 323-4-1 Cpen.

are integrated into the framework of the 2001 Convention on Cybercrime, which organizes police and judicial cooperation among signatory states to conduct transnational investigations and prosecutions in the face of equally globalized attacks. It should also be noted that this criminal protection of public digital systems may be accompanied by a technical response, since Article L.2321-2-1 of the French Defense Code allows ANSSI to take specific technical surveillance measures when it is "aware of a threat likely to undermine the security of the information systems of public authorities".

However, for some years now, cyberdefense has had other exceptional instruments, specifically designed to enable a technical and operational response, at its disposal. Three other actors are involved within the state in this "offensive" cyberdefense dimension. Let us mention, in a few words, the most discreet of these actors, namely, the French intelligence community. While we know that the specialized services have a mission to detect threats, including cyber threats, due to state defense secrecy we know less about their intrusive capacities (or their reactivity to an external attack). Only a sibylline penal provision indicates to us in Article 323-8 of the Criminal Code that it is not applicable to the measures implemented by the authorized agents of the state services designated, by order of the Prime Minister, among the specialized intelligence services mentioned in Article L.811-2 of the Internal Security Code, to ensure the protection of the fundamental national interests outside the national territory mentioned in Article L.811-3 of the same code.

One can logically conclude from the statement of this particular penal immunity that certain specialized services (first and foremost the French external intelligence and SIGINT agency, DGSE) can involve themselves in offensive operations against foreign digital systems for the highly strategic purposes of national security (since it specifically refers to the protection of national interests)[18].

More visible, in the texts of the last decade, has been the central role played by the Prime Minister with his armed wing in this area, ANSSI. As the national cybersecurity authority, ANSSI is the pivotal point around which the exceptional prerogatives conferred on the head of government by

---

18 See Chapter 3.

Article L. 2321-2 of the Defense Code are implemented[19]. Indeed, it is the Prime Minister, through ANSSI, who intervenes to "respond to a computer attack that targets information systems affecting the war or economic potential, or the security or survival capacity, of the nation". Here again, and despite the (unfortunate) disparity in terminology, it is a question of reacting to a threat to national security, to which the law will allow a response that can go as far as the penetration of adversary systems and their neutralization, using all manner of equipment or software similar to those used by cybercriminals (since they are described as being of a nature to "allow the realization of one or more of the offences provided for in Articles 323-1 to 323-3 of the Criminal Code"). The powers of the Prime Minister (and therefore ANSSI) go very far, since they even allow measures to be imposed on companies and private operators targeted by the cyber attack that they must implement[20].

However, the operational response can also be directed by COMCYBER (the Cyberdefense Command), within the armed forces, "when the computer attack is exclusively aimed at the operational capabilities of the armed forces or the defense chains of command". The competent authority is then "the cyberdefense operational command of the armed forces staff, in liaison with ANSSI" (SGDSN 2018, p. 48). Finally, and to complete our analysis of the levels of national security resources, the Ministry of the Armed Forces has made public its "public elements of military doctrine for offensive computer warfare"[21], which, although very general in their terminology, assert that the military action chain complements the protection, intelligence and judicial investigation chains[22] by practicing offensive computer warfare if necessary.

Although the armed forces logically remain very tight-lipped about the offensive operations that France could decide to launch in order to punish its aggressors and protect its digital infrastructure, the message is clear: the use of cyber weapons by French forces is not intended to only support traditional military operations (by neutralizing opposing digital systems), but could also be engaged in order to retaliate to a cyber attack. The preamble to the document

---

19 The application of which is the subject of a classified instruction of March 7, 2016 (see SGDSN 2018).

20 Article L. 1332-6-4 Cdef.

21 Department of the Army (2019), Public elements of military offensive computer warfare doctrine.

22 *Ibid.*, p. 4.

is, in this respect, very clear when it mentions the various cyber attacks "against Estonia in 2007, the electricity networks of Ukraine, TV5 Monde in 2015, the WannaCry ransomware in the spring of 2017 and also the NotPetya attack in June 2017, [which] illustrate the possible fields of action for attackers whose four major objectives are espionage, illicit trafficking, destabilization and sabotage"[23]. Further on, it is also mentioned that offensive cyber operations can be "carried out to support defensive computer warfare"[24]. Finally, it should be noted that the recent Military Programming Law also allowed for the extension of the "criminal excuse", already recognized for combatants in operations, to those of them who are involved in "digital actions"[25].

5.4. Conclusion

In conclusion, it appears that the very empirical system that has progressively emerged to combat new digital threats is declined according to a pyramid whose different levels are coherent with the way in which we can understand national security. While cyberdefense does not have a direct relationship with everyday cybersecurity (in the same way that national security has little to do with common public security missions), it is focused on the anticipation and treatment of major threats affecting national life. This, then, gives the public authorities derogatory prerogatives that can restrict certain freedoms (such as when ANSSI has the power to require private actors to implement a particular aspect of a cybersecurity reference framework or to install probes on networks). Beyond and within the limits of what the law of armed conflict and humanitarian law allow, cyberdefense may also include an extreme extension that could be offensive and military, thus manifesting, in the field of digital threat, the statement in the 2008 *Livre Blanc sur la Défense et la Sécurité Nationale* that "[the] objectives [of national security] are supported by defense policy, in its entirety". The graduality of cyberdefense resources and their doctrine of use are, therefore, part of the broader framework of permanent protection and, in a crisis, of national security.

---

23 *Ibid.*, p. 4.
24 *Ibid.*, p. 10.
25 Article L.4123-12 Cdéf, modified.

5.5. References

Assemblée nationale (2018). Rapport d'information sur la cyberdéfense. Document no. 1141, 4 July.

Ministère des Armées (2019a). Politique ministérielle de lutte informatique défensive (LID). Report.

Ministère des Armées (2019b). Politique ministérielle de lutte informatique offensive (LID). Report.

SGDSN (2018). Revue stratégique de cyberdéfense. Report, SGDSN.

Warusfel, B. (2014). L'entrée de l'Union européenne dans les champs de la défense et de la sécurité. *Cahiers de la sécurité et de la justice*, 27–28, 189–198.

Warusfel, B. (2018). Le contentieux de la sécurité nationale. In *Annuaire 2018 du droit de la sécurité et de la défense*, Warusfel, B., Baude, F. (eds). Mare et Martin, Paris.

6

Omnipresence Without Omnipotence: The US Campaign Against Huawei in the 5G Era

6.1. Introduction

As 5G networks are being deployed, policymakers are likely to be confronted with an expanded and multidimensional cyber-threat landscape. Admittedly, a lot of the often-quoted examples of use that this new generation of mobile networks could enable – such as autonomous vehicles, remote surgery, "smart" electric power grids and industrial processes – are still hypothetical. The profound legal, economic and social transformations needed for such innovations to find a viable market are rarely mentioned in the deterministic scenarios of both tech enthusiasts and cyber-doomsters. That said, 5G is undoubtedly going to expand the connectivity of modern societies, which will open up new areas of vulnerability. In addition, the extremely low levels of latency that this new generation is striving for will require network architectures to be increasingly "software-defined". This, in turn, will lead to heightened complexity – "the worst enemy of security" in the famous words of Bruce Schneier (2012).

Within this expanded threat landscape, much of the public debate on 5G security has focused quite narrowly on the issue of vendor trustworthiness. Such concerns are not new nor are they unique to telecommunication networks. IT systems have long been so complex that they exceed any

---

Chapter written by Mark CORCORAL.

human abilities for comprehensive analysis. This is broadly accepted insofar as products are subject to maintenance and software updates to correct any flaws that might be found during their lifecycle. However, it implies that products are vulnerable not only to potential failure or third-party exploitation, but also to manipulation by the vendor, bearing in mind that these three types of threats are often difficult to distinguish from one another in practice. Attributing intent, error or ignorance as being the cause of a system malfunctioning is really a matter of interpretation and judgment. In such complex systems, the existence of hidden functions deliberately planted by the vendor can rarely be proven or disproven from a purely technical standpoint. Moreover, the relationship between any buyer and vendor of IT equipment is both asymmetric – in terms of access to information and exposure to harm – and long term – given the vendor keeps communicating with the equipment for a long time after it has been installed. This means that any IT system may have a hidden functionality, which is why the problem fundamentally comes down to trust. Thus, as Olav Lysne (2018, p. 6) explains, "when we ask ourselves whether a [software and/or hardware] vendor can be trusted, we must ask ourselves whether we think the vendor will remain trustworthy throughout the lifetime of the product we are buying". Making such a judgment is therefore as much a matter of technical analysis as it is a matter of subjective beliefs. Given that telecommunication networks are deemed to be a critical infrastructure, this issue has, unsurprisingly, taken on a strong political dimension.

In this context, much of the attention has focused on Huawei. Established in 1987 in the Shenzhen Special Economic Zone, Huawei first made its mark on the Chinese domestic market by manufacturing switch systems for rural areas. Starting off with reverse-engineered equipment, the company grew by incrementally transforming its products through in-house R&D. Similarly, Huawei expanded abroad from the late 1990s by consistently penetrating low-end markets through imitation, before scaling up through customer-centric innovation (Nolan 2014, pp. 758–762; Barré 2016, pp. 139–143; Zhou et al. 2016). Still chaired by its founder, Ren Zhengfei, the company has become one of the world leaders in the telecommunications sector, particularly in the market of network equipment. In recent years, the company has demonstrated its innovative capabilities by taking on an unprecedented role in the 5G standardization process within the 3GPP[1]. This has made it an emblem of China's ambitions to upscale its industry – labeled "Made in China 2025" – and to increase its involvement in technical standardization processes – labeled "China Standards 2035" (Rühlig 2020).

As a backlash to its success, the company has faced strong political opposition from the United States. Initially characterized by domestic distrust and restrictions against the company, US actions have taken a decidedly more offensive turn since 2018, with the launch of a targeted political, legal, economic and diplomatic campaign. The purpose of this chapter is not to pass political judgment on this campaign, but to identify its origin, measure its scope, describe its mechanisms and identify some of its possible flaws. It will consist of two parts, beginning with an analysis of where this anti-Huawei campaign originated and what disprutive measures were taken by the United States government against the Shenzhen group. Given the insufficiency of these unilateral actions, the second part will look at the rhetorical tactics employed by American officials in pleading for a ban of the Chinese vendor's equipment to US partners and allies. It will show that, interestingly, US diplomacy sought to "rhetorically coerce" allies by framing the ban as an objective necessity rather than trying to rally them to a common cause against Huawei. We will see that while this diplomatic initative has succeeded in bringing the issue to the forefront of the international stage, its influence over US partners and allies must not be overstated. The conclusion will draw some broader lessons from the analysis above as regards the ability of the US government to articulate such diverse policy tools and, also, to mobilize its allies in the pursuit of its strategic goals.

6.2. The unilateral American offensive against Huawei: a disruptive campaign causing significant collateral damage

The intensity of the American campaign against Huawei cannot be fully understood if one does not take the perceptions that guided it into account. It

---

1 3GPP is a grouping of standardization entities. Its objective is to prepare, define, improve and maintain globally applicable technical standards for telecommunication devices. It is based on the voluntary participation of its members, which include companies, associated standards organizations and other entities. Decisions on technical standards are made through votes that are open to all members. Each quarter, 3GPP consolidates all technical standards produced by all of its working groups. This consolidated information is provided to the 3GPP member standards organizations, which then make it available to the entire telecommunications industry as formal standards.

is therefore appropriate to briefly outline them before analyzing the unilateral measures that constitute this offensive against the company.

6.2.1. *Huawei: an "unusual and extraordinary" threat to the United States' position in the international order*

Washington's distrust of Huawei is not new. As early as the mid-2000s, concerns were raised by the RAND Corporation (Medeiros *et al.* 2005, p. 218) and within the intelligence community (NSA 2008) about the group's alleged links to the Chinese authorities. These concerns were conveyed in political debates and were coupled with accusations of circumventing US sanctions and unfair trade practices (McCotter 2007). Several of the company's investment projects in the United States were then blocked by the Committee on Foreign Investment in the United States (CFIUS)[2], and major American telecom operators came under political pressure to refrain from purchasing Chinese-branded equipment (Weisman 2008; Segal 2016, p. 140). In 2012, the House of Representatives Permanent Select Committee on Intelligence publicly designated the company as a threat to US national security. Its investigative report on the two Chinese telecom giants – Huawei and ZTE – called for the group's exclusion from all government IT systems and "strongly encouraged" US companies to "consider the long-term security risks associated with doing business" with them and to "seek other vendors for their projects" (HPSCI 2012). At the risk of shifting the burden of proof, the report denounced Huawei's failure to demonstrate compliance with US sanctions on Iran, as well as its financial and managerial independence. Ren Zhengfei's past links with the People's Liberation Army and the existence of a Party Committee within the company were also pointed to as evidence of "influence, pressure and oversight of the company's activities" by the Chinese government (HPSCI 2012, p. 3). Last but not least, the report states that the commission had information showing that "Huawei exhibits a pattern of disregard for the intellectual property rights of other entities and companies in the United States" (HPSCI 2012, p. 31), an issue that was already the subject

---

2 The Committee on Foreign Investment in the United States (CFIUS) is an interdepartmental body established under the Gerald Ford presidency to "monitor the impact of foreign investment in the United States [...] and to coordinate the implementation of US policy with respect to such investment" (POTUS 1975). Since a 1988 amendment (known as the Exon-Florio Amendment), the President of the United States may, through CFIUS, block any foreign investment that may affect national security (Connell and Huang 2014, pp. 135–138).

of diplomatic tensions between China and the United States (Lindsay *et al.* 2015).

With the rollout of 5G approaching, and amidst a sharp deterioration in Sino-American relations, this distrust soon turned into outright hostility. In a leaked National Security Council (NSC) memorandum, Brigadier General Robert Spalding expressed concern that "the Chinese may be poised to lead in 5G" and warned that, even if they were to be completely excluded from the US market, "radio manufacturers other than Huawei and ZTE [would] face declining market share". He further expressed the view that America was "on the edge of a precipice" (NSC 2018)[3]. A year later, the executive order on "securing the information and communications technology and services supply chains" declared a "national emergency" on this issue and imposed a strict ban:

> The unrestricted acquisition or use in the United States of information and communications technology or services designed, developed, manufactured, or supplied by persons owned by, controlled by, or subject to the jurisdiction or direction of foreign adversaries […] constitutes an *unusual* and *extraordinary* threat to the national security, foreign policy, and economy of the United States. (POTUS 2019a)

Although this phrasing is tailored for legal purposes[4], it is also politically significant. As Attorney General William Barr made clear in a public speech, the issue with Huawei extends far beyond immediate security concerns about American networks:

> From a national security standpoint, if the industrial internet [enabled by 5G] becomes dependent on Chinese technology,

---

3 After his memorandum was leaked, Brigadier General Robert Spalding stepped down from his position at the NSC, due to the controversy over his call for the US government to administer the rollout of 5G "just like the Eisenhower Highway System" (referring to the interstate highway funding program implemented by the federal government in the 1950s). Seen as a proposal to nationalize mobile networks, the memorandum caused an outcry from regulators – most notably the Federal Communications Commission (FCC) – and telecom operators. The framing of the threat, however, seems not to have raised any eyebrows.

4 From a legal standpoint, the use of the phrase "*unusual and extraordinary threat to the national security, foreign policy, and economy of the United States*" allows the President to take economic measures to deal with it pursuant to the 1977 International Emergency Economic Powers Act.

China would have the ability to shut countries off from technology and equipment upon which their consumers and industry depend. The power the United States has today to use economic sanctions would pale by comparison to the unprecedented leverage we would be surrendering into the hands of China. (Barr 2020)

The stakes for American power are therefore extremely high: the technological supremacy of the United States is at risk which, in turn, could jeopardize its position in the international order. This is why the coming of 5G has marked a shift in Washington from a defensive posture – through CFIUS screening and political pressure on US operators – to a decidedly offensive posture as regards the Chinese vendor.

6.2.2. *A political, legal and economic offensive against Huawei, causing significant collateral damage*

The American offensive against Huawei is composed of multiple strands. From a purely political standpoint, the company is accused by the United States for supporting the repressive actions of authoritarian regimes. This refers primarily to actions attributed to the Chinese government against the Muslim Uighur minority in Xinjiang (Strayer 2019d) and against protesters in Hong Kong (Hendel and Farrell 2020). However, the company is also accused of having ties to the Iranian regime, which allegedly "received assistance" from Huawei in implementing "domestic surveillance actions, including during the protests in Tehran in 2009" (DOJ 2020). According to Christopher Krebs, who served as director of the Cybersecurity and Infrastructure Security Agency (CISA), the Huawei case is ultimately a question of values and political regimes:

> Ultimately what this is about – and 5G is just a proxy for a broader conversation – is defending democracy. […] We're at a pivotal moment where we can either allow autocratic states to proliferate their technologies […] or we can push our own solutions out there into the world. (Krebs 2019)

This political charge is supported by the legal strand of the offensive. In early December 2018, Meng Wanzhou, the Huawei CFO and daughter of the company's founder, was arrested in Canada at the request of the US Department of Justice. She is accused of participating in the circumvention of sanctions against Iran and of lying to several US financial institutions about it. Subsequently, the company has also been charged in the United States with intellectual property theft (DOJ 2019b), racketeering and violating sanctions against North Korea (DOJ 2020). In response to Huawei's accusations of this being a matter of "political persecution" (Huawei 2020), the Department of Justice (DOJ) has consistently claimed to be conducting its investigations and making decisions on indictments "independently from the White House" (Nakashima and Barrett 2019).

However, as is routine in national security cases, there is likely to have been some internal coordination in bringing these charges. The involvement of the National Security Division (NSD) in these proceedings is a further indication of this. Among other things, this division of the DOJ is "responsible for combating threats to critical infrastructure and the private sector from nation-states" (DOJ 2021). Since 2018, it has been leading a "China Initiative", which "reflects the [Justice] Department's strategic priority of countering Chinese national security threats and reinforces the President's overall national security strategy" (DOJ 2020). Created by the 2005 reauthorization of the Patriot Act, the NSD is one of the most successful institutional expressions of the hybridization between national security policy and law enforcement, often referred to as "lawfare" (Kittrie 2016; Estève 2018). Lawyers and prosecutors in this division have long defended criminal prosecutions as one of many strategic tools that can be used to serve national security policy (Lisa Monaco cited in Leithauser 2013). The testimony of the Deputy Assistant Attorney General for National Security, Adam Hickey, has offered some illuminating insights in this regard, framing national security prosecutions as following a three-step process. First, the DOJ's resources are to be prioritized in accordance with the US national security strategy, because it would be inappropriate for investigators to spread themselves thin by "going after threats that are not critical or critically important" (Hickey 2019). This is a "programmatic awareness" that all relevant prosecutors are expected to have. Second, as in any prosecution, the DOJ independently "chooses the individual targets, charges and which cases to bring". Last, but not least:

> The third stage is presenting an option to the intelligence community or the State Department, or indicating that we

intend to move forward [with prosecution] and then receiving feedback – whether it's about what sources and methods could be exposed, whether there are concerns about reciprocity, whether the timing of a charge or an arrest causes diplomatic or other policy concerns. And then those concerns are given to the Attorney General, who makes a decision about whether to move forward at his or her discretion. (Hickey 2019)

This process specifically allows for coordination on the timing of certain criminal proceedings to take the government's policy agenda into account[5]. In this case, after several years of investigations into certain facts dating back to 2007, it was only on the eve of the launch of the American diplomatic campaign on this subject that prosecutors sought an arrest warrant for Meng Wanzhou from a federal judge in Brooklyn. According to Adam Hickey, this fine balance between independence and coordination allows for strategic considerations to be incorporated into DOJ's actions "without compromising its independence or undermining the credibility of the tool" (Hickey 2019). However, in the Huawei case, that credibility was somewhat undermined by the US president himself, Donald Trump having said that he would "surely intervene" if he thought it would be "good for what will probably be the biggest trade deal ever", in the context of the ongoing "trade war" with China (Mason and Holland 2018).

That said, those criminal proceedings did help enable the third prong of the US offensive against Huawei, which involves economic measures. The indictment against Meng Wanzhou and her company was indeed used to justify Huawei's addition to the Commerce Department's Bureau of Industry and Security (BIS) Entity List in May 2019 (DOC 2019). This listing of Huawei imposed new restrictions on US products being exported to the Chinese telecom giant without a license issued by the BIS. Such restrictions have an extraterritorial scope in the sense that when certain regulated items – such as semiconductors[6] – are sold to a listed entity, if more than 25% of

---

5 Interview with Christopher Painter, March 2019.

6 Semiconductors are materials, usually silicon, whose electrical conductivity can be significantly increased by introducing a small amount of impurity at a chosen location. This process makes it possible to etch integrated circuits (the famous "electronic chips"), which concentrate a large number of logical functions in a small space, making semiconductors the basic element of modern electronics.

their total value is the product of American software or technology, they become subject to BIS controls, regardless of where they are manufactured.

However, it turned out that most of the semiconductors produced outside the United States that Huawei was using did not meet that threshold. This led to a quandry on whether to expand the export controls so that the US government could tighten its grip on the Shenzhen group's supply chains, even if that meant causing heavy losses for its US suppliers. This issue presented the Trump administration with a dilemma that, in some ways, echoed the debate that took place in the aftermath of the Cold War on how to maintain America's technological edge vis-à-vis China (Meijer 2016). This debate opposed the "Control Hawks", on the one hand, who wanted to prevent any transfer of sensitive technologies to China in order to keep it behind, to the "Run Faster" coalition, on the other hand, which was composed of officials who thought it was best to let US firms freely conquer markets abroad. That way, their dominant position would ensure that the US government had privileged access to cutting-edge technologies. Put differently, while the "Control Hawks" believed in the persistence of a trade-off between economic and national security interests as in the Cold War, the "Run Faster" coalition believed that the two were now aligned. This logic of alignment of interests seems to have become paroxysmal in President Trump's national strategy due to its embrace of the phrase "economic security is national security" (Trump 2017). Following this logic, Donald Trump initially opposed the expansion of export controls on Huawei, using Twitter to denounce those in his administration that invoked the "national security excuse" to promote a measure that he viewed as potentially disastrous for US companies' competitiveness (Trump 2020).

However, as things stood, the export controls only had a limited effect on their target and were, in some ways, counterproductive. For instance, US companies were obliged to apply for BIS licensing just to participate in standardization working groups. Such licenses being temporary, this ultimately threatened US companies with being excluded from standardization processes at the request of their own government, paving the way for their Chinese competitors to fill the gap. Several US Senators soon denounced the "economic and national security implications" of these restrictions (Cotton *et al.* 2020), prompting the Commerce Department to amend its rules (DOC 2020a).

More broadly, the United States has few options to promote alternatives to Huawei, which benefits from the path dependency that stems from its existing footprint in many telecom networks. The first phase of 5G deployments, known as "non-standalone" 5G (NSA 5G), does indeed rely heavily on the legacy infrastructure. This means that switching vendors for 5G first requires "ripping and replacing" existing equipment to maintain interoperability. The idea of having to undertake these costly and time-consuming operations can deter the operators from switching providers and the policymakers from requesting them to do so. Admittedly, in the United States, the Federal Communications Commission announced that incentives would be implemented to encourage small rural operators with Chinese-branded equipment to get rid of it (FCC 2019, 2020). Nonetheless, Huawei's prominence in the rest of the world is such that the additional cost involved with banning its equipment would be considerably higher.

To address this issue, some US government officials have stood for supporting the Open-RAN Alliance, a private initiative led by several transnational operators, such as AT&T, Verizon, Orange and Telefonica. The goal of this initiative is to modify the architecture of radio access networks in order to lower certain barriers to entry that exist in the equipment market (O-RAN Alliance 2019). With the initiative seen as a way to challenge Huawei and encourage the emergence of American competitors, two US senators introduced a bill in January 2020, the Utilizing Strategic Allied (USA) Telecommunications Act, which provides up to $750 million in funding for research in Open-RAN. That said, it is unlikely that this enterprise, backed by the US government and some transnational operators, will be able to offer a viable short-term alternative to Huawei[7]. Attorney General William Barr went as far as publicly dismissing Open-RAN as "a pie in the sky". Instead, he defended the idea of US equity investment in Huawei's main competitors, Nokia and/or Ericsson, "either directly [by the government] or through a consortium of US and allied private companies" (Barr 2020). This proposal seems rather at odds with the anti-statist impulse that inhabits US political culture and has long served to limit the assertiveness of its foreign policy (Friedberg 2012). Unsurprisingly, the idea of partial nationalization of European equipment manufacturers provoked an outcry in the White House. Disavowed by Vice President Mike Pence, this option was ruled out by Donald Trump's economic advisor, Larry Kudlow,

7 Interview with an operator representative, September 2020.

who stated that "the US government is not in the business of buying companies, whether domestic or foreign" (Shepardson 2020).

Faced with this impasse in the midst of the Covid-19 pandemic, President Trump eventually reversed his position by authorizing the expansion of BIS export controls. Following two sets of legal changes to the rules that apply to exports to Huawei (DOC 2020b, 2020c), the extraterritorial reach of BIS's controls extended to all semiconductors designed or manufactured with US technology anywhere in the world which, in effect, covers most of the market[8]. The aim of this move was made abundantly clear:

> [To] further restrict Huawei's ability to obtain foreign-made chips developed or produced using US software or technology to the same degree as for comparable US chips. (DOC 2020b, 2020c)

This amounts to weaponizing the lead that the US semiconductor industry has in order to contain Huawei's foothold on the market of 5G network equipment (Fox Business 2020). However, this action comes at a price. While the exact impact of these restrictions is unclear at the time of writing, US semiconductor industry representatives have stated that significant disruption is expected in this highly strategic sector of the economy (SIA 2020). Industry representatives have indeed warned the government that decoupling could be extremely perilous, in a statement underscoring the fact that "sales to China drive semiconductor research and innovation here in the United States" (SIA 2020). These concerns, echoed inside the government by the Department of Defense's Office of The Under Secretary of Defense for Research and Engineering (USD-R&E), could ultimately harm US technological leadership in the semiconductor industry.

While this political, legal and economic offensive has undoubtedly disrupted Huawei's business, it has also exhibited two serious limitations. On the one hand, mixed messaging within the US government has cast doubt on the independence of the American criminal justice system. On the other hand, decoupling Huawei from American companies and diversifying the

---

8 US companies Ansys, Cadence and Synopsys dominate the semiconductor design software market. LAM Research, Teradyne and Applied Materials also supply many of the critical machine tools to the foundries on which Huawei depends, such as the Taiwan Semiconductor Manufacturing Company (TSMC).

global telecoms equipment market have proven to be extremely difficult. In any case, the United States could not act alone in this endeavor. Hence, the fourth strand of the US campaign against Huawei, to which we now turn.

6.3. The American diplomatic offensive: the limits of American rhetorical coercion of their partners and allies

Since the Five Eyes summit[9] in Nova Scotia in the summer of 2018, US diplomacy has been working hard to convince its partners and allies to exclude Huawei from their 5G deployments. Potential risks of espionage and of network sabotage posed by Chinese equipment are at the forefront of this effort. Although Australia, Israel, Japan, the UK, Taiwan and Vietnam have announced such a ban, the European Union has remained very divided on this issue. To date, Estonia, Poland, Romania and Sweden are the only EU member states to have fully complied with the US demands. France, Germany, Italy, the Netherlands and the Czech Republic seem set to implement risk mitigation measures, but not a blanket ban against the Shenzhen group. Finally, bearing in mind that not all final decisions have been made at this point, there are indications that Austria, Bulgaria, Hungary, Ireland, Portugal and Spain do not intend to take restrictive measures against Huawei. Elsewhere, the company has faced relatively little resistance. With the notable exception of India – where the policy debate on this issue is still ongoing at the time of writing – Huawei's network equipment business has flourished in most of Asia, as well as in the Middle East, Africa and Latin America.

As previously noted, the costs and time-loss involved with any change of equipment supplier mean that convincing foreign governments to ban Huawei completely was a tall order from the start. In addition, diplomatic relations with partners and allies were put under severe strain under the Trump presidency. With that context in mind, the next section takes a look at the discursive tactics employed by US diplomacy to try to overcome these difficulties.

---

9 The Five Eyes refers to a signals intelligence sharing (SIS) cooperation that unites the dedicated services of the United States, the United Kingdom, Australia, Canada and New Zealand.

6.3.1. *Educating rather than persuading: an attempt to rhetorically coerce partners and allies*

Global in scope, the American diplomatic campaign has put forward a two-step argument. The first step is to call for the adoption of a "risk-based security framework" to assess vendors' trustworthiness. This must include, as a mandatory criterion, "the extent to which suppliers are subject to foreign government control" (Strayer 2019c). Obviously, this is a thinly veiled reference to Huawei, considered by US government officials as an "arm of the [Chinese] state – or, more precisely, the Chinese Communist Party" (Ford 2019). Equally, a lot of emphasis is placed on the existence of a National Intelligence Law which "obliges any company under [China's] jurisdiction to comply with the requests of the Chinese intelligence services" (Pai 2019), the implication being that the problem "cannot be resolved by the company itself" (Hendel and Farrell 2020).

The second step of the argument supports the claim that it is impossible to safely have Huawei equipment in non-sensitive parts of a 5G network because "there will no longer be a real distinction between a core and an edge network" (Strayer 2019d). This requires come clarification. The "edge" generally refers to the radio-access network, that is, an array of base stations which directly communicate with user equipment along radio frequencies. The "core" generally refers to much more sensitive network functions which also concentrate most of the network's processing power. The "core" is actually an amalgamation of two things: the control plane, which includes entities in charge of network access authorization, user authentication, session setups, mobility management and security functions; and the user plane, which is in charge of routing packets of data back and forth to deliver all the services requested by users' equipment (voice, text messages, web browsing, etc.). The important point is that, given 5G networks are meant to enable data transfers with a response time of a few milliseconds, achieving such low latency requires moving the processing power of the "core" closer to the "edge" of the network. To do so, networks need to be "virtualized". A "virtualized" network is one where network functions – previously implemented by dedicated equipment – are implemented by software applications running on generic off-the-shelf hardware. This means that (at least in theory) sensitive core functions could be pushed to the very edge, making it difficult to ensure that there is a separation between sensitive and non-sensitive parts of a network. Thus, American diplomats have argued that "you can't protect yourself by just having unreliable vendors at the edge. You can't have them anywhere in your network" (Strayer 2019d).

To sum up, according to this two-step argument, if a government fails to ban Huawei completely, it is essentially providing an "arm of the Chinese Communist Party" with the ability to compromise the security of its critical infrastructure and citizens' data. Compelling in its internal logic, the American argument is also threatening in its implications. Among many other high-ranking Trump administration officials, Defence Secretary Mark Esper warned allies that failing to prohibit Huawei "could jeopardise our intelligence-sharing and communications capabilities and, by extension, our alliances" (DOD 2020).

What is striking about this campaign is that it does not so much seek to persuade allies of the righteousness of the US struggle against Huawei as to deprive them of the possibility of constructing a politically viable objection. This is what Ronald Krebs and Patrick Jackson (2007) call "rhetorical coercion". In the words of Hélène Dufournet, the aim is to establish a "standard of discourse that restricts the possibilities of expressing opposition" (Dufournet 2015, p. 265). Ideally, this process is so restrictive that it results in a "non-choice" (Mattern 2005, p. 606) or at least a "narrowing of the space of possibilities" (Dufournet 2015, p. 265), so that the target acquiesces to save face regardless of what it thinks of the argument's merits. These tactics are clearly at play in the way US diplomacy has sought to frame its argument as a factual finding from which the choice to exclude Huawei necessarily follows. Robert Blair, the White House special representative on telecom issues at the end of the Trump presidency, has stated that the role of the US government in this controversy is one of an "educator" which is trying "to share what it knows about the risks that unsecured and untrustworthy equipment can pose" (Hendel and Farrell 2020). Similarly, Ambassador Robert Strayer has made clear that the goal of this global campaign is to "start educating" (Strayer 2019a) allies about the objective situation – not to persuade them to join a political cause against Huawei. To be effective, however, this discourse needs to resonate with the target's audience – which is far from obvious.

6.3.2. *Successful agenda setting but limited rhetorical coercion*

It is perhaps an exaggeration to say, as Robert Strayer (2020) did, that "hardly anyone" had taken the risks posed by Huawei equipment into account before the US diplomatic campaign had drawn attention to it. In France, for example, for the past decade state authorities have prevented Huawei equipment from being installed in operators' core networks as well as in radio access networks in areas considered to be sensitive[10]. The Chinese vendor has been excluded from the Australian broadband network and has been subject to restrictions in Taiwan and Israel since 2013. It also came under intense scrutiny from the UK government, which set up a dedicated Huawei Cyber Security Evaluation Centre (HCSEC) in 2010, as will be further discussed later on in this chapter.

That said, there is no denying that the US diplomatic campaign has had a strong impact, bringing the issue of equipment vendors' trustworthiness to the forefront of the international stage. It sparked intense controversy at the Shangri-La Dialogue, in May 2019, and at the Munich Security Conference, in February 2020, as well as in domestic political debates in both Europe and the Asia–Pacific. Most notably, the risk assessment criterion put forward by the United States – namely, the extent to which suppliers are subject to foreign government control – has been much more broadly accepted than it was before. For instance, the Prague "5G Security Conference", which hosted delegations from 31 states, the European Union (EU) and NATO in May 2019, concluded with a final declaration calling on governments to "take into account the rule of law, the security environment, vendor malfeasance, and compliance with open, interoperable, secure standards, and industry best practices" in decision-making processes (Government of the Czech Republic 2019)[11]. US diplomacy also welcomed the fact that the "EU Coordinated Risk Assessment" mentioned "the likelihood that a supplier will be subject to interference from a non-EU country" (NIS Cooperation Group 2019, p. 22), in an implicit reference to the Chinese equipment manufacturer. Bilaterally, the United States also secured a formal commitment from

---

10 Interview with a representative of a French telecom operator, September 2020.

11 It should be noted, however, that this declaration did not have the scope that American diplomacy, co-chairing the conference, had hoped for. Indeed, the Europeans were opposed to this declaration being considered as a series of "Prague principles", binding on all participants, in order not to render European coordination initiatives on this issue meaningless. These principles thus became "Prague proposals", binding only on the conference presidency.

Poland, Estonia, the Czech Republic and Romania to consider whether suppliers have "a transparent ownership structure", are "subject to foreign government control" and comply with "a legal regime that enforces transparent corporate practices". Despite these four countries all being members of the 17+1 dialog platform with China and having all been subject to Chinese diplomatic efforts for them to take a stand against any "discriminatory practices based on country of origin"[12], clearly their attachment to the alliance with the United States outweighed other considerations.

Despite these elements of success, one should not overstate the campaign's influence. For instance, Australia's decision to ban Huawei equipment, announced at the end of August 2018, is hardly attributable to the American diplomatic initiative[13]. In Israel and Taiwan, the ban was also decided before its launch. The same is true in Vietnam, where Viettel, the main national operator, has been working on developing its own equipment and software for years (Zhong 2019), while still using Huawei in other countries where it operates, such as Laos and Cambodia. Moreover, certain US allies in Asia have refrained from restricting Huawei's involvement in the deployment of their mobile networks, such as Thailand, where the company began its globalization in 1997 (Barré 2016, p. 139); the Philippines, where the group provides a surveillance camera system as part of President Duterte's "public safety" campaign (Huong 2019, pp. 41–42); and, most notably, South Korea. Many governments in the region have discarded US allegations as unfounded or have considered the risks posed by Huawei equipment to be acceptable. While acknowledging the risks involved, former Malaysian Prime Minister Mahathir Mohamad viewed them as being irrelevant, his country being "too small to have an effect on a company like Huawei" and being an "open book" to any kind of espionage (quoted in Huong 2019, p. 42). Under such conditions, US pressure has gained little traction. For example, although the topic of 5G security was raised at the ASEAN-US Cyber Policy Dialogue, the aforementioned risk assessment criterion was not included in the meeting's final declaration (DOS 2019). Consequently, despite the tone adopted by US diplomacy, in

---

12 Interview with a French diplomat, July 2020.

13 The Australian authorities' distrust of Huawei stretches back more than a decade. A national security review of its involvement in the rollout of Australia's fiber network was conducted as early as 2008, leading to its exclusion from the project in 2012 and a limitation on its involvement in mobile networks.

many cases it has failed to bring about the desired change. An exception worth noting is of course Japan, where operators SoftBank, Docomo and KDDI all announced a move away from Huawei, despite having established commercial relationships with the group for 4G and preliminary 5G testing. This followed the release of 13 conditions by the Ministry of Internal Affairs and Communication, one of which required operators to "take sufficient cybersecurity measures in supply chain management" (cited in Duchâtel 2020).

In Europe, this security imperative is frequently invoked, but it is rarely viewed as meaning that a blanket ban should be enforced against the Chinese vendor. In this sense, the American attempt to rhetorical coerce its allies has only had limited success. To be fully successful, the coercer must be able to find resonance with the target's audience, such that its reputation is put on the line. To do so, the coercer needs to be able to count on "rhetorical commonplaces" that "represent the boundaries of legitimate framing" for any given situation (Krebs and Jackson 2007). In other words, the coercer needs to impose a norm of discourse that deprives the target of the possibility of formulating a politically tenable objection. If successful, the target will find itself rhetorically entraped, forcing it to validate the coercer's discourse, regardless of its actual merits. In making its case against Huawei, the challenge for US diplomats has been twofold. First, on a subject as complex as 5G, there is no obvious "commonplace" that can be used to rhetorically entrap partners and allies. While US officials have long supported the idea that a 5G-induced overlap between the core and the edge of a network means that the decision as regards Huawei equipment comes down to a "for-or-against" binary choice, several European governments, including France, do not look at the issue "from an American angle"[14]. Asked about American claims as regards the core and edge distinction collapsing in 5G, Guillaume Poupard, the Director of the French Cybersecurity Agency, dismissed them by saying that "it's all much more complicated than that [...] There are still places in a telecoms network that are more sensitive than others" (Poupard 2019). The idea behind this objection is that, although 5G standards make it technically possible to run sensitive functions at the very edge of the network, so far there are no foreseeable use cases that make it imperative to do so. This implies that managing the risks posed by Huawei equipment does not necessarily boil down to an all-or-nothing decision. Settling this argument is beyond the scope of this chapter. The fact remains, however,

14 Interview with a French diplomat, February 2020.

that the idea of the core and edge distinction disappearing in 5G did not provide US diplomacy with the "rhetorical commonplace" it was hoping for. Instead, it gave European governments rhetorical leeway to oppose a general ban while also recognizing the seriousness of the issue at stake.

The second hurdle facing American diplomats has to do with their perceived lack of legitimacy. The United States has indeed been accused of trying to subordinate its allies in a trade war that "is not theirs" (Senate 2019). Assurances that this would have "nothing to do with trade issues" (Hendel and Farrell 2020) and that the United States would have "nothing to gain" commercially from anti-Huawei bans (Strayer 2020) are often seen as lacking credibility in the chancelleries of Europe, given how extensive the China–US trade conflict is[15]. The United States has also been accused of hypocrisy: while Edward Snowden's revelations have shown that the NSA uses the products of American equipment manufacturers, such as Juniper and Cisco, for intelligence purposes, the American government is now warning its allies against China using telecom equipment for the very same reasons. This equivalence was notably made by Peter Altmaier, the German Economy Minister, who said that Germany had no reason to ban Huawei since it had not "called for a boycott [against US equipment] after the NSA case either" (AFP 2019).

6.3.3. *American rhetorical coercion in the special relationship*

In addition to the technical debate, which is devoid of a "rhetorical commonplace" due to the complexity of the subject matter, the resonance achieved by the American discourse has varied depending on the targeted state's political and strategic culture. A government that has very close ties to the United States has fewer argumentative resources that it can use to resist rhetorical entrapment. In this respect, the United Kingdom, linked to the United States by a "special relationship" (Reynolds 1985), the Five Eyes alliance and NATO, is worthy of attention.

At the time of 4G rollouts, the UK made a clear distinction between ZTE – a Chinese state-owned company excluded from UK mobile networks – and Huawei – a private company allowed to enter on the condition that it accepted increased oversight from the Huawei Cyber Security Evaluation

---

15 Interview with a French diplomat, February 2020.

Centre (HCSEC). Created in 2010 as the result of an agreement between the company and the UK government, the HCSEC is a hybrid organization that is owned by the Chinese vendor but that has a supervisory board which is chaired by the director of the National Cyber Security Centre (NCSC) and includes officials from the Government Communications Headquarters (GCHQ) and from other government agencies. Its stated purpose is "to mitigate any perceived risk from Huawei's involvement in parts of the United Kingdom's critical national infrastructure" (HCSEC Oversight Board 2019, p. 2). This means that, despite being considered as a "high-risk vendor", Huawei's equipment has long been tolerated even in the core networks of some operators, such as BT and Vodafone, provided that the company fully complied with HCSEC oversight. The board's annual reports were reassuring until 2017 (HCSEC Oversight Board 2017, p. 4), but a remarkable change in tone later occurred (HCSEC Oversight Board 2018, pp. 3–4), to the extent that the 2019 report warned that "it will be difficult to properly manage the risks of future [Huawei] products in the context of [upcoming] UK [5G] deployments" (HCSEC Oversight Board 2019, p. 4).

In late January 2020, after intense US diplomatic efforts, the UK government announced the exclusion of "high risk suppliers" from network cores and limited their presence to 35% of equipment at the edge (Raab 2020). Most notably, the government cited "ownership and location considerations" of the supplier as a risk factor (Raab 2020). The UK Telecoms Supply Chain Review Report – published six months earlier – also cited China's 2017 National Intelligence Law as a prime example of such risk (DCMS 2019, p. 25). Nonetheless, Ian Levy, the technical director of the NCSC, insisted that these "restrictions and controls [...] give us a way to minimize the risk of using a vendor [...] like Huawei" (Levy 2020a). At that point, a total ban was not deemed necessary.

This decision caused great discontent in Washington, and not only within the Trump administration. Following the announcement, a bipartisan group of US senators wrote an open letter to members of the House of Commons, asking them to develop "a comprehensive phase-out strategy to remove Huawei" from UK networks (Sasse et al. 2020). Finding strong resonance, this call for action sparked a rebellion among Conservative Party "backbenchers" led by Iain Duncan Smith, who was leader of the opposition during Tony Blair's premiership, a cabinet minister in David Cameron's government and the manager of Boris Johnson's 2019 leadership campaign. These "rebels" accused the UK government of practicing a "semi-defense of the realm" and leaving the country "friendless among [its] allies" (UK Parliament 2020). Taking place shortly after the UK's formal withdrawal from the European Union, this rebellion placed the theme of Britain's potential isolation from its allies of the so-called "Anglosphere" at the heart of its argument, as illustrated by many of Iain Duncan Smith's speeches on this matter:

> The Canadians, Americans, Australians and New Zealanders all disagree with us ... As smart, as brilliant, as great as our security and cybersecurity services are, how come we are right and everyone else is wrong? [...] We are alone on this. (UK Parliament 2020)

Politically, this argument has proven to be very powerful. Given how invested the UK is in its alliance with the United States, through the Five Eyes, NATO and a unique cooperation on nuclear capabilities, the boundaries of acceptable discourse are somewhat narrower than in other Western European countries. For example, it would be difficult for a British Minister to claim that the government has no reason to ban Huawei since it did not "call for a boycott [against American equipment] after the NSA affair", as the German Minister Peter Altmaier did. Establishing an equivalence between the People's Republic of China and the United States would be contrary to the most fundamental principles of British foreign policy since the Suez crisis of 1956.

Evidently, the pressure from the Conservative rebels left the government with few options to articulate a viable objection. In March 2020, the 35% cap, initially presented as a satisfactory way to contain risk and avoid over-reliance, became an interim step toward "a situation where [the UK] no longer needs to use any high-risk vendors for [its] telecoms networks *at all*" (UK Parliament 2020). At that point, it was only a partial concession, in the sense that the government conditioned the achievement of this goal on "market diversification", and refused to set a precise timetable[16]. However, it was still a significant step in the sense that the debate about Huawei had shifted from ends – "should Huawei be excluded?" – to means and timeframes – "how and when should Huawei be excluded?" – thus leading to the

---

16 This refusal led to the tabling of an amendment by the "rebels", which was eventually won by the government, although 38 Conservative MPs voted in favor of it.

"narrowing of the space for possibilities" that is essential to rhetorical coercion (Dufournet 2015, p. 265).

In the Spring of 2020, two additional events terminanted the UK government resistance to a blanket ban. On the one hand, as the COVID-19 pandemic started to unfold, hawkishness vis-à-vis China grew, leading to an increase in the number of Conservative MPs that were prepared to rebel against the Johnson government on the Huawei issue. On the other hand, the NCSC decided to modify its recommendations to the government following the new measures announced by the US Department of Commerce in May, based on the fact that the reliability of the components used by Huawei could be put at risk (Levy 2020b). It is this combination of political pressure and technical uncertainty that eventually led to the UK government to announce the total withdrawal of Huawei equipment from all national mobile networks by 2027. While the scale of the resources expended to achieve that outcome certainly raises questions, the success of the American campaign in the United Kingdom seems quite clearly established.

6.4. The anti-Huawei offensive: a barometer of American power?

This offensive by the US government demonstrates both its ability to harm Huawei and its inability to curb the rise of the Chinese vendor alone. It also shows its strong influence in setting the international agenda and the limits thereof in convincing its allies of the appropriate course of action. The fact that, in the final weeks of the Trump presidency, Secretary of State Mike Pompeo decided to unilaterally demand a "clean path" for data traffic to US diplomatic facilities, in the name of an extraterritorial application of the 2019 National Defense Authorization Act (DOS 2020), attests to this difficulty. At the end of the day, this campaign reveals the unparalleled reach of American foreign policy, as well as the limits to its effectiveness. It is this paradox that the Huawei affair brings to light.

The multiplicity of instruments mobilized in this offensive illustrates this perfectly. America's legal resources has allowed it to initiate timely and strategically targeted proceedings against the company. Its commercial levers have enabled it to rapidly deprive the group of some of its supplies without delay. Its diplomatic network and public relations resources have also made the anti-Huawei campaign difficult to ignore. Nonetheless, this can also lead to a fragmentation of the policy process, which in turn risks losing coherence (Meijer and Jensen 2018). Since each vector – law enforcement, economic policy, diplomacy – falls under separate institutional structures, these may collide with one another, particularly when political coordination and messaging at the White House is in disarray. For instance, Donald Trump's statements that he would "surely intervene" if he thought it would be "good for what will probably be the biggest trade deal ever" (Shepardson 2020) certainly harmed the credibility of the DOJ's claims to prosecutorial independence and discredited the State Department's efforts to dissociate this campaign from the "trade war" with China. Thus, as the policy toolbox expands, strategic coherence is increasingly difficult to achieve and its effectiveness is uncertain. At the same time, the combination of diplomatic efforts and trade sanctions did end up tipping the scales in favor of a ban in the United Kingdom, the Johnson government having gradually aligned its position with that of the United States. It remains to be seen whether this outcome was worth the expended resources.

Moreover, the Huawei affair embodies, in a new form, what Colin Dueck (2008) calls the dilemma of the "reluctant crusader", that runs through the history of American foreign policy. On the one hand, the undertaking of a vast diplomatic initiative to "educate" its partners on 5G security is in line with America's "hegemonic" impulse, which constitutes the first legacy of its strategic culture (Layne 2007). On the other hand, the outright rejection of the US government taking a stake in one of Huawei's competitors illustrates the "burden aversion", or even the "anti-statism" (Friedberg 2012), which constitutes the second legacy of American strategic culture. While these two tendencies appear to be reconcilable long term in supporting the Open-RAN alliance, which aims to increase market diversification, this solution does not address the immediate issue at stake with respect to Huawei's participation in 5G deployments. This difficulty in finding an alternative solution that would break the path dependency enjoyed by the Chinese vendor indicates that the American offensive has essentially taken negative forms; hence the discursive tactics employed toward its allies, centered on a form of "rhetorical coercion" that can only succeed if there is "at least some shared understanding of the limits of acceptable discourse" (Krebs and Jackson 2007, p. 55). However, given the complexity of a topic like 5G, it is difficult to put a target's reputation on the line through purely objective technical arguments. Under these conditions, US diplomatic discourse can only resonate where attachment to the alliance with the United States is most deeply entrenched, namely, the Five Eyes, Japan and in certain Eastern European countries. Elsewhere, the United States has faced a lack of legitimacy and trust in making its case, partly as a result of the Snowden revelations and the US–China "trade war".

These difficulties faced by the US government in convincing its allies and pursuing a coherent strategy raise questions that are relevant in many other areas of international relations. In this respect, the specificity of cybersecurity issues and their "revolutionary" nature (Kello 2013, 2017) should be put into perspective: the Huawei affair is less the symptom of a revolution than it is a magnifier of pre-existing tendencies in world politics.

6.5. References

AFP (2019). Huawei : l'ambassadeur américain accuse Berlin d'avoir insulté les USA. *Le Figaro* [Online]. Available at: www.lefigaro.fr/flash-eco/huawei-l-ambassadeur-americain-accuse-berlin-d-avoir-insulte-les-usa-20191125 [Accessed on 31 March 2020].

Barr, W. (2020). Attorney General William Barr's Keynote Address: China Initiative Conference. *CSIS* [Online]. Available at: www.csis.org/analysis/attorney-general-william-barrs-keynote-address-china-initiative-conference [Accessed on 31 March 2020].

Barré, G. (2016). *Quand les entreprises chinoises se mondialisent : Haier, Huawei et TCL*. CNRS Éditions, Paris.

Connell, P. and Huang, T. (2014). An empirical analysis of *CFIUS*: Examining foreign investment regulation in the United States. *Yale J. Int'l L.*, 39, 135–138.

Cotton, T., Cornyn, J., Inhofe, J.M., Crapo, M., Rubio, M., Young, T. (2020). Letter to Secretary of Commerce on 5G standards. US Senate [Online]. Available at: www.inhofe.senate.gov/imo/media/doc/20200414%20Letter%20to%20Secretary%20of%20Commerce%20on%205G%20Standards%20FINAL.pdf [Accessed on 24 June 2020].

DCMS (2019). Telecoms supply chain review. Department for Culture, Media and Sport [Online]. Available at: www.gov.uk/government/publications/telecoms-supply-chain-review-terms-of-reference [Accessed on 31 March 2020].

DOC (2019). Addition of entities to the entity list. Department of Commerce, Federal Register [Online]. Available at: www.govinfo.gov/content/pkg/FR-2019-05-21/pdf/2019-10616.pdf [Accessed on 23 September 2020].

DOC (2020a). Commerce clears way for U.S. companies to more fully engage in Tech Standards-Development Bodies. Department of Commerce [Online]. Available at: www.commerce.gov/news/press-releases/2020/06/commerce-clears-way-us-companies-more-fully-engage-tech-standards [Accessed on 24 June 2020].

DOC (2020b). Commerce addresses Huawei's efforts to undermine entity list, restricts products designed and produced with U.S. technologies. Department of Commerce [Online]. Available at: www.commerce.gov/news/pressreleases/2020/ 05/commerce-addresses-huaweis-efforts-undermine-entity-list-restricts [Accessed on 10 September 2020].

DOC (2020c). Commerce department further restricts Huawei access to U.S. technology and adds another 38 affiliates to the entity list. Department of Commerce [Online]. Available at: www.commerce.gov/news/press-releases/ 2020/08/commerce-department-further-restricts-huawei-access-us-technology-and [Accessed on 10 September 2020].

DOD (2020). As prepared remarks by Secretary of Defense Mark T. Esper at the Munich Conference. Department of Defense [Online]. Available at: www. defense.gov/Newsroom/Speeches/Speech/Article/2085577/as-prepared-remarks-by-secretary-of-defense-mark-t-esper-at-the-munich-security/ [Accessed on 31 March 2020].

DOJ (2019a). Chinese telecommunications conglomerate Huawei and Huawei CFO Wanzhou Meng charged with financial fraud. Department of Justice [Online]. Available at: www.justice.gov/opa/pr/chinese-telecommunications-conglomerate-huawei-and-huawei-cfo-wanzhou-meng-charged-financial [Accessed on 31 March 2020].

DOJ (2019b). Chinese telecommunications device manufacturer and its U.S. affiliate indicted for theft of trade secrets, wire fraud, and obstruction of justice. Department of Justice [Online]. Available at: www.justice.gov/opa/pr/chinese-telecommunications-device-manufacturer-and-its-us-affiliate-indicted-theft-trade [Accessed on 30 September 2020].

DOJ (2020). Chinese telecommunications conglomerate Huawei and subsidiaries charged in racketeering conspiracy and conspiracy to steal trade secrets. Department of Justice [Online]. Available at: www.justice.gov/opa/pr/chinese-telecommunications-conglomerate-huawei-and-subsidiaries-charged-racketeering [Accessed on 31 March 2020].

DOJ (2021). Information about the Department of Justice's China initiative and a compilation of China-related prosecutions since 2018. Department of Justice [Online]. Available at: www.justice.gov/nsd/information-about-department-justice-s-china-initiative-and-compilation-china-related [Accessed on 1 April 2021].

DOS (2019). Co-chairs' statement on the inaugural ASEAN-U.S. cyber policy dialogue. Department of State [Online]. Available at: www.state.gov/co-chairs-statement-on-the-inaugural-asean-u-s-cyber-policy-dialogue/ [Accessed on 31 March 2020].

DOS (2020). Senior State Department Official on State Department 2019 successes on cybersecurity and 5G issues. Department of State [Online]. Available at: www.state.gov/senior-state-department-official-on-state-department-2019-successes-on-cybersecurity-and-5g-issues/ [Accessed on 31 March 2020].

Duchâtel, M. (2020). Japan's 5G: A mirror for Europe. Institut Montaigne [Online]. Available at: www.institutmontaigne.org/en/blog/japans-5g-mirror-europe [Accessed on 31 March 2020].

Dueck, C. (2008). *Reluctant Crusaders: Power, Culture, and Change in American Grand Strategy*. Princeton University Press, Princeton.

Dufournet, H. (2015). Le piège rhétorique : une contrainte par la morale ? *Revue française de science politique*, 65(2), 261–278.

Estève, A. (2018). Le "lawfare" ou les usages stratégiques du droit. In *L'Enjeu mondial. Guerres et conflits armés au XXIᵉ siècle*, Pelopidas, B., Ramel, F. (eds). Presses de Sciences Po, Paris.

FCC (2019). FCC bars use of universal service funding for equipement & services posing national security risks. Federal Communications Commission [Online]. Available at: www.docs.fcc.gov/public/attachments/DOC-360976A1.pdf [Accessed on 27 September 2020].

FCC (2020). FCC designates Huawei and ZTE as national security threats. Federal Communications Commission [Online]. Available at: www.docs.fcc.gov/public/attachments/DOC-365255A1.pdf [Accessed on 27 September 2020].

Ford, C.A. (2019). Huawei and its siblings, the Chinese Tech Giants: National security and foreign policy implications [Online]. Available at: www.state.gov/huawei-and-its-siblings-the-chinese-tech-giants-national-security-and-foreign-policy-implications/ [Accessed on 31 March 2020].

Fox Business (2020). Commerce Department adding 38 affiliates to restricted entity list: Commerce Secretary Wilbur Ross explains how these additional measures will help protect American national security from Huawei [Online]. Available at: www.video.foxbusiness.com/v/6181801166001/#sp=show-clips [Accessed on 15 September 2020].

Friedberg, A.L. (2012). *In the Shadow of the Garrison State: America's Anti-statism and its Cold War Grand Strategy*. Princeton University Press, Princeton.

Government of the Czech Republic (2019). Prague 5G Security Conference announced series of recommendations: The Prague Proposals [Online]. Available at: www.vlada.cz/en/media-centrum/aktualne/prague-5g-security-conference-announced- series-of-recommendations-the-prague-proposals-173422/ [Accessed on 31 March 2020].

HCSEC Oversight Board (2017). Huawei cyber security evaluation centre: Oversight board annual report 2017 [Online]. Available at: www.gov.uk/government/publications/huawei-cyber-security-evaluation-centre-oversight-board-annual-report-2017 [Accessed on 31 March 2020].

HCSEC Oversight Board (2018). Huawei cyber security evaluation centre oversight board: Annual report 2018 [Online]. Available at: www.gov.uk/government/publications/huawei-cyber-security-evaluation-centre-oversight-board-annual-report-2018 [Accessed on 31 March 2020].

HCSEC Oversight Board (2019). Huawei cyber security evaluation centre oversight board: Annual report 2019 [Online]. Available at: www.gov.uk/government/publications/huawei-cyber-security-evaluation-centre-oversight-board-annual-report-2019 [Accessed on 31 March 2020].

Hendel, J. and Farrell, M. (2020). Questions for Robert Blair, Trump's Point Man on 5G. *Politico* [Online]. Available at: www.politico.com/news/agenda/2020/02/25/questions-for-robert-blair-trumps-point-man-on-5g-106364 [Accessed on 31 March 2020].

Hickey, A. (2019). ICCE 2019 – panel two – enforcing norms: Cyber diplomacy & law enforcement. Atlantic Council [Online]. Available at: www.youtube.com/watch?v=N-DdPin223g [Accessed on 31 March 2020].

HPSCI (2012). Investigative report on the U.S. national security issues posed by Chinese Telecommunications Companies Huawei and ZTE. US Congress, House Permanent Select Committee on Intelligence [Online]. Available at: www.intelligence.house.gov/news/documentsingle.aspx?DocumentID=96 [Accessed on 31 March 2020].

Huawei (2020). Huawei statement on US Justice Department Indictment [Online]. Available at: www.huawei.com/en/press-events/news/2020/2/huawei-statement-on-us-justice-department-indictment [Accessed on 31 March 2020].

Huong, L.T. (2019). A collision of cybersecurity and geopolitics: Why Southeast Asia is wary of a Huawei Ban. *Global Asia*, 14(3), 41–42.

Kello, L. (2013). The meaning of the cyber revolution: Perils to theory and statecraft. *International Security*, 38(2), 7–40.

Kello, L. (2017). *The Virtual Weapon and International Order*. Yale University Press, New Haven.

Kittrie, O. (2016). *Lawfare: Law as a Weapon of War*. Oxford University Press, Oxford.

Krebs, C. (2019). 5G innovation and security [Online]. Available at: www. csis.org/events/5g-innovation-and-security [Accessed on 31March 2020].

Krebs, R.R. and Jackson, P.T. (2007). Twisting tongues and twisting arms: The power of political rhetoric. *European Journal of International Relations*, 13(1), 35–66.

Layne, C. (2007). *The Peace of Illusions: American Grand Strategy from 1940 to the Present*. Cornell University Press, Ithaca.

Leithauser, T. (2013). Justice Department creates cyber unit to address "National Security" threats. Cybersecurity policy report.

Levy, I. (2020a). The future of telecoms in the UK. *NCSC* [Online]. Available at: www.ncsc.gov.uk/blog-post/the-future-of-telecoms-in-the-uk   [Accessed   on 10 September 2020].

Levy, I. (2020b). Summary of the NCSC analysis of May 2020 US sanction. *NCSC* [Online]. Available at: www.ncsc.gov.uk/report/summary-of-ncsc-analysis-of-us-may-2020-sanction [Accessed on 10 September 2020].

Lindsay, J., Cheung, T.M., Reveron, D. (2015). *China and Cybersecurity: Espionage, Strategy, and Politics in the Digital Domain*, Oxford University Press, New York.

Lysne, O. (2018). *The Huawei and Snowden Questions: Can Electronic Equipment from Untrusted Vendors be Verified? Can an Untrusted Vendor Build Trust Into Electronic Equipment?* Springer, Cham.

Mason, J. and Holland, S. (2018). Exclusive: Trump says he could intervene in U.S. case against Huawei CFO. *Reuters* [Online]. Available at: www.reuters. com/article/us-usa-trump-huawei-tech-exclusive-idUSKBN1OA2PQ [Accessed on 25 September 2020].

Mattern, J.B. (2005). Why soft power isn't so soft: Representational force and the sociolinguistic construction of attraction in world politics. *Millennium*, 33(3), 583–612.

McCotter, T. (2007). Communist China and CIFUS: Dropping the Shark. *Congressional Record*, 153(149), 11226–11227.

Medeiros, E.S., Cliff, R., Crane, K., Mulvenon, J.C. (2005). *A New Direction for China's Defense Industry*. RAND Corporation, Washington D.C.

Meijer, H. (2016). *Trading with the Enemy: The Making of US Export Control Policy toward the People's Republic of China*. Oxford University Press, Oxford.

Meijer, H. and Jensen, B. (2018). The strategist's dilemma: Global dynamic density and the making of US "China policy". *European Journal of International Security*, 3(2), 211–234.

Nakashima, E. and Barrett, D. (2019). Justice Dept. charges Huawei with fraud, ratcheting up U.S.-China tensions. *The Washington Post* [Online]. Available at: www.washingtonpost.com/world/national-security/justice-dept-charges-huawei-with-fraud-ratcheting-up-us-china-tensions/2019/01/28/70a7f550-2320-11e9-81fd-b7b05d5bed90_story.html [Accessed on 31 March 2020].

NIS Cooperation Group (2019). Report on EU coordinated risk assessment of 5G [Online]. Available at: www.ec.europa.eu/commission/presscorner/detail/en/IP_19_6049 [Accessed on 31 March 2020].

Nolan, P. (2014). Globalisation and industrial policy: The case of China. *The World Economy*, 37(6), 747–764.

NSA (2008). PRC information warfare & Huawei [Online]. Available at: https://theintercept.com/document/2019/01/23/prc-information-warfare-huawei/ [Accessed on 2 July 2020].

NSC (2018). The Eisenhower National Highway System for the information age [Online]. Available at: www.docs.house.gov/meetings/IF/IF16/20180130/106810/HHRG-115-IF16-20180130-SD1011-U1011.pdf [Accessed on 31 March 2020].

O-RAN Alliance (2019). O-RAN alliance [Online]. Available at: www.o-ran.org [Accessed on 31 March 2020].

Pai, A. (2019). Geopolitics and the 5G supply chain [Online]. Available at: www.wilsoncenter.org/event/geopolitics-and-the-5g-supply-chain [Accessed on 31 March 2020].

POTUS (1975). Executive Order 11858 of May 7, 1975, 40 Federal Register 20263, 3 Code of Federal Regulations, 1971–1975 Comp., 990.

POTUS (2019a). Executive order on securing the information and communications technology and services supply chain. Presidency of the United States [Online]. Available at: www.whitehouse.gov/presidential-actions/executive-order-securing-information-communications-technology-services-supply-chain/ [Accessed on 31 March 2020].

POTUS (2019b). Remarks by President Trump on United States 5G deployment. Presidency of the United States [Online]. Available at: www.whitehouse.gov/briefings-statements/remarks-president-trump-united-states-5g-deployment/ [Accessed on 31 March 2020].

Poupard, G. (2019). L'État et la sécurité des systèmes d'information. France Culture [Online]. Available at: www.franceculture.fr/emissions/soft-power/soft-power-le-magazine-des-internets-emission-du-dimanche-24-novembre-2019 [Accessed on 31 March 2020].

Raab, D. (2020). Foreign Secretary's statement on Huawei [Online]. Available at: www.gov.uk/government/speeches/foreign-secretary-statement-on-huawei [Accessed on 31 March 2020].

Reynolds, D. (1985). A "special relationship"? America, Britain and the international order since the Second World War. *International Affairs*, 62(1), 1–20.

Rühlig, T. (2020). Technical standardisation, China and the future international order. *Heinrich Böll Stiftung* [Online]. Available at: www.eu.boell.org/en/2020/03/03/technical-standardisation-china-and-future-international-order [Accessed on 31 March 2020].

Sasse, B., Markey, E.J., Tillis, T., Coons, C.A., Rubio, M., Van Hollen, C., Moran, J., Gillibrand, K., Burr, R., Warner, M., Cruz, T., Blumenthal, R., Thune, J., Romney, M., Scott, R., Hawley, J., Blackburn, M., Young, T. (2020). Bipartisan letter calling for UK to reconsider Huawei decision. US Senate [Online]. Available at: www.democrats.senate.gov/newsroom/press-releases/schumer-and-sasse-lead-bipartisan-letter-calling-for-uk-to-reconsider-huawei-decision [Accessed on 25 September 2020].

Schneier, B. (2012). Complexity the worst enemy of security. *Computer World* [Online]. Available at: www.computerworld.com/article/2493938/complexity-the-worst-enemy-of-security.html [Accessed on 31 March 2020].

Segal, A. (2016). *The Hacked World Order*. Public Affairs, New York.

Senat (2019). Commission des affaires économiques : compte rendu de la semaine du 3 juin 2019 [Online]. Available at: www.senat.fr/compte-rendu-commissions/20190603/eco.html [Accessed on 31 March 2020].

Shepardson, D. (2020). White House dismisses idea of U.S. buying Nokia, Ericsson to challenge Huawei. *Reuters* [Online]. Available at: www.fr.reuters.com/article/idUSKBN2012A5 [Accessed on 25 September 2020].

SIA (2020). SIA statement on export control rule changes. Semiconductor Industry Association [Online]. Available at: www.semiconductors.org/sia-statement-on-export-control-rule-changes-2/ [Accessed on 15 September 2020].

Strayer, R. (2019a). Press briefing with Deputy Assistant Secretary Robert Strayer [Online]. Available at: www.state.gov/telephonic-press-briefing-with-deputy-assistant-secretary-robert-strayer-cyber-and-international-affairs-and-information-policy-bureau-of-economic-and-business-affairs/ [Accessed on 31 March 2020].

Strayer, R. (2019b). 5G: National security concerns, intellectual property issues, and the impact on competition and innovation [Online]. Available at: www.judiciary. senate.gov/meetings/5g-national-security-concerns-intellectual-property-issues-and-the-impact-on-competition-and-innovation [Accessed on 31 March 2020].

Strayer, R. (2019c). Press briefing with Deputy Assistant Secretary Robert Strayer – Translations [Online]. Available at: www.translations.state.gov/2019/07/11/press-briefing-with-deputy-assistant-secretary-robert-strayer/ [Accessed on 31 March 2020].

Strayer, R. (2019d). U.S. policy on 5G technology [Online]. Available at: www.state.gov/US-Policy-On-5g-Technology [Accessed on 31 March 2020].

Strayer, R. (2020). Top US cybersecurity official warns of threat posed by China's Huawei. *France 24* [Online]. Available at: www.youtube.com/watch?v=wMud 4gvNgMs [Accessed on 31 March 2020].

Trump, D. (2017). National Security Strategy of the United States of America [Online]. Available at: https://trumpwhitehouse.archives.gov/wp-content/uploads/ 2017/12/NSS-Final-12-18-2017-0905.pdf [Accessed on 30 August 2021].

Trump, D. (2020). Tweet from 18 February, 2020, at 9:37 AM [Online]. Available at: www.thetrumparchive.com/?dates=%5B%222020-02-17%22%2C%222020-02-19%22%5D [Accessed on 1 April 2021].

UK Parliament (2020). Huawei and 5G [Online]. Available at: www. hansard.parliament.uk/Commons/2020-03-04/debates/9023564F-30E1-40C4-A9DE-E19DB8139E02/HuaweiAnd5G [Accessed on 31 March 2020].

Weisman, S.R. (2008). Sale of 3Com to Huawei is derailed by U.S. security concerns. *The New York Times* [Online]. Available at: www.nytimes.com/2008/02/21/business/ worldbusiness/21iht-3com.1.10258216.html [Accessed on 3 September 2020].

Zhong, R. (2019). Is Huawei a security threat? Vietnam isn't taking any chances. *The New York Times* [Online]. Available at: www.cn.nytimes.com/technology/ 20190719/huawei-ban-vietnam/en-us/ [Accessed on 25 September 2020].

Zhou, Y., Lazonick, W., Sun, Y. (2016). Catching up and developing innovation capabilities in China's telecommunication equipment industry. *China as An Innovation Nation*. Oxford University Press, New York.

The Issue of Personal and Sovereign Data in the Light of an Emerging "International Law of Intelligence"

> *Starting in 2020, the process of creating, collecting and processing data has become the main obsession of the whole of society and everyone has ended up benefitting from it.*

Marc Dugain, *Transparence*, 2019, p. 32

7.1. Introduction

On the whole, it is easy to understand the nature of data, the unit of measurement of which is the byte: "A piece of data is an elementary description, typically numerical for us, of a reality" (Abiteboul 2012)[1]; or even: "The basic element that can be processed or produced by a computer to convey information" (Schmitt 2017). On the other hand, when we focus on the status and functions of data, which are precisely what public international law might be concerned with, the questioning becomes more complex.

Chapter written by Fabien LAFOUASSE.

1 Compare this definition with the definition of "computer data" given in Article 1 of the Budapest Convention on Cybercrime (Council of Europe 2001): "Any representation of facts, information or concepts in a form suitable for computer processing […]."

First, the status of data is generally determined according to three states: the data may be in transit, in use or stored. In this case, the location (*ratione loci*) of data at a given moment is the predominant criterion in any analysis of data capture by an intelligence service on the basis of the principle of territoriality; indeed, cyberspace does not escape the territorial link by the very virtue of its physical composition[2]. In addition, there is the thorny question of where data are used, as opposed to where they have been collected. Moreover, data captured may be content or connection data[3], sovereign (Faure-Muntian 2018)[4] or personal[5] data, primary or processed[6] data. As a result, at least four points from various branches of international law can be highlighted: the territorial integrity of the state whose data have been intercepted when this operation is accompanied by an unconsented intrusion into a space under national sovereignty; the immunity of the state's property, particularly when it is not on the territory of the state to which it belongs; the secrecy of correspondence (international communications law); and the right of respect for private life (international and European human rights law). In the absence of a legally established semantic distinction between information and data, it is appropriate, as Vadillo suggests, to opt for the

---

2 On this notion, see Chapter 1.

3 Connection data refers to the "container" allowing the routing of an electronic communication (Commission nationale de contrôle des techniques de renseignement 2015–2016), as opposed to the content of correspondence exchanged or information viewed. Connection data is the correct technical name for metadata (or data about data), "the cross-checking of which, especially because it is massive, may lead to the identification of a person" (Norodom 2014, p. 734).

4 Where sovereign data is understood as follows: "[The] sovereignty of a piece of geographic data is therefore defined by its destination or use, which is to serve as a direct support for the decisions of the public power. A piece of data is therefore only sovereign if its availability conditions the very possibility of a public decision, that is to say, if it is truly critical for the public power".

5 "Personal" data is defined in Article 4.1 of the General Data Protection Regulation (GDPR) as "any information relating to an identified or identifiable natural person […]; an 'identifiable natural person' is one who can be identified, directly or indirectly, in particular by reference to an identifier, such as a name, an identification number, location data, an online identifier, or to one or more factors specific to his or her physical, physiological, genetic, mental, economic, cultural or social identity".

6 For example, in its "Principles relating to remote sensing of the Earth from outer space", adopted on December 3, 1986, the United Nations General Assembly defines primary data as "the raw data collected by sensors on board a space object and transmitted or communicated to the ground from space by telemetry in the form of electromagnetic signals […]" and processed data as "the products of the processing of the primary data necessary to make the data usable" (Principle 1, A/RES/41/65).

following gradation: "Information includes intelligence, which, in turn, includes data" (Vadillo 2020, p. 62).

Cyberespionage refers to any act undertaken clandestinely or under false pretenses, which uses digital capabilities to collect, or attempt to collect, information. Thus, the capture of data flows in cyberspace, however massive (Basdevant and Mignard 2018, p. 11) and fluid they may be, falls under the category of traditional intelligence gathering under the rules of public international law. Indeed, the intersection between the espionage vector used and the space in which the clandestine intelligence operation takes place leads once again to a distinction between, on the one hand, acts of espionage associated with an internationally wrongful act (constituted by the infringement of the territorial sovereignty of the spied-upon state, for example a spy plane penetrating, without its consent, the national airspace of the spied-upon state) and, on the other hand, unfriendly acts (Salmon 2001, p. 28) of espionage committed in or from international spaces (high seas, international airspace, outer space – in the image of an intelligence vessel collecting data from the high seas) (Lafouasse 2012).

In fact, it is necessary to distinguish between, on the one hand, a manifest violation of territorial integrity, which in itself generates an internationally wrongful act, whether or not it is accompanied by an act of espionage, and, on the other hand, an act of espionage per se, which, in the absence of customary and treaty rules, is not wrongful under public international law, a reasoning that is applicable to acts of cyberespionage. To precisely illustrate this last point, we can consider that the lawfulness of the interception of an undersea communication cable depends, among other things, on whether the operation takes place within or outside the territorial waters of the coastal state (Schmitt 2017, pp. 168–170)[7].

The collection of personal and sovereign data (Faure-Muntian 2018, pp. 14–15)[8] without the knowledge of their owners leads us first to identify the

---

7 Rule 32 ("Peacetime cyber espionage") of the *Tallinn Manual 2.0 on the International Law Applicable to Cyber Operations* states: "Although peacetime cyber espionage by States does not per se violate international law, the method by which it is carried out might do so."

8 Sovereign data refers to data for which the state and its administrations are the exclusive holders, such as the so-called "sovereignty database", and the sole decision-makers as to their level of accessibility to third parties; thus, under the terms of Article 14 of Law No. 2016-1321 of October 7, 2016, for a Digital Republic, reference (public) data is public information that "constitutes a common reference for naming or identifying products, services, territories

legal rules mobilized both in the corpus of international and European human rights law and in the body of customary norms on which the territorial sovereignty of states is based (section 7.2). Then, an approach centered on data localization considerations at the time of their capture sheds new light on the interactions between public international law and an emerging international law of intelligence (section 7.3).

7.2. The legal rules invoked in the collection of personal and sovereign data

If we look at Article 2 of the decree establishing, in France, a general data administrator[9], we can observe that, in the missions entrusted to him or her, he or she must organize the best use of the administrations' data and its widest circulation, "while respecting the protection of personal data and secrets protected by law". We can summarize here, in a few words, the two main categories of data that can be distinguished in a legal analysis of their collection by a foreign state, namely, personal data, the protection of which is based on the conventional rules of international human rights law (section 7.2.1), and sovereign data, the collection of which may infringe on the customary rules relating to the territorial integrity of the state to which they belongs (section 7.2.2).

7.2.1. *Right to privacy versus general communications surveillance*[10]

The definition of personal data that we adopt is deliberately broad and encompasses all of an individual's digital activities, which constitute, so to speak, their digital private sphere. The right to privacy, which includes the

---

or persons". On the other hand, other sovereign data, due to their very sensitivity, remain not publicly accessible.

9 Decree No. 2014-1050 of September 16, 2014, establishing a general data administrator (Legifrance 2014).

10 The terminology "general communications surveillance" is used by the Fundamental Rights Agency (FRA), which states: "Intelligence can be collected with technical means and at large scale. This surveillance technique is referred to in different ways, including 'signals intelligence', 'strategic surveillance', 'bulk investigatory powers', 'mass digital surveillance' and 'storage of data on a generalised basis'. Whenever possible, FRA uses the national laws' terminology, but also uses, as a generic encompassing term, 'general communications surveillance'" (Fundamental Rights Agency 2017).

protection of personal data, is a pillar of the European Convention on Human Rights and is enshrined in its Article 8. However, we should not make the mistake of considering that this convention is the only instrument codifying the right to privacy[11], even if we must admit that European case law is by far the most abundant. This is why any examination of the jurisprudence on the right to privacy from the European Court of Human Rights (ECtHR) here must focus solely on requests with an international dimension in the implementation of "secret surveillance measures"[12] – in this case, the interception of communications, which, it should be remembered, consists of content and connection data – as opposed to the more frequent simple requests from citizens subjected to such measures in the context of cases under criminal law. Strictly speaking, there have been four ECtHR judgments to date that meet this international criterion:

– *Weber and Saravia v. Germany* (June 29, 2006): The two applicants, a German national and a Uruguayan national, resident in Uruguay, challenged the extension of the powers of the German intelligence service (BND) to record telecommunications during so-called "strategic" surveillance;

– *Liberty and Others v. United Kingdom* (July 1, 2008): Three civil liberties groups (one British and two Irish) alleged that in the 1990s the British Ministry of Defence used an "electronic monitoring device" capable of simultaneously intercepting 10,000 telephone calls from Dublin to London or the continent;

– *Centrum för Rättvisa v. Sweden* (June 19, 2018 and May 25, 2021, the Grand Chamber): A foundation alleged that legislation allowing mass interception of electronic signals in Sweden for foreign intelligence purposes had infringed its right to privacy;

– *Big Brother Watch and Others v. United Kingdom* (September 13, 2018 and May 25, 2021, the Grand Chamber): British journalists and civil liberties organizations filed a complaint against three surveillance regimes, namely: the mass interception of communications, the sharing of information with foreign states and the obtaining of communications data from communications service providers.

---

11 The International Covenant on Civil and Political Rights (ICCPR) and the American Convention on Human Rights are two other examples.

12 In its judgment in *Klass and Others v. Germany* (September 6, 1978), the ECtHR used, for the first time, the complete formula of "secret surveillance measures" (paragraph 49), which includes the interception of communications.

It is interesting to note that, on February 5, 2019, the panel of the Grand Chamber accepted referrals to the Grand Chamber at the request of the applicants in the last two cases, who were dissatisfied with some of the Court's conclusions. Indeed, in *Centrum för Rättvisa*, the Court unanimously found no violation of Article 8, insofar as Swedish legislation and practice in the field of electromagnetic intelligence offered adequate and sufficient safeguards against arbitrariness and the risk of abuse. In contrast, in *Big Brother Watch and Others*, where the applicants believed that, by the very nature of their activities, their communications could have been intercepted by the British intelligence services, the Court held that the bulk interception regime did violate Article 8, although it recognized that the use of such a regime did not in itself violate the Convention. What do these cases have in common? The defendant states were being challenged for their use of international communications surveillance systems, which were allegedly massive (at least in the last three cases). In these cases, however, the Court considered that, subject to the application of six "minimum guarantees"[13] by the states parties, the existence per se of these surveillance systems was legitimate (it could have added, moreover, as judged in *Weber and Saravia*, that these devices did not infringe the territorial sovereignty of the foreign states to which the said communications were linked). It is clear that the interception of content and connection data relating to these international communications, not to mention their retention (Kittichaisaree and Kuner 2015), constitutes a legal issue which, beyond the jurisprudence of the ECtHR and other courts dedicated to human rights, extends beyond the strict framework of respect for privacy to touch on international telecommunications law (especially the secrecy of correspondence) and, through this, the rules of territorial and digital sovereignty of states. Finally, as Buchan reminds us, when a state commits an act of cyberespionage against an individual located on its own territory both the European Convention on Human Rights and the ICCPR apply, insofar as this individual is both on its territory and *ipso facto* subject to its jurisdiction, even if the data collected are stored on cyberinfrastructures located outside the said territory (Buchan

---

13 These six minimum guarantees are: the nature of the offences that may give rise to an interception warrant; the definition of the categories of persons who may be wiretapped; the setting of a limit on the duration of the measure; the procedure to be followed for the examination, use and conservation of the data collected; the precautions to be taken for the communication of the data to other parties; and the circumstances under which the deletion or destruction of the recordings may or must take place.

2019, p. 97)[14]. Thus, while the location of intercepted data is not a major obstacle to the application of human rights in terms of privacy protection, it remains central in terms of the possible infringement of territorial sovereignty.

7.2.2. *Violation of territorial sovereignty versus cyberespionage*

In the current state of public international law, the principle of territoriality remains predominant in any analysis of incidents affecting state sovereignty. This is the case for acts of espionage committed by an intelligence service of state A (spying state) against the fundamental interests of state B (spied-upon state): either these acts of espionage are accompanied by a violation of the territorial integrity of the spied-upon state, because the vector used for this purpose has penetrated, without its consent, the spaces under its national sovereignty, or they are carried out from or in international spaces[15] and do not, in this case, violate the territorial integrity of the spied-upon state.

In the first configuration, the infringement of the territorial sovereignty of the spied-upon state undoubtedly constitutes an internationally wrongful act; in the second, in the absence of such an infringement, the act of espionage in question would be represented as an unfriendly act. In fact, it is necessary to distinguish, on the one hand, between a manifest violation of territorial integrity, which in itself constitutes an internationally wrongful act, whether or not it is accompanied by an act of espionage, and, on the other hand, the act of espionage per se, which, in the absence of customary and treaty rules, is not wrongful under public international law.

This territorialist reasoning would, at first glance, be undermined in the context of acts of cyberespionage[16] (Buchan 2019, p. 13), where the violation of the borders of the spied-upon states is less tangible than in cases of acts of espionage using physically visible vectors. It is true that we have

---

14 Russell Buchan, Senior Lecturer in Law at the University of Sheffield, has written the first book devoted entirely to the relationship between acts of cyberespionage and international law, in which he cites and analyzes the extensive international and domestic case law involved.

15 Not to mention the acts of espionage committed from strictly national spaces, such as the interception of international communications by ground antennas from the national territory of the spying state.

16 A cyberespionage operation is based on four constituent elements: the non-consensual (1) copying of confidential (2) data that is in cyberspace (3) or in transit (4) through it.

been witnessing a deterritorialization of espionage since the mid-1950s, with the placing in orbit of the first imaging and then communications interception satellites, in the sense that spying states whose technological capacities enable them to have recourse to such technical resources seek, as soon as possible, to free themselves precisely from the territorial constraints of spied-upon states and their legal consequences in order to covertly collect intelligence. For all that, it has also been verified that this deterritorialization does not mean a dematerialization of espionage, including in cyberspace, which would mean ignoring the physical or material layer of cyberspace, made up of the infrastructures that support all the interconnected networks (transit networks, servers, data farms, submarine cables, etc.), in addition to its software and cognitive layers. Consequently, cyberspace is a territorialized space, with part of its infrastructures located in spaces under national sovereignty. In other words, cyberspace is the sum of "physical and non-physical components characterized by the use of computers and the electromagnetic spectrum to store, modify and exchange data using computer networks" (Schmitt 2017, p. 564).

In these circumstances, although cyberspace per se may have been considered, ultimately erroneously, as an exclusively international space, there is sufficient evidence from state practice to demonstrate that cyberinfrastructures located on land, in internal waters and territorial seas, as well as in national airspace, are not beyond the territorial sovereignty of states or the execution of their jurisdiction; furthermore, even though cyber activities may cross multiple borders or take place in international waters, international airspace, or outer space, the fact remains that they are all carried out by individuals or entities subject to the jurisdiction of one or more states, regardless of whether the cyberinfrastructures involved are owned by states, private companies or individuals (Schmitt 2017, pp. 11–13).

It has been written that the new relationships with classical institutional territories induced by the datasphere[17] proceed from a phenomenon of detachment from these territories, insofar as "the collection, processing and

17 "The notion of the datasphere [...] allows us to encompass in the same concept the strategic issues linked to cyberspace but also those linked to the geography of flows and the control of data, the understanding of the informational space, the mapping of topological networks, the fusion of geolocalized and non-spatialized data" (Douzet and Desforges 2018, pp. 87–108).

circulation of these data in a dematerialized form creates situations detached from classical territories", and insofar as "[the] localization criteria are altered from the perspective of the datasphere" (Bergé and Grumbach 2016, p. 5). However, the capture of a piece of data, in transit or stored in cyberinfrastructures, by an espionage vector is still physically linked to a place that itself belongs to a space with an internationally recognized legal regime. To take the reasoning further, the challenges posed by the technologies of data circulation, and even of the non-territoriality of this data, which call into question the traditional distinction between "here" and "there" (Daskal 2015, p. 329), which obviously should not be denied, are not such as to undermine the cross-analysis between the attack vector and the space in which (or from which) the collection of data takes place.

In support of these arguments, we can refer to the doctrine of the French Ministry of the Armed Forces, which defines cyberspace as "the communication space constituted by the global interconnection of infrastructures and equipment for the automated processing of digital data and by the objects connected to them and the data processed therein", in which "the principle of sovereignty applies" (Ministère des Armées 2019, pp. 7 and 18). It follows that cyberespionage does not escape a "territorialist" approach, which certainly does not enjoy consensus (Daskal 2018, pp. 179–240). The data collected in cyberspace (a technique described as "digital intelligence" (DIGINT)[18] or "cyber intelligence" (CY(B)INT)[19] (Klimburg 2016)), regardless of their volume, are the same, legally speaking, as the information collected by other spy techniques: the place where the collection of these data takes place is decisive in establishing a possible violation of the territorial sovereignty of the state whose data are collected. While it appears, given the state of knowledge available in open sources and particularly through the revelations of Edward Snowden, that the cyberespionage techniques used are mostly deployed from spaces outside the sovereignty of spied-upon states, acts of cyberespionage associated with an

---

18 The DIGINT technique, mentioned in the reports of the Intelligence and Security Committee of Parliament (2009–2010, p. 10; 2011–2012, p. 60), involves "systems for the collection and analysis of electronically collected information", incorporating the technological specifics of the massive digitization of data and, as a corollary, the technically conceivable capture of "megadata".

19 The term CYBINT is a subcategory of SIGINT, referring to the collection of information in cyberspace (Buchan 2019, p. 16).

intrusion into a space under national sovereignty should not be systematically dismissed.

The criterion of *ratione loci* is essential in the legal understanding of the cyberespionage act, and no less so than for other acts of espionage. Moreover, this criterion is not only important as to the place where the collection of the data takes place, but also as to their place of exploitation. Thus, a Canadian judge, in the CSIS Act case (October 5, 2009), mentioned "a number of American decisions in which US courts of appeal have ruled that a judge has the power to authorize the interception of communications when the first place where the communication will be listened to is within the judge's jurisdiction" and found this reasoning compelling and applicable to the Canadian case[20].

7.3. Data localization in the light of international intelligence law

It is stimulating to observe the concomitant emergence of debates on interception, protection, retention and localization of data (section 7.3.1), on the one hand, and on "international intelligence law", on the other hand, as if one feeds into the other (section 7.3.2).

7.3.1. *Data fluidity versus data storage*

The case involving the US government and Microsoft (*Microsoft Ireland Warrant*) is a perfect legal illustration of the issue of data localization and therefore access to that data. The facts, as summarized by Christakis (2017, p. 18), are as follows:

> In December 2013, a US judge ordered Microsoft to turn over to US authorities, in the context of a drug trafficking case, a suspect's emails that were on a Microsoft server located in Ireland. The search warrant for the email account was issued by the judge under the Stored Communications Act (SCA) of 1986. Microsoft, however, refused to turn over the contents of that email, arguing that the data in question was located in its

---

20 X (RE), 2009 CF 1058, [2010] 1 R.C.F.460, Federal Court, Ottawa, paragraphs 53 and 58, October 5, 2009.

data center in Ireland and that the SCA did not apply extraterritorially. In a decision issued on July 14, 2016, a US Court of Appeals (Second Circuit) held that the US government could not compel a company to turn over customer emails stored on servers located outside the United States. The court found that Congress had not given the provisions of the SCA extraterritorial application and that a warrant under the SCA "can only apply to data stored within the United States". The US government challenged this decision in the Supreme Court, which agreed in October 2017 to hear the case.

The Supreme Court issued its decision (*United States v. Microsoft*) on April 17, 2018, ruling that the case had become moot after the passage of the Clarifying Lawful Overseas Use of Data (CLOUD) Act on March 23, 2018, section 103(*a*)(1) of which authorizes the transmission of data to the US government, regardless of its location. It should be noted that the United States and the United Kingdom entered into a data-sharing agreement on October 7, 2019, after four years of negotiation, to facilitate cross-border access to data for the purpose of combating serious crime, this agreement being the first to emerge from the provisions of the CLOUD Act (Christakis 2019).

In this groundbreaking case, two opposing positions were defended by the parties to the proceedings: for Microsoft, given the extraterritorial scope of the US government's request for data stored in Ireland, the determining criterion was the place where the data were stored, for which the US authorities could make a request to the Irish authorities within the framework of existing mutual legal assistance mechanisms. For the US government, on the other hand, as long as the data in question were accessible from the United States (even if stored in Ireland), everything happened on US soil, especially since Microsoft employees working in the United States could retrieve them from their offices; the only relevant criterion in this case was therefore the location from which the data were accessible. Washington argued that the data were "highly mobile and fluid", whereas Microsoft considered the location of storage to be of great technical significance, since the data did have a "physical location" and were stored using hard drives located in data centers in specific countries.

In this respect, the study conducted by the 35 *amici curiae*, or high-level experts, at the request of Microsoft is particularly rich in information. The main thrust can essentially be drawn from the following paragraph:

While "the cloud" is not a physical thing, data stored "in the cloud" does have at least one identifiable physical location. The cloud is merely an abstraction related to data access. The underlying data, however, is stored using traditional physical media, typically on hard drives in servers within large data centers like Microsoft's[21].

The conclusion of this opinion was also given to the Court:

Amici respectfully submit that the resolution of this appeal should take into account the fact that web-based email and other data stored "in the cloud" has at least one identifiable, physical location, and that the content of customer emails is securely stored as the confidential property of the account holder[22].

Thus, it is technically and legally arguable that stored data hold a physical location, which includes "the cloud" (Woods 2016, pp. 729–789; Woods 2018, pp. 328–406), and that the underlying problem is really how to access that data, especially when it is located outside the territory of the requesting state. In a judicial context, the requesting government may take its action in the context of a possible mutual legal assistance agreement with the requested state or even, for states parties to the 2001 Budapest Convention on Cybercrime, in the form of a "production order"[23]. Of course, in the case of an intelligence operation aimed at recovering such data without the consent of the state in whose territory it is located, the point of law at issue is the possible infringement of the territorial sovereignty of the victim state, depending on whether or not the act of cyberespionage – which is not a cyber attack – is accompanied by a territorial intrusion[24]. Under these

---

21 Warrick (2014), Brief for *Amici Curiae* Computer and Data Science Experts in Support of Appellant Microsoft Corporation (In the Matter of a Warrant to Search a Certain E-mail Account Controlled and Maintained by Microsoft Corporation, *Microsoft Corporation v. USA*), December 15, p. 11.

22 *Ibid.*, p. 23

23 Article 18.1.b of the Budapest Convention allows states to enact legislation requiring service providers to disclose "subscriber data" when ordered to do so by authorities, regardless of where it is stored (Council of Europe 2001).

24 The French position on this point is as follows: "Any unauthorized penetration of French systems by a state or any production of effects on French territory by a digital vector may constitute, *a minima,* a violation of sovereignty" (Ministère des Armées 2019, p. 6).

conditions, states pay particular attention to the degree of protection afforded to their sovereign data, beyond the rules of immunity of state property.

7.3.2. *Datasphere versus international intelligence law*

The best illustration of the issue of sovereign data protection is certainly the agreement on hosting data and information systems concluded between Estonia and Luxembourg on June 20, 2017, under the terms of which Estonian data are stored in a data center located in Luxembourg; the Estonian government sees this agreement as the creation of the first digital embassy, which would be granted traditional diplomatic privileges and immunities on the same level as a physical embassy[25], and acknowledges that Luxembourg was chosen because it has highly secure (certified tier IV[26]) state data centers, which would allow the Estonian authorities to continue to use the data even in case of major disruptions in the normal functioning of its institutions. The respective parliaments of the two states ratified this agreement and it entered into force in March 2018. Thus, digital sovereignty, the exclusive jurisdiction that a state has over its sovereign data, regardless of where it is stored, including in the cloud, and regardless of the conventional rules on immunity and inviolability of diplomatic property (Robinson *et al.* 2019)[27], remains a major objective of states, just like, more

---

25 As with the data centers of international organizations already installed in Luxembourg, the installation of an Estonian data center is part of the strategy that seeks to make Luxembourg a center of digital trust in Europe, and even worldwide. This is the first data center of a foreign state located in Luxembourg, granting Estonia the appropriate guarantees with regard to the security and inviolability of its premises and data; privileges and immunities similar to those covering diplomatic missions are provided for in this agreement, even though this data center cannot be qualified as an embassy from the point of view of public international law (see *Annales du droit luxembourgeois* (2017–2018), vol. 27–28, section 6.1)

26 The Uptime Institute, an independent advisory body, classifies data centers into four tiers: I, II, III and IV. Each tier takes the characteristics of the previous tier and adds supplementary enhancements. The objective is to evaluate the quality and reliability of a data center's hosting capabilities.

27 These authors conclude their analysis as follows: "This paper has identified that the Vienna Convention is not deemed presently suitable for the protection and inviolability of data and information systems outside of the traditional diplomatic mission. In this exploratory research, the case of the Estonian Data Embassy in Luxembourg has shown that although the Vienna Convention may be applicable in this context, a key challenge emerges in that it is yet to be tested in any given scenario and thus lacks a degree of legal precedent. In this case, an extralegal

broadly, their territorial sovereignty, given that this is the version of territorial sovereignty that is adapted to the digitization of data. Therefore, the application of classical rules of public international law to issues of non-consensual access to a third state's sovereign data is valid.

There is a growing tendency for states to control and restrict the flow of data out of their territory, using coercive approaches of varying degrees: emblematically, Russia is developing a "Ru.Net" (Ristolainen 2017, pp. 113–131), aimed at better controlling the Russian segment of the internet in case of disconnection from the global internet (legislation signed in May 2019 and effective in November of the same year), following on from the law on personal data protection, adopted in July 2014 and effective on September 1, 2015, which obliges companies to store personal data of Russian citizens on servers based in Russia. Other countries impose restrictions on data storage, such as the United States, which requires cloud providers working for the Department of Defense to store data in the United States or Indonesia, where data must be stored in servers physically located on Indonesian territory (The Centre for Internet and Society (India) 2019, pp. 49–60). For its part, the International Court of Justice (ICJ) came close to issuing a landmark ruling on the seizure of sovereign data by a foreign intelligence service in the case of *Timor-Leste v. Australia* (International Court of Justice 2014a)[28], but the two parties ultimately decided to settle their dispute amicably by asking the Court to strike the case from its list after Australia returned the documents and data it had seized to Timor-Leste in May 2015. Timor-Leste's main argument was the existence of a fundamental rule of customary international law, recognizing the immunity and

layer in the form of a bilateral agreement was found to be sufficient, affording similar powers and immunities to both the 'sending' and 'receiving' states. As it seems at present, there is significant progress to suggest that the Vienna Convention could be extended in its current form to incorporate the protection of data and information systems outside the traditional diplomatic mission. Indeed, as other states may follow Estonia's lead, the re-assessment of international law and the Vienna Convention may prove a beneficial solution."

28 On December 17, 2013, Timor-Leste filed a lawsuit against Australia regarding the seizure, and subsequent detention, by Australian agents of documents, data and other property belonging to Timor-Leste, or which Timor-Leste was entitled to protect under international law. Timor-Leste contended that these items were taken from the business premises of one of its legal advisers in Narrabundah, Australian Capital Territory.

inviolability of the state and its property[29], of which the documents and data in question were certainly a part; the requesting state considered that:

> [...] the rights it seeks to protect are the property rights it holds in respect of the seized items, which include the rights to inviolability and immunity of such property (and, in particular, documents and data) to which it is entitled as a sovereign state, as well as its right to confidentiality of any communication with its legal advisers[30].

Although the case was not judged on its merits, the Court, in its order for provisional measures, referred to the "plausible right" of any state to have its documents and data exchanged with its counsel protected[31].

State property, traditionally kept exclusively in the territory of the state of ownership, is now partly outside that territory. Thus, the general prohibition of interference in the territory of another state, which was previously sufficient to protect such state property, is no longer sufficient; furthermore, the specific protections granted to a certain category of sovereign property (such as diplomatic property through the relevant provisions of the Vienna Convention on Diplomatic Relations, or state vessels, aircraft and satellites through ad hoc conventions) constitute a piecemeal approach that actually shows the absence of a "general right to state property" (Tzeng 2016, pp. 1805–1819). In the wake of the Snowden revelations, particularly those relating to the interception of the communications of foreign heads of state (such as the Brazilian president and the German chancellor), it became clear that, beyond the customary protests of victim states, the content of the telephone conversations of heads of state intercepted by a foreign intelligence service was not specifically protected by any customary or treaty rule, and that this act of espionage did not constitute an internationally wrongful act under public international law.

Within the ecosystem of intelligence law (see the Appendix), there is an international law of intelligence which, since the mid-2000s, has emerged

---

29 See the legal reasoning developed by the requesting state (International Court of Justice 2014b, pp. 32–40, paragraphs 5.15–5.49).

30 International Court of Justice (2014a), p. 9, para. 24.

31 *Ibid*, paragraph 27, p. 10.

from the body of public international law: it is both affiliated with the other branches of international law that are, in turn, invoked on the occasion of the commission of an act of espionage between states (Lafouasse 2018) (the violation of the territorial waters of a coastal state for espionage purposes thus falls under Article 19, part 2, of the United Nations Convention on the Law of the Sea; the declaration of *persona non grata* for an intelligence officer under diplomatic cover is codified in Article 9, part 1, of the Vienna Convention on Diplomatic Relations), and backed up by a *lex specialis*, in the sense of a special norm governing a given branch of international law (International Law of Intelligence), which some Anglo-Saxon authors believe to be discernible in the "regulated" conduct of espionage operations.

Thus, according to Buchan, who notes that states are now mature enough to officially recognize that intelligence is an integral part of the game of international relations, as well as a public policy in its own right, the time is right to develop, through the adoption of a treaty or, more progressively, through customary law, an international law of intelligence containing tailor-made rules that would delimit, in particular, the circumstances under which the collection of confidential information is acceptable (Buchan 2019, pp. 192–195). For his part, Lubin, a law professor at Yale University who specializes in intelligence and national security issues, has constructed a trinitarian approach to the regulation of intelligence activities: first, states would consider themselves bound by the rules relating to the right to launch an espionage operation, based essentially on two customary grounds, namely, national security and international security, stability and cooperation (*jus ad explorationem*); second, there would be the rules relating to the choice of resources and targets in the conduct of espionage operations, with particular reference to the emerging body of case law relating to respect for the right to privacy and general communications surveillance (*jus in exploratione*); third, there would be the rules triggered once the espionage operation has been completed and relating to the responsibility of states, this category nevertheless coming up against the absence of a general principle for a recognized law of transparency in national security cases (*jus post explorationem*) (Lubin 2019, pp. 1–45). This crystallizing *lex specialis* would find a model in European human rights law, with the ECtHR having identified such a three-stage system in its *Roman Zakharov v. Russia* judgment[32]: "Review and supervision of secret surveillance measures may take place at three stages: when the surveillance is ordered, while it is being carried out, or after it has ceased" (European Court of Human Rights 2015, paragraph 233).

7.4. Conclusion

International communications surveillance is an area that, in the coming years, is likely to be the subject of conventionally accepted regulation by states, on the dual basis of the increasing number of national laws on intelligence and the abundant case law from adjudicative human rights bodies on so-called mass surveillance. It is this juxtaposition between national intelligence laws and an emerging international law of intelligence that is described in the intelligence quadrants in the Appendix, with each state simultaneously assuming the posture of the spied-upon state, with legislation and jurisdictional powers to repress acts of espionage committed against it, and of the spying state, deploying its intelligence officers and espionage vectors abroad, while at the same time supervising the intelligence activities it conducts on its own territory. The regulatory function of international communications surveillance, which would obviously not mean banning it, could include a body of common rules governing secret surveillance operations conducted by states parties and targeting their nationals as well as foreigners (individuals as well as official representatives), regulating in particular the issue of access to, and storage of, sovereign and personal data; in 2018, at a purely national level, the United Kingdom thus adopted five "codes of good practice" within the framework of the Investigatory Powers Act (Kahn 2018). However, first, potential state parties will have to balance the expected gain against the cost incurred by shaping such a (non-legally binding) "code of conduct", if not a (legally binding under treaty law) convention. Data are more than ever at the center of a "big game", the boundaries of which do not have the delineated contours of traditional borders, leading states to simultaneously integrate the jurisprudential line of

---

32 In this December 4, 2015, judgment, the applicant, a Russian national and editor-in-chief of a publishing house in Russia, alleged that the system of secret interception of cell phone communications in Russia did not comply with the requirements of Article 8. The Court found that Russia had violated Article 8, ruling that the domestic legal provisions governing the interception of communications did not contain adequate and effective safeguards against arbitrariness and the risk of abuse.

digital *habeas corpus* advocated by the EU[33] and the controversies over the concepts of *data liberum/data clausum*, according to the *mare liberum/mare clausum* model that has historically shaped state approaches to public international law.

7.5. Appendix: the quadrants of intelligence law

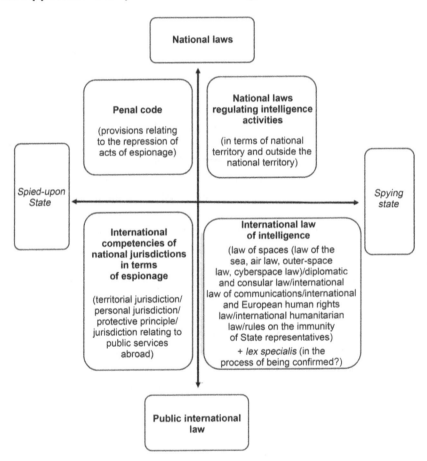

Figure 7.1. *The quadrants of intelligence law*

33 In its resolution on mass electronic surveillance of EU citizens from March 12, 2014, following the Snowden affair, the European Parliament decided "to launch a European digital *habeas corpus* protecting fundamental rights in the digital age" (Official Journal of the European Union 2014, paragraphs 131–132).

7.6. Sources and references

7.6.1. *Sources*

Commission Nationale de Contrôle des Techniques de Renseignement (2015–2016). Activity report, CNCTR.

Council of Europe (2001). Convention on Cybercrime. Budapest, 23 November.

European Court of Human Rights (1978). *Klass and others v. Germany*. Judgment of 6 September.

European Court of Human Rights (2006). *Weber and Saravia v. Germany*. Judgment of 29 June.

European Court of Human Rights (2008). *Liberty and Others v. United Kingdom*, Judgment of 1 July.

European Court of Human Rights (2015). *Roman Zakharov v. Russia*. Judgment of 4 December.

European Court of Human Rights (2018a). *Centrum för Rättvisa v. Sweden*. Judgment of 19 June.

European Court of Human Rights (2018b). *Big Brother Watch and Others v. United Kingdom*. Judgment of 13 September.

Fundamental Rights Agency (2017). Surveillance by intelligence services: Fundamental rights safeguards and remedies in the EU, vol. 2: Field perspectives and legal update.

Intelligence and Security Committee of Parliament (2009–2010). Annual Report.

Intelligence and Security Committee of Parliament (2011–2012). Annual Report.

International Court of Justice (2014a). Questions relating to the Seizure and Detention of Certain Documents and Data. *Timor-Leste v. Australia*, Order on Provisional Measures. ICGJ 472, 3 March.

International Court of Justice (2014b). Questions relating to the Seizure and Detention of Certain Documents and Data. *Timor-Leste v. Australia*, Memorial of the Democratic Republic of Timor-Leste. 1, 28 April.

Legifrance (2014). Decree No. 2014-1050 of September 16, 2014, establishing a general data administrator.

Ministère des Armées (2019). Droit international appliqué aux opérations dans le cyberspace.

Official Journal of the European Union (2014). European Parliament resolution of 12 March 2014 on the US NSA surveillance programme, surveillance bodies in various Member States and their impact on EU citizens' fundamental rights and on transatlantic cooperation in Justice and Home Affairs (2013/2188(INI)).

Official Journal of the European Union (2016). Regulation (EU) 2016/679 of the European Parliament and of the Council of 27 April 2016 on the protection of natural persons with regard to the processing of personal data and on the free movement of such data, and repealing Directive 95/46/EC (General Data Protection Regulation).

Republic of Estonia and the Grand Duchy of Luxembourg (2017). Agreement between the Republic of Estonia and the Grand Duchy of Luxembourg on the hosting of data and information systems. 20 June.

United Nations (1961). Vienna Convention on Diplomatic Relations. Vienna, 18 April.

United Nations (1982). United Nations Convention on the Law of the Sea. Montego Bay, 10 December.

Warrick, P. (2014). Brief for *Amici Curiae* computer and data science experts in support of appellant Microsoft Corporation (in the matter of a warrant to search a certain e-mail account controlled and maintained by Microsoft Corporation). *Microsoft Corporation v. United States of America*, 15 December.

X (RE) [also known as the CSIS Act] (2009). 2009 CF 1058, [2010] 1 R.C.F.460. Federal Court, Ottawa, 5 October.

7.6.2. *References*

Abiteboul, S. (2012). Sciences des données : de la logique du premier ordre à la Toile. Chair of Computer and Digital Sciences, inaugural lecture, March 8.

Basdevant, A. and Mignard, J.-P. (2018). *L'Empire des données*. Don Quichotte, Paris.

Bergé, J.-S. and Grumbach, S. (2016). La sphère des données et le droit : nouvel espace, nouveaux rapports aux territoires. *Journal du droit international*, 4.

Buchan, R. (2019). *Cyber Espionage and International Law*. Hart Publishing, Oxford.

Christakis, T. (2017). Données, extraterritorialité et solutions internationales aux problèmes transatlantiques d'accès aux preuves numériques. Avis juridique sur l'affaire Microsoft Ireland. CEIS.

Christakis, T. (2019). 21 thoughts and questions about the UK/US CLOUD Act agreement (and an explanation of how it works – with charts). *European Law Blog* [Online]. Available at: www.europeanlawblog.eu/2019/10/17/21-thoughts-and-questions-about-the-uk-us-cloud-act-agreement-and-an-explanation-of-how-it-works-with-charts [Accessed 21 August 2021].

Daskal, J. (2015). The un-territoriality of data. *The Yale Law Journal*, 125(2), 326–398.

Daskal, J. (2018). Borders and bits. *Vanderbilt Law Review*, 71, 179–240.

Douzet, F. and Desforges, A. (2018). Du cyberespace à la datasphère. Le nouveau front pionnier de la géographie. *Netcom*, 31(1/2) [Online]. Available at: https://journals.openedition.org/netcom/3419.

Faure-Muntian, V. (2018). Les données géographiques souveraines : rapport au gouvernement. Report, July.

Kahn, M. (2018). Documents: UK investigatory powers codes of practice. *Lawfare* [Online]. Available at: www.lawfareblog.com/documents-uk-investigatory-powers-codes-practice.

Kittichaisaree, K. and Kuner, C. (2015). The growing importance of data protection in public international law. *European Journal of International Law* [Online]. Available at: www.ejiltalk.org [Accessed 21 August 2021].

Klimburg, A. (2016). Shades of cyber grey: Espionage and attack in cyberspace. *The Fletcher Forum of World Affairs* [Online]. Available at: http://www.fletcherforum.org/home/2016/8/15/shades-of-cyber-grey-espionage-and-attack-in-cyberspace [Accessed 21 August 2021].

Lafouasse, F. (2012). *L'Espionnage dans le droit international*. Nouveau Monde Éditions, Paris.

Lafouasse, F. (2018). Droit international du renseignement. JurisClasseur communication, fascicule 1200.

Lubin, A. (2019). The liberty to spy. *Harvard International Law Journal*, 61(1), 1–45.

Norodom, A.-T. (2014). Le droit international et Internet après l'"affaire Snowden" : la recherche de nouveaux équilibres. *Annuaire Français de Droit International*, 60, 731–753.

Ristolainen, M. (2017). Should "RuNet 2020" be taken seriously? Contradictory views about cyber security between Russia and the West. *Journal of Information Warfare*, 16(4), 113–131.

Robinson, N., Kask, L., Krimmer, R. (2019). The Estonian Data Embassy and the applicability of the Vienna Convention: An exploratory analysis. *Proceedings of the 12th International Conference on Theory and Practice of Electronic Governance*, Melbourne, Australia, April 3–5.

Schmitt, M. (ed.) (2017). *Tallinn Manual 2.0 on the International Law Applicable to Cyber Operations*. Cambridge University Press, Cambridge.

The Centre for Internet and Society (India) (2019). The localisation gambit. Unpacking policy measures for sovereign control of data in India [Online]. Available at: www.cis-india.org/internet-governance/resources/the-localisation-gambit.pdf.

Tzeng, P. (2016). The state's right to property under international law. *The Yale Law Journal*, 125(6), 1805–1819.

Vadillo, F. (2020). Une seconde loi renseignement ? Pour une main tremblante mais des idées claires. *L'Hétairie*, 12.

Woods, A. (2016). Against data exceptionalism. *Stanford Law Review*, 68, 729–789.

Woods, A. (2018). Litigating data sovereignty. *The Yale Law Journal*, 128, 328–406.

International Cybersecurity Cooperation

This chapter takes the form of an interview, conducted in October 2020, with the director of France's ANSSI, Guillaume Poupard, who has headed the agency since 2014.

8.1. Current attack trends

– Sébastien-Yves Laurent (S.-Y.L.)[1]: What are the main cyberattacks observed by ANSSI and what are the orders of magnitude of the types of attacks you have detected, based on the nature of the victims?

– Guillaume Poupard (G.P.): At ANSSI, we are always a little wary of quantitative indicators for cyber attacks, because they generally lead to the aggregation of events of quite different types, scales or severities. We must keep in mind that certain aspects of a cyber attack, such as its purpose or origin, are sometimes difficult to establish, which necessarily limits the relevance of such indicators. We therefore prefer to identify trends.

One of the most significant trends is the current explosion of ransomware, which is now the main cyber threat to companies, local authorities and public entities, such as hospitals, for example. The groups behind these attacks have gradually become more organized and professional, and some of them have even become cybercrime multinationals, making huge profits. Some of them

---

Chapter written by Guillaume Poupard.

1 The coordinator of the book thanks General Emmanuel Germain, former Deputy Director General of ANSSI.

now specialize in "big game" hunting, by attacking, after meticulous preparation and reconnaissance, large companies that are able to pay sizeable ransoms, sometimes in the millions of dollars.

Another major source of concern is the risk of espionage, which remains very high for companies and administrations, especially those who operate in strategic fields. Some states are indeed developing increasingly stealthy and sophisticated capabilities in order to capture information that could give them a competitive advantage, whether in the technological, strategic or diplomatic fields. A cyberattack tactic that is now frequently observed, when the objective is to break into the relatively well-protected network of a strategic entity, is to conduct a rebound attack from the information system of one of its subcontractors, which is generally much less well equipped in terms of cybersecurity:

– S.-Y.L.: In terms of R&D, in cybersecurity, what are the main challenges today, for the public and private sectors?

– G.P.: Research and innovation in cybersecurity are very dynamic, both in the public and private sectors, there is still a lot to build. From ANSSI's point of view, there are three fundamental issues:

- first, the functionality of solutions: today, all too often, cybersecurity is carried out at the expense of users and becomes a burden. It is therefore essential for cybersecurity solutions to become easier to use, especially for users with specific needs, either by their nature or by their size. The solution offered to a small company must not be too technical and must be fully integrated to facilitate its deployment and its use. It must also protect the company against the threats it really faces. The level of cybersecurity expected for an SME cannot be the same as for defense companies, ministries or large banks;

- then there is the challenge of managing this ecosystem: in France, and also in Europe, many small but very well-performing actors exist and the ground is rich enough to have global ambitions in the field of cybersecurity. However, we will need to forge closer links between companies, with public services involved in cybersecurity as well as with education and research organizations. This is the purpose of the "Campus Cyber" project starting in the autumn of 2021, which will be a unique place that will bring together all the players in French cybersecurity in order to encourage the development of synergies and the construction of tomorrow's cybersecurity solutions, by meeting all the technological and human challenges;

- finally, the last issue is digital sovereignty: R&D, in cybersecurity and also in digital technology, must enable us to take our digital destiny into our own hands and reduce dependencies that are harmful to Europe and France. Although this issue is not strictly limited to cybersecurity, I am convinced that there can be no sustainable cybersecurity without digital sovereignty.

8.2. The multiple paths of international cooperation

– S.-Y.L.: How is international cooperation in the field of cyberdefense constructed? Does it tend to be bilateral or multilateral?

– G.P.: As a result of historical choices, the French cybersecurity model strictly separates offensive and defensive activities. The creation of ANSSI, the French national authority for cyberdefense and cybersecurity, in 2009, confirmed this cardinal principle, as did the more recent 2018 *Revue stratégique de cyberdéfense*[2]. The agency therefore ensures the cybersecurity of all public administrations and critical operators as well as the nation. Within the framework of these missions, it also maintains cooperation with many foreign partners, who are only occasionally immediate counterparts, due to the originality of the French model. Although the French model has become more widespread over the last few years, with the adoption of similar organizations in Israel, Singapore and Japan, other organizational models exist, such as the affiliation of cybersecurity to a ministry, for example, the Ministry of the Interior in Germany, the Defense or the Economy and Telecommunications ministries in other countries. Another type of organization is based on the integration of offensive and defensive missions within a single organization, following the example of Anglo-Saxon technical intelligence agencies, such as the NSA in the United States or the British Government Communications Headquarters (GCHQ). However, the UK chose to create a separate branch dedicated to cybersecurity issues, the National Cyber Security Centre (NCSC), in order to develop closer relations with the sector. Finally, there is a last type involving fragmentation of cybersecurity missions, all endorsed by the agency in France, among several organizations with various supervisory authorities. While they must be taken

---

2 See SGDSN (2018). Revue stratégique de cyberdéfense, February 12.

into account, these differences between models do not prevent the construction of fruitful international cooperation at all levels – technical, diplomatic and strategic. The strength of ANSSI in the development of international cooperation stems directly from its strictly defensive mission, which makes it easy to identify common interests in favor of the stability of cyberspace.

As in all fields, cooperation is both bilateral and multilateral, with the two frameworks complementing and reinforcing each other. In this respect, ANSSI maintains both bilateral and multilateral relations, at both the technical and political levels. Among the multilateral cooperation frameworks, the European Union is the most relevant instance for ANSSI. It has been built around a common regulatory framework that is progressively becoming denser, notably with the Network and Information Security Directive[3], adopted in 2016, and the Cybersecurity Act[4], adopted in 2019. The Cybersecurity Act gives a permanent mandate to ENISA, the European cyber security agency[5], which does not replace national entities, but rather works on networking and coordinating the capabilities of EU Member States. Member states have created the Cyber Crisis Liaison Organisation Network (CyCLONe)[6] to increase their cooperation, particularly by creating a shared crisis management mechanism. This network, which brings together the directors of European cybersecurity agencies, illustrates the dynamism of European cooperation in cybersecurity.

– S.-Y.L.: An organization like ANSSI is involved in international cooperation on a daily basis, as are its counterparts: is not there a risk of becoming dependent on foreign partners and ultimately of losing sovereignty?

– G.P.: Cooperation does not necessarily lead to dependency, as long as it is based on mutually beneficial exchanges. This is how we approach all our international cooperation at ANSSI. This makes it essential to preserve effective and sovereign cyber capabilities.

---

3 See www.eur-lex.europa.eu/legal-content/FR/TXT/?uri=CELEX:32016L1148.

4 See www.ec.europa.eu/digital-single-market/en/eu-cybersecurity-act.

5 See www.enisa.europa.eu.

6 See www.enisa.europa.eu/news/enisa-news/blue-olex-2020-the-european-union-member-states-launch-the-cyber-crisis-liaison-organisation-network-cyclone.

At a time when the balance of power in cyberspace is taking shape, France is indeed faced with a choice concerning its place among these powers. While some countries choose to entrust their protection to other more powerful states, French sovereignty in cyber matters has been reaffirmed, thanks to substantial investments in this field. However, being a cyber power is a daily challenge. As technologies and their uses are constantly evolving, keeping up with the state of the art requires us to constantly seek out new skills, develop new techniques, constantly reinvent ourselves and rely on external relays to scale up our action. This is the ongoing effort that ANSSI has been undertaking for several years and which must continue. This is the price of our sovereignty in cyber matters.

– S.-Y.L.: What are the practices or customs that govern international exchanges between cyberdefense organizations, and, as director of ANSSI, is it easy to cooperate internationally with organizations that are very often from the private sector?

– G.P.: I am going to disappoint you, but cooperation between cyberdefense agencies is quite standard. I imagine that a meeting between two directors of cybersecurity agencies, let us say a Frenchman and a German, is very similar to a meeting between two directors of environmental protection or economic development agencies... We take turns visiting each other, signing cooperation protocols and publishing news on our respective websites. That is not to say that it lacks dynamism, quite the contrary, but the practices of this cooperation are not fundamentally different from any other international cooperation.

Cooperation between CERTs (Computer Emergency Response Teams) operates at a completely different pace. Built around the sharing of technical information, these cooperations are structured around a continuous flow of exchanges. Whether they are bilateral or within a CERT network, these cooperations can take place between governmental CERTs (the European CSIRTs Network) or between public CERTs and private CERTs (with INTERCERT-FR, on a national scale, or FIRST and IWWN, on an international scale). In order to enable cooperation between such different entities, dedicated mechanisms must be put in place. For example, a sensitivity scale dedicated to exchanges between CERTs allowing the transmission of sensitive elements, but of shared interest, has been widely adopted by CERT networks. This protocol, called the Traffic Light Protocol (TLP), provides the possibility of sharing information based on a red, amber, green and white light system. TLP:WHITE information can thus be widely shared, whereas TLP:RED information cannot be shared beyond its immediate recipients. This type of mechanism makes it possible to overcome the possible differences between organizations, particularly the distinction between private and public, so that everyone contributes to the stability of cyberspace.

– S.-Y.L.: Could you talk about the normative role of the agency you manage, which works in conjunction with the diplomatic apparatus to prepare French positions in international forums?

– G.P.: As the rise of offensive actors in cyberspace has accelerated and has been posing an increased threat to cyberspace stability, the classical tools of international law and diplomacy have had to be fully mobilized to address this new struggle. As far as ANSSI is concerned, it is therefore particularly encouraging that cybersecurity is now perceived as being equal to the more traditional security issues and that it is fully taken into account in international forums: the European Union, the United Nations (UN), G7, G20, the Organisation for Economic Co-operation and Development (OECD), the Organization for Security and Co-operation in Europe (OSCE), the North Atlantic Treaty Organization (NATO) and so on. While everyone's interests and priorities may differ, France is promoting the development of a secure, stable, prosperous and open cyberspace, in which each actor identifies and assumes its share of responsibility as soon as possible. In this respect, France refutes the structuring of a digital Wild West and calls for the development of responsible standards of behavior for both states and private companies. This is the crux of the Paris Call for trust and security in cyberspace, launched by French President Emmanuel Macron on November 12, 2018, on the occasion of the 13th edition of the Internet Governance Forum.

In order to defend this particular vision of cyberspace at the international level, ANSSI is working in close collaboration with the Ministry of Europe and Foreign Affairs to determine French positions regarding the stability of cyberspace. The fundamental principles defended by the agency in this aspect are (1) prevention, with the enactment of norms, standards and measures to prevent the occurrence of disputes in cyberspace; (2) cooperation, to facilitate the peaceful resolution of disputes and to quickly stop the consequences of a serious incident, in particular through the principle of due diligence; and finally (3) prohibition, for non-state actors, to conduct offensive activities in cyberspace. ANSSI is also working, notably within OECD, to make private actors, especially systemic actors, more accountable in the design and maintenance of their digital products and services, in order to avoid the development of large-scale vulnerabilities, and the associated risk of compromise.

8.3. The issue of attack attribution

– S.-Y.L.: France defends the principle that the attribution of an attack is political. However, do not you think it would be possible – if the source is certain – to make a purely geographical attribution ("The attack originated in such and such a territory", without mentioning whether it was the state or a private actor), without indicating the nature of the perpetrator?

– G.P.: Attribution, which is indeed a political act by nature, is only of interest if it offers a response to aggression, by activating certain levers available to the political level with regard to the perpetrators: public attribution in the form of "name and shame", economic sanctions and so on. Therefore, there would be little interest in designating a geographical area. Moreover, it is generally very difficult to univocally link an attack to a precise territorial origin, because an attacker of a given nationality can, from a third country, use an attack infrastructure located anywhere. So it is easy to see that linking an attack to a territory does not really make sense in practice.

– S.-Y.L.: What is the segment that ANSSI investigates in attack attribution procedures?

– G.P.: Attribution is not ANSSI's responsibility. Nevertheless, the technical understanding that ANSSI might have of an attack, because it has conducted investigations on the victim's information system when it provided assistance, constitutes an element that may, if necessary, feed the investigations conducted for attribution purposes.

– S.-Y.L.: In January 2020, you stated that France was not far from participating in collective attribution. Is the political authority ready for this?

– G.P.: We were indeed not far from doing it and it is now done, since the Council of the European Union adopted a first package of sanctions against perpetrators of cyberattacks on July 30, 2020. Four individuals and a government entity from Russia, a company and two individuals from China and a North Korean entity were unanimously found guilty of certain cyber attacks that harmed the interests of the Union and its Member States. France had been one of the most active supporters of the establishment of this European cyber sanctions regime, which was officially created in May 2019.

– S.-Y.L.: Defense implies knowing the means of attack and therefore either testing or investigating potentially adversary systems – this therefore implies a bit of offense, reverse engineering and intelligence. Since ANSSI's mission is defensive, how do you resolve these conflicts?

– G.P.: Indeed, offensive and intelligence capabilities are not part of ANSSI's mission. However, knowledge of the means of attack, which is essential for effective defense, does not necessarily require the use of these capabilities. Also, intervention with victims, analysis of malicious codes and exchanges with cybersecurity editors are all ways for ANSSI to understand the means of attack used. To do this, it relies on extremely specialized expertise, including code analysis and reverse engineering.

Cyberdefense and Cybersecurity Regulations in the United States: From the Failure of the "Comprehensive Policy" to the Success of the Sectoral Approach

9.1. Introduction

While, a few years ago, the study of cyber remained discreet, this new topic is becoming more widely discussed in the literature, especially in political science. In addition to the productions surrounding the strategic analysis of cyberwarfare and the appearance of this new means of waging war, notably through the writings initiated by Arquilla and Ronfeldt (1993), several reflections have appeared (including in France) that analyze cyber through the prism of international relations or geopolitics. Most of these studies tend to show how much this "new threat" impacts the way States (inter)act (modifying their international policies in the process), as well as our pre-existing analytical concepts. In this regard, Lucas Kello (2014) indicates that while theorists of international relations traditionally consider States as the principal and irreducible actors to which all other national and international agents are subordinate, and that relations between them are governed by strict rules allowing for the moderation of rivalries, the cyber phenomenon challenges traditional explanatory models. The emergence of new actors, especially private, on the international scene is redrawing interstate relations. Other authors, such as Chris Demchak (2011), suggest that cyber has

Chapter written by Adrien MANNIEZ.

profoundly modified State defense policies, and each state must now urgently develop "cyber power" in order to maintain its status as a great military power.

However, while we are regularly interested in the way in which cyber can modify our political science analytical frameworks, as well as the way in which States produce their defense policies, few, if any, works focus on the way in which the political variable can modify the form that the cyber topic[1] will take within each country. Thus, developing some of the material and reflections from a thesis written by the author on the comparative analysis of cyberdefense policies in France and in the United States, we show how internal state-specific logics can modify the contours of cyber policies. In this case, we show that, by using some of the tools of classical public policy analysis, and by focusing on the process of the emergence of the threat within the State, the construction of the "problem" by its promoters, and also the emergence of policy windows, or the weight of certain actors and the capacity of institutions to impose their decisions, it is possible to better understand the importance and the shape of cyberdefense and cybersecurity policies in a given country. Thus, we observe how and why cyber regulations in the United States seem to have systematically failed over the last 25 years. This may come as a surprise, especially when we know how certain powers, such as France, have managed to develop occasionally strong regulatory policies in this area.

9.2. The identification of a new threat and the impact of cyber on how US security and defense policies are designed

The first questions that need to be asked are: when did the State become interested in this cyber topic, when was it identified as a threat and how did it become a new problem that might require its intervention?

Apart from the National Security Decision Directive (NSDD)-145 of 1984, proposed by Ronald Reagan, it is really only since 1995 that the American federal government has seemed to be interested in the question of the security of the territory in the face of the threat of a computer attack. Indeed, following the terrorist attack in Oklahoma City in 1995 (which was a chemical explosion, not virtual or cyber), President Bill Clinton launched several initiatives aimed at producing reflections and reports on the security of American critical infrastructures. In July 1996, the President's

---

1 With the notable exception of Chapter 2 of this volume.

Commission on Critical Infrastructure Protection (PCCIP) task force was launched, with the mission of producing a complete report on possible attacks on these infrastructures. It was within the report produced by this group that the United States discovered the existence of a "cyber problem". The chairman of the PCCIP commission said at the time:

> We found all our infrastructures increasingly dependent on information and communications systems that criss-cross the nation and span the globe. That dependence is the source of rising vulnerabilities and, therefore, it is where we concentrated our effort. We found no evidence of an impending cyberattack which could have a debilitating effect on the nation's critical infrastructures. While we see no electronic disaster around the corner, this is no basis for complacency. We did find widespread capability to exploit infrastructure vulnerabilities. The capability to do harm – particularly through information networks – is real; it is growing at an alarming rate; and we have little defense against it.[2]

The significance of the cyber issue (unprecedented at the time) in the report[3] appeared to surprise White House advisors (Kaplan 2016, pp. 39–40), who discovered on reading it that more than half of the PCCIP's recommendations targeted not physical vulnerabilities (for which the report had been commissioned) but virtual ones. The document then indicated that it was "urgent" to take action on what they described as "cybersecurity" (PCCIP 1997). However, in addition to revealing the existence of a new threat, the PCCIP report also introduced several elements that would change the way the United States would henceforth produce its security and defense policies.

The first notable element was the distinction that would now be made between, on the one hand, threats from physical attacks and, on the other hand, from virtual attacks, which could particularly affect critical infrastructures (PDD 1995; PCCIP 1997)[4]. The report introduced this new dichotomy for the

---

2 General Marsh, Chair of the PCCIP Committee, in his introductory message to the report (PCCIP 1997, p. 5).

3 To illustrate its importance, the term cyber is cited 162 times in the 192 pages of the report.

4 Note here that this document is still partly classified; however, its contents are repeated in an official summary of the 1998 PDD-62 (PDD 1998a) which states that, "Moreover, easier access to sophisticated technology means that the destructive power available to terrorists is greater

first time and indicated that, henceforth, each type of threat would have to be dealt with in a specific way, using different solutions and tools.

The second major contribution of the report was that it mentioned the need to modify the way in which the State must consider the protection of these critical infrastructures by developing new methods of action, such as the implementation of a public/private partnership. In this regard, the report indicated that:

> Because the infrastructures are mainly privately owned and operated, we concluded that critical infrastructure assurance is a shared responsibility of the public and private sectors Therefore, in addition to our recommendations about improving our government's focus on infrastructure assurance in the Information Age, you will find some recommendations for collaborative public and private organizational arrangements that challenge our conventional way of thinking about government and private sector interaction[5].

It should be noted here that the report did not indicate full government responsibility for securing these infrastructures from cyber threats, but created a "shared" responsibility between the public and private sectors, without defining the terms. The formalization of this approach, embodied in the findings of the PCCIP report, is important when considering the actions taken by the federal government over the following two decades. This is because it referred to the idea that, while cyber risk certainly represents a threat to the State (which could legitimately lead to the idea that the State should produce a public policy to respond to it), it turned out that, in many cases, infrastructure security would in fact be the responsibility (and, in fact, at the total discretion) of private companies. Subsequently, as we shall see, given the responsibility that was partially transferred to private partners, no strong policy would immediately emerge. Only initiatives based on the voluntary participation of private actors would emerge.

---

than ever. Adversaries may thus be tempted to use unconventional tools, such as weapons of mass destruction, to target our cities and disrupt the operations of our government. They may try to attack our economy and critical infrastructure using advanced computer technology". Available at: www.au.af.mil/au/awc/awcgate/ciao/62factsheet.htm. Note: A more complete version of the PDD-39, which does not appear to be partly blacked out, is available from January 2019 at: www.clinton.presidentiallibraries.us/items/show/12755.

5 General Marsh, Chair of the PCCIP Committee for the report (PCCIP 1997, p. 5).

Finally, the last contribution of the report produced by the PCCIP was the discovery that cyber had redefined the way in which States should henceforth conceive the production of their security and defence policies. While, up to that point, it was sovereign power that ensured the full and complete protection of the territory against external aggression, the State now found itself "forced" to deal with private actors to ensure its own security, as critical infrastructures were not under its control. In this context, the American approach induced by the PCCIP indicated that:

> Our new thinking must accommodate the cyber dimension. One of the most important is recognizing that the owners and operators of our critical infrastructures are now on the front lines of our security effort. They are the ones most vulnerable to cyber attacks. And that vulnerability jeopardizes our national security, global economic competitiveness and domestic well being[6].

Thus, cyber was transforming the way in which States (in this case the United States) created and developed their security and defence policies. In this case, this "change" described by the PCCIP brought civilian, private operators to the forefront, where previously it was the military or public organizations in the context of interstate confrontation. The US federal government found itself having to deal with the existence of a threat to the nation, but whose weakest links (critical infrastructures) were in the hands of private companies. Beyond the changes that cyber had brought to US defense policies, it is interesting to note that the conclusions of the PCCIP would have a profound impact on all subsequent US cyber policies. Indeed, the report produced the basis for an "ideological framing" of this "new public problem", as seen by the measures taken by the authorities, as we will now demonstrate.

9.3. From the impact of cyber on policy to the impact of politics on cyber

While it is undeniable, as we have just seen, that cyber has had an impact on the way defence policies are conceived on the other side of the Atlantic, it is also interesting to note, conversely, the impact that political logics have had

---

6 General Marsh, Chair of the PCCIP Committee (PCCIP 1997, p. 5).

on the way the subject of cyber has been treated. Thus, by studying the addition of the cyber problem to the United States agenda, we realize how much classical logics – as well as observable logics in other subjects of study – have been able to impact and shape this new problem. We therefore observe here how much the weight of political logics, of ideological choices, as well as the framing operated by certain actors on this cyber problem impact the form of the measures taken by governments on the subject.

We mentioned earlier that the PCCIP marked a turning point in the way of thinking about policies aimed at securing the US territory. Following the report, in order to implement this "new thinking" by taking into account the cyber dimension, and thus integrate private operators into US security and defense policies, the White House quickly appointed a national cybersecurity coordinator, Richard Clarke. He therefore became the first "Cyber Tsar", a position that would be almost systematically renewed within the White House staff, starting with the Clinton administration. However, while the establishment of this new position seems to be a strong act, the document at the origin of his nomination remains clear: the Tsar is in reality only a coordinator with no real power, authority, decision-making capacity or competence in terms of regulation, for instance (PCCIP 1997, p. 109). Moreover, despite the conclusions of the PCCIP report, and the creation of a national advisor on cyber issues, no cyberdefense or cybersecurity policy would see the light of day, despite the insistence of the president's new personal advisor. Richard Clarke would later describe how the issue of implementing cyber policies would become one of the sticking points between him and some of the president's advisors, with the core of the discussion being whether or not to implement federal regulatory policies on private actors with critical infrastructures. The absence of security measures represented a risk for the State in case of an attack and Bill Clinton ended up ruling on the issue, by officially indicating his refusal of the idea of any regulation or imposition of security standards on companies in the National Plan for Information Systems Protection (NPISP):

> We cannot mandate our goals through Government regulation. Each sector must decide for itself what practices, procedures and standards are necessary for it to protect its key systems. As part of this partnership, the federal government stands ready to help. (Clinton 2000)

Thus, the State chose to simply place itself as a potential aid available to companies aiming, on a voluntary basis, to protect their computer networks in order to defend themselves (and, by the same token, the United States) against offensive cyber actions. The president also specified the implementation of public/private partnerships (the new tools recommended by the PCCIP), which would primarily be realized by the holding of discussion forums between actors, information sharing and good practices. It should be noted that the subtitle of the NPISP was "an invitation to dialogue", thus implying the implementation of simple soft measures, based mainly on voluntary action. This choice of refusing to implement coercive policies in cyber matters would then be repeated many times over the next two decades.

In yet another attempt, Cyber Tsar Richard Clarke tried again, during the Clinton administration, to integrate the idea of a federal policy to regulate companies and infrastructures in the face of the cyber threat, as evidenced by a preliminary (but ultimately unadopted) version of PDD-63 (PDD 1998b), which stated that "the Federal Government shall serve as a model to the private sector on how infrastructure assurance is best achieved and shall, to the extent feasible, distribute the results of its eandeavors" (Kaplan 2016, p. 98). This regulation project wanted by Clarke was leaked to the press, provoking "panic in the business world and an outcry from some members of Congress" (Kaplan 2016, p. 101). When confronted with the proposal, some members of Congress spoke of measures that would undermine civil liberties, while influential business actors referred to the government's regulatory policy as "the incarnation of their worst nightmares" (Kaplan 2016, p. 101). In the wake of this outcry, and in the face of President Clinton's outright refusal, proponents of the "regulatory approach" to cybersecurity (led by Clarke) would have to wait for the next administration for a new window of opportunity to emerge.

Richard Clarke was reappointed as Cyber Tsar by President Bush in 2001 and the NPISP resumed with his teams, trying to introduce the previously rejected measures (Clarke and Knake 2010, p. 113). The result was the National Strategy to Secure Cyberspace, which was signed by President Bush in February 2003 (Clarke and Knake 2010). However, issues of regulatory policy were once again strongly resisted by both White House advisors and the newly elected president. Richard Clarke would later state on this subject:

Substantively, there was little difference between the Clinton and Bush approaches, except that the Republican administration not only continued to eschew regulation, they downright hated the idea of the federal government issuing any new regulations on anything at all. (Clarke and Knake 2010, p. 113)

The main argument put forward by White House advisors to justify the refusal to regulate seems to be the fear of seeing the innovation of large US IT companies drastically curbed, and also the fact that this would have a strong impact on the country's economy, which had already been badly affected by the September 11 attacks (Clarke and Knake 2010). Some large Silicon Valley companies have not hesitated in mobilizing their political resources in order to avoid the appearance of such measures in federal policy, according to Richard Clarke:

Bush's personal understanding and interest in cybersecurity early in his administration were best summed up by a question he asked me in 2002. I had gone to him in the Oval Office with news of a discovery of a pervasive flaw in software, a flaw that would allow hackers to run amok unless we could quietly persuade most major networks and corporations to fix the flaw. Bush's only reaction was: "What does John think?" John was the CEO of a large information technology company and a major donor to the Bush election committee. (Clarke and Knake 2010, p. 113)

We see here how certain logics, which we regularly observe in other subjects, impacted the first American cyber initiatives. This choice of the occupants of the White House to reject any initiative aiming at producing regulatory policies seems to have been common to all administrations (transcending political and partisan cycles) and would quickly end up being truly characteristic of US cyber policy, as we will see. Faced with these multiple refusals, Richard Clarke resigned at the beginning of 2003, considering that he had not succeeded in convincing the staff members of the importance of the idea of a cyber regulation policy for future security (Clarke and Knake 2010, p. 113).

In 2007, having fallen virtually to the bottom of the government's list of concerns, the issue of US cyberdefense resurfaced during a National Security Council held by George W. Bush in the presence of Mike McConnell, then

Director of National Intelligence, who was able to capture the president's attention on the importance of the threat[7]. After briefing the White House on the cyber threat, especially from an economic point of view, McConnell asked for "strong" actions on the matter:

> Bush said, "I want it fixed. I want a plan, soon, real soon." The result was the Comprehensive National Cybersecurity Initiative (CNCI) and National Security Presidential Decision 54. Neither has ever become public. (Clarke and Knake 2010, p. 114)

The CNCI is interesting because it revealed a broad ambition for the White House, that of putting in place a comprehensive policy, including both private and public actors, with a view to securing the entire national territory[8]. We can see here the formalization of the desire, underpinned by the PCCIP a decade ago, to rethink security and defense policies, including cyber risk. However, although the subject of cyber has been brought back to the forefront by the US intelligence services[9], the question of setting up regulatory policies to protect companies remains, once again, tainted by a certain political taboo. Indeed, the primary objective of the CNCI was to be global and comprehensive and, therefore, to strengthen the resilience of not only military and government networks, but also of private companies and infrastructures. However, it became apparent that this policy would, once again, not be integrated into the plan at that time. The global nature of the

---

7 While the existence of this meeting is confirmed by several sources, the exact date is sometimes given as May 16, 2007, under the definition "NSC 05/16/2007 – Cyber Terror", which is available from the George W. Bush Presidential Library at: www.georgewbushlibrary. smu.edu/Research/Digital-Library. For more details on the content of this meeting and the exchanges that took place, we refer the reader to the speeches reported in particular in the book by Richard Clarke and Fred Kaplan.

8 It should be noted here that the content of these two documents is still largely classified, so it was not possible for us to consult them. Only the information from the interviews we conducted enabled us to study the subjects covered. However, it is clear from the interviews that the initial idea of creating a broad cyberdefense program, including military and government networks, as well as those of the private sector, will ultimately be limited to the protection of the first two. What was supposed to be a national and comprehensive policy will be much narrower than expected.

9 We deal with the reasons for this takeover of the subject by the intelligence services in more detail in our previously mentioned thesis work.

policy would only be an announcement, since the measures would be limited to the strict perimeter of public infrastructures. A White House cyber advisor during the Obama administration told us about this:

> In 2008, with the CNCI, they tried to create something like a "comprehensive cyber security initiative". And in speaking to people who worked in the administration whom I knew, I asked 'em, "Why did you call that comprehensive", because it's not really comprehensive. And they said they didn't call it comprehensive but the press office had put comprehensive in front because it sounded better. That was the initial effort to come up with a "national strategy" within the constraints... the ideological constraints that the Bush administration faced[10].

It should also be noted that the question of excluding measures aimed at companies seemed to be more a matter of political choice than of financial or technical resources, since the Presidency had stated that it wanted to commit considerable resources to the CNCI:

> In the weeks leading up to the directive, McConnell stressed that the plan would be expensive; Bush waved away the warning, saying that he was willing to spend as much money as Franklin Roosevelt had spent on the Manhattan Project. (Kaplan 2016, p. 178)

Once again, the private sector was excluded from US cyber policies. The CNCI rejected the idea of regulation, a taboo subject for more than 10 years, which provoked the astonishment of President George W. Bush's former Cyber Tsar, who became the cyber special advisor of the Democratic candidate Barack Obama, in the middle of the presidential campaign:

> Both documents [CNCI and NSPD 54] called, appropriately enough, for a twelve-step plan. They focused, however, on securing the government's networks. Oddly, the plan did not address the problem that had started the discussion in the Oval Office, the vulnerability of the financial sector to cyberwar. [...] the initiative did not address vulnerabilities in the private sector, including in our critical infrastructures. That tougher problem

---

10 Interview conducted at CSIS Headquarters in Washington, DC, December 2015.

was left to the next administration. (Clarke and Knake 2010, p. 114)

Thus, beyond the comprehensive character described by the CNCI, which was intended to be a strong policy integrating companies and private actors in the defense policy against virtual aggressions targeting the national territory, it appears from a more in-depth study that it was actually more of an announcement effect than real concrete measures imposed by the State. The issue of regulation had, once again, been pushed aside by the presidency and the security of critical infrastructures in the face of cyber threats had once again been left to the mercy of private actors. The logic that had existed since the Clinton era was maintained during President Bush's two terms of office. From 2008, we saw the US presidential campaign taking up the subject of cyber, at least in the Democratic camp. The future 44th president would indicate in his Purdue speech:

As President, I'll make cybersecurity the top priority that it should be in the 21st century. I'll declare our cyber infrastructure a strategic asset, and appoint a National Cyber Advisor who will report directly to me. We'll coordinate efforts across the federal government, implement a truly national cybersecurity policy and tighten standards to secure information – from the networks that power the federal government, to the networks that you use in your personal lives. (Obama 2008)

The issue of critical infrastructure security in the face of cyber attacks, highlighted by the 1996 PCCIP, had resurfaced. A reading of the speech clearly suggests that the future tenant of the White House wanted to appoint a dedicated cyber advisor (Cyber Tsar) back on his team, thus regaining control over security and defense policies in this area. It also underlined a desire to integrate critical infrastructures (and therefore, the companies that own them) into the system. In this vein, the Purdue speech appeared to encourage innovation in the way the United States should act in this matter. On this subject, a cyber advisor to the US President recounted:

For some reason, Obama was always interested in cybersecurity, so he took it seriously from the start before he was president. And I think that means, when he came in, he wanted to see some kind of better approach than the Bush people had done. What Bush had done was quite inadequate and so Obama wanted to do something a little bit more comprehensive, a little more organized[11].

The Democratic candidate's strong interest in the security of companies and infrastructures can be explained, in particular, by the composition of his campaign teams; indeed, it was Richard Clarke, former cyber advisor to Bill Clinton, then to George W. Bush, who assumed the position of national security and cybersecurity advisor throughout the entire campaign. On this subject, he indicated:

> Although I had signed on to the campaign as a terrorism advisor, I used that access to pester the candidate and his advisors about cyber war. It was not surprising to me that Obama got the issue, since he was running the most technologically advanced, cyber-dependent presidential campaign in history. (Clarke and Knake 2010, p. 116)

Given the former Cyber Tsar's commitment to the idea of imposing a cyber regulation policy on private companies, and that every attempt to convince sitting presidents had ended in failure, we can understand the direction taken by Barack Obama just before his election victory. However, again, the proponents of cyber regulation policies (led by Clarke) were not able to impose their ideas once the candidate had been elected. Richard Clarke remembers:

> Shortly before the inauguration, Paul Kurt and I provided the new White House team with a draft decision document to formalize the proposals Obama had advocated in the Purdue speech. We argued that if Obama waited, people would come out of the woodwork to try to stop it. Although the most senior White House staff understood that problem and wanted a quick decision, it was, understandably, not a high priority for them. Instead, the new Obama White House announced a Sixty Day Review and asked one of the drafters of Bush's CNCI to run it. (Clarke and Knake 2010, p. 118)

The resulting report, once again, buried any desire to put in place a real global cyber policy that would be imposed on private actors. This result was

11 Interview conducted at CSIS Headquarters in Washington, DC, December 2015.

not surprising, given that exactly the same teams that had worked on the CNCI during the previous administration were in charge of working on the future cyber vision of the Obama era. Here, again, we see the ideology imposed since the Clinton administration, leaving companies to implement measures on a voluntary basis, with support (especially technical support) from the government if necessary, but without it being imposed. A Pentagon cyber advisor said on this subject:

> All in all, all this work to develop a strategy for cyberspace [the respondent is referring to the Sixty Days Review announced by Obama once in office] was the recycling of the clichés of the last twelve years[12].

At the end of the Sixty Days Review, President Obama, who had declared his interest in the protection of private critical infrastructures during the Purdue speech and his willingness to renew the US vision in this matter, finally showed very clearly his opposition to the idea of creating a global cyber policy. In the same way, no imposition of a regulatory policy on companies would be on the agenda (despite Richard Clarke's lobbying of the Democratic candidate during the campaign), as the newly elected president indicated: "So let me be very clear: my administration will not dictate security standards for private companies" (New York Times 2009). He preferred to "strengthen the public/private partnerships that are critical to this endeavor" (New York Times 2009), in the image of the methods already developed and used since the Clinton era. The new administration justified its decision not to regulate in order to avoid penalizing the American economy, which had just been hit hard by the subprime[13] crisis.

There are several lessons to be learned here. First of all, we can clearly see the importance of certain key actors in the promotion of the cyber subject to the presidency, particularly Richard Clarke, but also Mike McConnell, who were both able to draw the White House's attention to this new threat. They were the true proponents of the cyber problem, trying to put forward their vision and defending their approaches, as was the case for the regulatory issues. However, certain actors and ideological choices would stop any will to

---

12 Interview with a Pentagon special advisor on cyber matters, conducted in Washington, DC, November 2015.

13 "We're working to recover from a global recession while laying a new foundation for lasting prosperity".

establish global cyber policies within the private sphere, thus returning to the more neutral vision already outlined in the PCCIP report.

9.4. From a comprehensive cyber policy to a sectoral approach: the success of an undeclared regulatory policy

As we have just seen, the United States has been marked by a long political tradition of rejecting the idea of a global cyber regulation policy imposed on both public and private actors. Is the United States, which is considered one of the greatest military (cyber) powers, a leaden-footed colossus, with strong offensive capabilities but incapable of imposing any defensive measures on private actors present on its territory? The question is all the more relevant when we compare the American case with that of France, which, through the work of ANSSI, seems to be able to impose important cyber regulation measures on its operators of vital importance (OIVs). While the resistance to regulation in the United States seems to be an inextricable situation, it is necessary to look beyond President Obama's simple announcement, indicating a refusal to dictate any security standards to private companies, and analyze the reality of the actors' practices.

Indeed, in order to avoid an outcry, such as the one the federal government experienced when Richard Clarke's project was leaked to the press a few years ago, the Obama White House is developing a strategy based on sectoral regulation, which will replace the previous failed comprehensive policy projects. The main tool of this approach is the National Institute of Standards and Technology (NIST), an agency of the Department of Commerce, whose mission is to create standards to promote and secure the US economy in all its domains (other than cyber). The standards set by NIST aim to take measures to ensure the security of facilities (such as during physical attacks), the continuity of certain services and infrastructures and the security of financial transactions. These standards are then imposed by the department concerned on health organizations, industrial companies, private companies and even certain entire sectors such as finance. From the start, NIST has become a central resource for the government in the field of cybersecurity, including, implicitly, computer risks. Although no government initiative bearing the label of cyber policy is actually being enacted by the Obama administration, the sectoral approach allows each department to adapt standards and preventive measures against this new risk on a case-by-case basis. As a result, contrary to a global cyber policy, which would have been specifically created and overseen by the Department of Homeland Security (Homeland Security Act 2002)[14] (as was the case in many previous projects), State actors are finally mobilizing a complete mesh of existing standards (sometimes even prior to the appearance of this new cyber threat). Through the sectoral approach, more than 20 departments have been involved in the application of standards related (indirectly) to cybersecurity (Leclair 2013, p. 5), each of them applying the measures originally defined by NIST for entirely different reasons, but ultimately having applications in cybersecurity. In this regard, a cyber advisor to President Barack Obama told us:

> That comes from NIST, it produces a framework that any company can follow... They are not bound by law, it's voluntary, with the following exception that if you're a regulatory agency... if you are a regulated sector, and your regulatory agency says, "you might have to do this", then it's no longer voluntary[15].

As a result, a two-tiered cyber defense policy is emerging in the United States. While some sectors escape government control due to the absence of a global cyberdefense policy (and the simple recourse to voluntary measures), other sectors that are already regulated in other areas are subject to new (cyber) standards, in addition to the pre-existing standards. Moreover, the various US departments regularly develop or reuse standards that were not originally designed to deal with cyber attacks, but which are used as such. Thus, in the case of the financial sector, for example, which is highly regulated without any cyber measures (Bris 2007), certain requirements, such as the multiplication of backups and access media in order to secure financial transactions, may prove to be useful in the event of a cyber attack aiming to delete or modify certain data on a server (Leclair 2013, p. 115). In this sense, the banking sector perfectly illustrates the reuse strategy developed by the Treasury Department. According to a Pentagon cyber advisor:

---

14 In accordance with the Homeland Security Act, which states that the Department of Homeland Security is responsible for conducting US cyber policy. Cybersecurity is addressed in section 225 of the Homeland Security Act. See, in this regard, the Homeland Security Act (2002), Pub. L. No. 107-296, 116 Stat. 2135.

15 Interview conducted at CSIS Headquarters in Washington, DC, December 2015.

You can't meet the banks and say "you should have such and such IT system", it's just unthinkable here in the United States. So, the governors are on the outside looking in, but the United States Government has a lot of places to be on the outside, right? So for instance, let's consider the banking sector: banks are overseen by States, banks are overseen and controlled by the Treasury. For instance, let us say a bank loses money because of a hack, it has to report it, but by whose rules? I think federal rules, OK? But here is also a Security Exchange Commission. In theory every time you have an incident that could affect our stock price you have to report it to our Security Exchange Commission[16].

The protective measures provided to mitigate certain risks, including financial risks, are used by the federal government to secure markets in the event of a cyber attack. In the same way, other sectors considered "at risk" are the subject of a profound framework, particularly with regard to the risks that may result from accidents or physical harm. This is the case in the chemical industry, which has become the focus of numerous security standards, particularly following the New York attacks of 2001 (Leclair and Ramsay 2013, pp. 40–41). For example, the American government mobilized a multitude of texts, such as the Chemical Facility Anti-Terrorism Standards (CFATS) and the Ammonium Nitrate Security Program (ANSP), both of which (originally) had anti-terrorist aims, but which are capable of being reused in the framework of cyber protection (Leclair and Ramsay 2013, pp. 40–41). The use of this type of standard thus allowed the Department of Commerce to secure nearly 10,000 companies in the chemical industry in cyber matters in 2013 (Leclair and Ramsay 2013, p. 31). Finally, the reuse of pre-existing standards defined by the NIST also makes it possible to apply a cybersecurity policy in sectors that, at first glance, seem to have little, if any, connection with cyber risk. Thus, we find cybersecurity-related standards aimed at occasionally unexpected sectors, such as the agrifood industry, but also American agriculture (Cooper 2013, p. 141).

As a result, although the United States has not been able to develop a global regulatory policy dedicated to cyber, the re-use of pre-existing texts

---

16 Interview with a Pentagon special advisor on cyber matters, conducted in Washington, DC, November 2015.

or standards developed for other purposes does not just allow the government to act in this area; the use of a sectoral approach is even more interesting in cyber matters, since it allows the government to go beyond what could have been envisaged in the framework of a global cyber policy. On this subject, a cyber advisor within the Obama administration told us:

> Sony! Sony is not a critical infrastructure, so there is no ability to say to Sony, "You should take the following actions to protect yourself." So you can put all this stuff under "best practices", under "guidelines", you could put out... you know that's all nonsense and people aren't gonna do it[17].

Indeed, Executive Order 13636 of 2013 calls for companies to make critical infrastructures cyber-secure. However, this definition tends to cover only a portion of the companies at risk, by means of a division into 18 sectors (Libicki 2016, p. 77), the term "critical infrastructure" having been originally conceived and defined by the Department of Homeland Security to deal with the threat of a physical bomb explosion, for example, and not a logical bomb introduced into a computer system through a virus (Libicki 2016, p. 77).

In this way, US sectoral policy not only allows it to extend beyond simple voluntary measures for certain sectors, but also to extend cyber policy to private entities that it would not otherwise have had access to. Rather than attempting to regulate companies labeled as critical infrastructure (which does not always cover the necessary reality), the use of the sectoral approach and the reuse of undeveloped standards for cyber purposes ultimately allow the state to compensate for the absence of a regulatory policy in cyber matters, thus turning the opposition to any attempt at a comprehensive policy by the White House against resistance from Congress and the lobbyists mentioned above. However, such a system also has some pitfalls, particularly with respect to the ability of some departments to enforce the standards for which they are responsible. A cyber advisor to President Barack Obama told us:

> well that's why it varies from sector to sector and that's not the most efficient model. The people, the agencies that regulate the banks have a lot of authority so they can compel the banks to do things. The agencies that regulate electrical companies don't have a lot of authority. They can't compel electrical companies

---

17 Interview conducted at CSIS Headquarters in Washington, DC, December 2015.

to do that much. It's historic and it varies from agency to agency... The OCC, the Office of the Comptroller of the Currency, was created right after the Great Depression: people were very worried about financial stability, so they created a very powerful agency. So it's this "mélange" of agencies, it's both a strength, but it's also a weakness[18].

Thus, it appears that whereas the Treasury Department is able to enforce strong cybersecurity standards, due to its significant regulatory power, other departments such as the Energy Department are challenged by their lack of overall authority, making it difficult to regulate the sector for which it is responsible. The combination of a lack of a comprehensive policy and the sectoral approach produces a disparity in the State's ability to impose its cybersecurity policy on the private sphere. According to our respondent:

Well, now you could think of laws that could be useful, but, the current approach is "OK, you have the executive order," but the executive order cannot create "new authorities"; it can allow the president to extend actual authorities in a new way. So the president can't announce, you know, "I want to do something that Congress doesn't authorise me to do" but he can use his existing authorities and that is just what he did, to go to these sector-specific agencies and say, "Now when you regulate companies, make sure that you consider their cybersecurity. And use this NIST framework as a way to measure how well they are doing." You could say it's not perfect because differents agencies vary widely in their authority... The electrical regulation agency is a very weak agency[19].

In short, while the idea of a global cyber policy focused on regulation could not be implemented for the reasons mentioned above, it eventually led to an adaptation of the actors, who then developed a sectoral approach. The reuse of pre-existing security texts and standards allows for the implementation of a cyber regulation policy "that dares not say its name". While this certainly makes it possible to circumvent certain difficulties and systematic opposition, it also has consequences, such as a certain disparity in the effectiveness of the system, since some sectors are better protected than

18 Interview conducted at CSIS Headquarters in Washington, DC, December 2015.
19 Interview conducted at CSIS Headquarters in Washington, DC, December 2015.

others. This disparity is not a function of the importance of the threat or the critical nature of the sector, but rather of institutional logic.

9.5. Conclusion

The cyber topic, although recent, is still mostly studied through the prism of international relations, reflections centered on geopolitics, or its impact on the strategic conduct of war. As we have seen, while cyber certainly brings about changes in the way States conceive and produce their security and defence policies, we also thought it would be interesting to examine the change(s) that the internal political variables specific to each State may effect in the cyber topic. In this case, by developing part of the approach from our thesis work in this chapter, we wanted to show why regulation policies in the United States have (unlike France) systematically failed over the last 25 years.

Moreover, it was also an opportunity for us to show that, in addition to the contribution that cyber can make to our classical analytical tools from political science[20], the analytical tools of political science (such as those used for public policy analysis) can, in return, modify our understanding of the cyber phenomenon. From this point of view, this chapter was an opportunity for us to show that, although coercive policies have seemingly never been officially applied to the private sector in the United States, we realize that the development of the sectoral approach in the United States seems to be, in itself, a regulatory policy in all but name. We therefore consider that, in the face of cyber policies, it is necessary to go beyond appearances and announcements, by focusing specifically on the process of the emergence of the cyber threat within the State, the construction of the problem by its promoters, the emergence of windows of opportunity, the weight of certain actors and the capacity of institutions to impose their decisions. Thus, if we analyze cyberdefense policies as classical public policies, we realize that it is possible to explain the form of the different cyber policies within each State and to understand the specificities of the different cyber policy models.

---

20 In the introduction, we mentioned the sometimes major impact that cyber could have on the classical analytical frameworks in the field of international relations.

9.6. References

Arquilla, J. and Ronfeldt, D. (1993). *Cyberwar is Coming!* RAND Corporation, Santa Monica.

Bris, A. (2007). Managing complexity in the financial services industry. In *Managing Complexity in Global Organizations*, Maznevski, M., Steger, U., Amann, W. (eds), Wiley, Chichester.

Clarke, R.A. and Knake, R.K. (2010). *Cyberwar: The Next Threat to National Security and What to do About it*. Ecco Harper Collins Publisher, New York.

Clinton, B. (2000). Defending America's Cyberspace, National Plan for Information Systems Protection Version 1.0 – An Invitation to a Dialogue. The White House.

Cooper, C. (2013). Cybersecurity and food and agriculture. In *Protecting our Future: Educating a Cybersecurity Workforce – Volume 2*, Leclair, J., Ramsay, S. (eds). Hudson Whitman Excelsior College Press, London.

Demchak, C.C. (2011). *Wars of Disruption and Resilience: Cyber Conflict, Power and National Security*. University of Georgia Press, Athens.

Homeland Security Act (2002). Pub. L. No. 107-296, 116 Stat. 2135.

Kaplan, F. (2016). *Dark Territory: The Secret History of Cyber War*. Simon & Schuster, New York.

Kello, L. and Richard, T. (2014). Les Cyberarmes : dilemmes et futurs possibles. Report, Institut français des relations internationales (IFRI).

Leclair, J. and Ramsay, S. (2013). *Protecting our Future: Educating a Cybersecurity Work-force – Volume 2*. Hudson Whitman Excelsior College Press, London.

Leclair, J. and Rumsfeld, D. (2013). *Protecting our Future: Educating a Cybersecurity Work-force – Volume 1*. Hudson Whitman Excelsior College Press, London.

Libicki, M. (2016). *Cyberspace in Peace and War*. Naval Institute Press, Annapolis.

National Security Decision Directive Number 145 (1984). National Policy on Telecommunications and Automated Information Systems Security. September 17.

New York Times (2009). Obama's remarks on cyber-security [Online]. Available at: www.nytimes.com/2009/05/29/us/politics/29obama.text.html.

Obama, B. (2008). Speech. Perdue University, 16 July.

PCCIP (1997). Critical Foundations: Protecting America's Infrastructures. Report, President's Commission on Critical Infrastructure Protection.

PDD (1995). Presidential Decision Directive 39 (PDD-39): U.S. Policy on Counterterrorism.

PDD (1998a). Presidential Decision Directive 62 (PDD-62): Combating Terrorism.

PDD (1998b). Presidential Decision Directive 63 (PDD-63) on Critical Infrastructure Protection.

List of Authors

Mark CORCORAL
Sciences Po
Paris
France

Alix DESFORGES
University Paris 8
France

Frédérick GAGNON
Chaire Raoul-Dandurand
Université du Québec à Montréal
Canada

Fabien LAFOUASSE
IDEST
Jean Monnet University
Saint-Étienne
France

Sébastien-Yves LAURENT
IRM
University of Bordeaux
France

Adrien MANNIEZ
CEPEL
University of Montpellier
France

Guillaume POUPARD
ANSSI
Paris
France

Alexis RAPIN
Chaire Raoul-Dandurand
Université du Québec à Montréal
Canada

Bertrand WARUSFEL
CRJP8
University Paris 8
France

Marc WATIN-AUGOUARD
CREOGN
Melun
France

Index

Other titles from

in

Computer Engineering

2021

DELHAYE Jean-Loic
Inside the World of Computing: Technologies, Uses, Challenges

DUVAUT Patrick, DALLOZ Xavier, MENGA David, KOEHL François,
CHRIQUI Vidal, BRILL Joerg
*Internet of Augmented Me, I.AM: Empowering Innovation for a New
Sustainable Future*

HARDIN Thérèse, JAUME Mathieu, PESSAUX François,
VIGUIÉ DONZEAU-GOUGE Véronique
*Concepts and Semantics of Programming Languages 1: A Semantical
Approach with OCaml and Python*
*Concepts and Semantics of Programming Languages 2: Modular and
Object-oriented Constructs with OCaml, Python, C++, Ada and Java*

MKADMI Abderrazak
*Archives in The Digital Age: Preservation and the Right to be Forgotten
(Digital Tools and Uses Set – Volume 8)*

TOKLU Yusuf Cengiz, BEKDAS Gebrail, NIGDELI Sinan Melih
*Metaheuristics for Structural Design and Analysis (Optimization Heuristics
Set – Volume 3)*

2020

DARCHE Philippe
Microprocessor 1: Prolegomena – Calculation and Storage Functions –
Models of Computation and Computer Architecture
Microprocessor 2: Core Concepts – Communication in a Digital System
Microprocessor 3: Core Concepts – Hardware Aspects
Microprocessor 4: Core Concepts – Software Aspects
Microprocessor 5: Software and Hardware Aspects of Development,
Debugging and Testing – The Microcomputer

LAFFLY Dominique
TORUS 1 – Toward an Open Resource Using Services: Cloud Computing
for Environmental Data
TORUS 2 – Toward an Open Resource Using Services: Cloud Computing
for Environmental Data
TORUS 3 – Toward an Open Resource Using Services: Cloud Computing
for Environmental Data

LAURENT Anne, LAURENT Dominique, MADERA Cédrine
Data Lakes
(Databases and Big Data Set – Volume 2)

OULHADJ Hamouche, DAACHI Boubaker, MENASRI Riad
Metaheuristics for Robotics
(Optimization Heuristics Set – Volume 2)

SADIQUI Ali
Computer Network Security

VENTRE Daniel
Artificial Intelligence, Cybersecurity and Cyber Defense

2019

BESBES Walid, DHOUIB Diala, WASSAN Niaz, MARREKCHI Emna
Solving Transport Problems: Towards Green Logistics

CLERC Maurice
Iterative Optimizers: Difficulty Measures and Benchmarks

GHLALA Riadh
Analytic SQL in SQL Server 2014/2016

TOUNSI Wiem
Cyber-Vigilance and Digital Trust: Cyber Security in the Era of Cloud Computing and IoT

2018

ANDRO Mathieu
Digital Libraries and Crowdsourcing
(Digital Tools and Uses Set – Volume 5)

ARNALDI Bruno, GUITTON Pascal, MOREAU Guillaume
Virtual Reality and Augmented Reality: Myths and Realities

BERTHIER Thierry, TEBOUL Bruno
From Digital Traces to Algorithmic Projections

CARDON Alain
Beyond Artificial Intelligence: From Human Consciousness to Artificial Consciousness

HOMAYOUNI S. Mahdi, FONTES Dalila B.M.M.
Metaheuristics for Maritime Operations
(Optimization Heuristics Set – Volume 1)

JEANSOULIN Robert
JavaScript and Open Data

PIVERT Olivier
NoSQL Data Models: Trends and Challenges
(Databases and Big Data Set – Volume 1)

SEDKAOUI Soraya
Data Analytics and Big Data

SALEH Imad, AMMI Mehdi, SZONIECKY Samuel
Challenges of the Internet of Things: Technology, Use, Ethics
(Digital Tools and Uses Set – Volume 7)

SZONIECKY Samuel
Ecosystems Knowledge: Modeling and Analysis Method for Information and Communication
(Digital Tools and Uses Set – Volume 6)

2017

BENMAMMAR Badr
Concurrent, Real-Time and Distributed Programming in Java

HÉLIODORE Frédéric, NAKIB Amir, ISMAIL Boussaad, OUCHRAA Salma, SCHMITT Laurent
Metaheuristics for Intelligent Electrical Networks
(Metaheuristics Set – Volume 10)

MA Haiping, SIMON Dan
Evolutionary Computation with Biogeography-based Optimization
(Metaheuristics Set – Volume 8)

PÉTROWSKI Alain, BEN-HAMIDA Sana
Evolutionary Algorithms
(Metaheuristics Set – Volume 9)

PAI G A Vijayalakshmi
Metaheuristics for Portfolio Optimization
(Metaheuristics Set – Volume 11)

2016

BLUM Christian, FESTA Paola
Metaheuristics for String Problems in Bio-informatics
(Metaheuristics Set – Volume 6)

DEROUSSI Laurent
Metaheuristics for Logistics
(Metaheuristics Set – Volume 4)

DHAENENS Clarisse and JOURDAN Laetitia
Metaheuristics for Big Data
(Metaheuristics Set – Volume 5)

2014

BOULANGER Jean-Louis
Industrial Use of Formal Methods: Formal Verification

BOULANGER Jean-Louis
Formal Method: Industrial Use from Model to the Code

CALVARY Gaëlle, DELOT Thierry, SÈDES Florence, TIGLI Jean-Yves
Computer Science and Ambient Intelligence

MAHOUT Vincent
Assembly Language Programming: ARM Cortex-M3 2.0: Organization, Innovation and Territory

MARLET Renaud
Program Specialization

SOTO Maria, SEVAUX Marc, ROSSI André, LAURENT Johann
Memory Allocation Problems in Embedded Systems: Optimization Methods

2011

BICHOT Charles-Edmond, SIARRY Patrick
Graph Partitioning

BOULANGER Jean-Louis
Static Analysis of Software: The Abstract Interpretation

CAFERRA Ricardo
Logic for Computer Science and Artificial Intelligence

HOMES Bernard
Fundamentals of Software Testing

KORDON Fabrice, HADDAD Serge, PAUTET Laurent, PETRUCCI Laure
Distributed Systems: Design and Algorithms

KORDON Fabrice, HADDAD Serge, PAUTET Laurent, PETRUCCI Laure
Models and Analysis in Distributed Systems

LORCA Xavier
Tree-based Graph Partitioning Constraint

TRUCHET Charlotte, ASSAYAG Gerard
Constraint Programming in Music

VICAT-BLANC PRIMET Pascale *et al.*
Computing Networks: From Cluster to Cloud Computing

2010

AUDIBERT Pierre
Mathematics for Informatics and Computer Science

BABAU Jean-Philippe *et al.*
Model Driven Engineering for Distributed Real-Time Embedded Systems

BOULANGER Jean-Louis
Safety of Computer Architectures

MONMARCHE Nicolas *et al.*
Artificial Ants

PANETTO Hervé, BOUDJLIDA Nacer
Interoperability for Enterprise Software and Applications 2010

SIGAUD Olivier *et al.*
Markov Decision Processes in Artificial Intelligence

SOLNON Christine
Ant Colony Optimization and Constraint Programming

AUBRUN Christophe, SIMON Daniel, SONG Ye-Qiong *et al.*
Co-design Approaches for Dependable Networked Control Systems

2009

FOURNIER Jean-Claude
Graph Theory and Applications

GUEDON Jeanpierre
The Mojette Transform / Theory and Applications

JARD Claude, ROUX Olivier
Communicating Embedded Systems / Software and Design

LECOUTRE Christophe
Constraint Networks / Targeting Simplicity for Techniques and Algorithms

2008

BANÂTRE Michel, MARRÓN Pedro José, OLLERO Hannibal, WOLITZ Adam
Cooperating Embedded Systems and Wireless Sensor Networks

MERZ Stephan, NAVET Nicolas
Modeling and Verification of Real-time Systems

PASCHOS Vangelis Th
Combinatorial Optimization and Theoretical Computer Science: Interfaces and Perspectives

WALDNER Jean-Baptiste
Nanocomputers and Swarm Intelligence

2007

BENHAMOU Frédéric, JUSSIEN Narendra, O'SULLIVAN Barry
Trends in Constraint Programming

JUSSIEN Narendra
A TO Z OF SUDOKU

2006

BABAU Jean-Philippe *et al.*
From MDD Concepts to Experiments and Illustrations – DRES 2006

HABRIAS Henri, FRAPPIER Marc
Software Specification Methods

MURAT Cecile, PASCHOS Vangelis Th
Probabilistic Combinatorial Optimization on Graphs

PANETTO Hervé, BOUDJLIDA Nacer
Interoperability for Enterprise Software and Applications 2006 / IFAC-IFIP I-ESA'2006

2005

GÉRARD Sébastien *et al.*
Model Driven Engineering for Distributed Real Time Embedded Systems

PANETTO Hervé
Interoperability of Enterprise Software and Applications 2005

Printed and bound by CPI Group (UK) Ltd, Croydon, CR0 4YY

27/10/2024

14580726-0003